SWORN ON THE ALTAR OF GOD

LIBRARY OF RELIGIOUS BIOGRAPHY

available

Billy Sunday and the Redemption of Urban America
by Lyle W. Dorsett

Liberty of Conscience: Roger Williams in America
by Edwin S. Gaustad

The Divine Dramatist:
George Whitefield and the Rise of Modern Evangelicalism
by Harry S. Stout

William Ewart Gladstone:
Faith and Politics in Victorian Britain
by David Bebbington

Aimee Semple McPherson: Everybody's Sister
by Edith Blumhofer

Sworn on the Altar of God:
A Religious Biography of Thomas Jefferson
by Edwin S. Gaustad

forthcoming

Charles G. Finney and the Spirit of American Evangelicalism
Charles Hambrick-Stowe

Emily Dickinson: The Fate of Theology in American Culture
Roger Lundin

Sworn on the Altar of God

A Religious Biography of Thomas Jefferson

Edwin S. Gaustad

WILLIAM B. EERDMANS PUBLISHING COMPANY
GRAND RAPIDS, MICHIGAN / CAMBRIDGE, U.K.

© 1996 Wm. B. Eerdmans Publishing Co.
255 Jefferson Ave. S.E., Grand Rapids, Michigan 49503 /
P.O. Box 163, Cambridge, CB3 9PU U.K.

Printed in the United States of America

01 00 99 98 97 96   7 6 5 4 3 2 1

Library of Congress Cataloging-in-Publication Data

Gaustad, Edwin S. (Edwin Scott)
    Sworn on the altar of God: a religious biography
of Thomas Jefferson / Edwin S. Gaustad.
        p.   cm.
    Includes bibliographical references and index.
    ISBN 0-8028-0156-0 (pbk.: alk. paper)
    1. Jefferson, Thomas, 1743-1826 — Religion. 2. Presidents —
United States — Biography. I. Title.
E332.2.G38   1995
277.3'081'092 — dc20
    [B]   95-47720
                                                        CIP

For Susan
who likewise
"cannot live without books"

Contents

Foreword

Unlike those of all but a small handful of his fellow Founding Fathers, Thomas Jefferson's name has not faded into the mists of time. When the producers of a recent film, *Jefferson in Paris*, chose to play fast and loose with his character and what he had done in his years as the new American ambassador to France, discomfited pundits joined angry scholars in vigorous protest. A phrase from one of Jefferson's letters concerning a "wall of separation" between church and state has been for the past fifty years at the forefront of constitutional discussion on sensitive questions about the proper place of religion in public life. (Nor is it irrelevant to note that reader demand prompts new editions of his many and always interesting letters.) Jefferson's words in many significant documents — especially the Declaration of Independence — remain a focus for diligent historical research into the moral as well as political world in which the United States came into existence. His presence on the nickel, as a revered icon for Democratic politicians at Jefferson-Jackson dinners, and more recently as an inspiration for Republican congressional leaders who invoke his sentiments on the danger of big government — all this and more testifies to Jefferson's continuing power in American memory.

The great achievement of Edwin S. Gaustad's biographical study of Jefferson is its demonstration of how religious concerns were central to many of Jefferson's main preoccupations. That achievement requires, by the nature of the case, great nuance, for Jefferson is a type of person who has become considerably more difficult to assess in the twentieth century than he was in his own day. He was sincerely, even profoundly, religious, and yet he also repudiated many of the doctrines, attitudes, and convictions of traditional Christianity. The Jefferson who read the New Testament (often in Greek or Latin) almost every day for the last fifty years of his life also prepared two different editions of the Gospels for his own use so that he could read about Jesus with the miraculous bits cut away. The Jefferson who cooperated with his friend James Madison in passing a landmark bill separating church and state in Virginia (thereby helping almost immediately Baptists, Presbyterians, and several feisty Protestant sects) also blithely predicted that most of the country would soon become Unitarian. The Jefferson who contributed money on at least one occasion to a Bible society also railed against the tyranny of New England–based religious voluntary societies. The Jefferson who intensely disliked the moral economy of slavery himself kept slaves. The Jefferson who distrusted any large-scale concentration of power nevertheless expressed nearly unbounded confidence in the moral potential of the monolithic educational system he proposed for Virginia. This is, in other words, a complicated person whose religious opinions and practices need every bit of the cautious wisdom that Gaustad devotes to his subject in the pages that follow.

Good historical studies do not necessarily have to speak directly to the present. But because this religious biography pays such close attention to a person whose ideals remain so important in American life, it becomes something of a challenging tract for the times as well as a luminous historical study. Readers who ponder Gaustad's picture of Jefferson's friendships with Madison, John Adams, and Benjamin Rush will be tempted to ask why today's partisan political differences exhibit so much less intelligence and so much more meanspiritedness. Those who take seriously Gaustad's contention that modern conservative evangelicals have as much to learn from Jefferson as to scorn will be in a better position to discriminate between essentials and nonessentials in contemporary culture wars. Those who note the resemblance between Jefferson's views and those of Jonathan Edwards on the subject of God's providential care for the world may find themselves more willing to seek wisdom in political opponents as well as in political friends. And those who, with the editors of this series, think that Jefferson went too far in critiquing the Puritan heritage or that he overestimated the virtues of French political life while underestimating the residual value of British politics should nonetheless find some attractive surprises in Gaustad's portrait. The book, in short, embodies many of its subject's virtues and, from any point on the political spectrum — from the start of the nineteenth century to the end of the twentieth — that is a substantial recommendation indeed.

Mark A. Noll
Nathan O. Hatch

Preface

Thomas Jefferson (1743-1826) is a many-sided, much-studied American icon. His many-sidedness is a large part of his lasting appeal, since he displayed an intellectual appetite and engaging virtuosity that flabbergasts an age given over more to specialization, method, and technique. From architecture and archaeology through classical languages and literature into history, law, and politics, on to music, rhetoric, and science — his quest seemed boundless. And in so much of this, his interests were far more than merely academic: in field after field, he proved to be a most highly skilled practitioner, a most remarkable contributor. To be sure, he was a patron of the arts and the sciences, but he surged far beyond patronage to a striking and enduring participation.

So many sides appear to require so many books, especially as we turn and return to Jefferson for definitions of ourselves and of what America is all about. As recently as 1993, with the celebration of the 250th anniversary of his birth, the reading and the viewing public witnessed another burst of academic essays and media notices. It is as though the nation, with all its collective energies and intellect, would hope to match those found in the life and thought of a single president. Biographers have found much to criticize as well as to praise, weighing and judging the mixed legacy of a complex man. But whatever the final academic judgments, the fact remains that we as American citizens refuse to let Thomas Jefferson go.

One "side" of Jefferson requires renewed attention — namely, his involvement, at both a practical and a theoretical level, with religion. While many arguments for such attention may be made, I limit myself to four bald categorical assertions, each of which will, I trust, become more fully clothed in the chapters that follow. First, Thomas Jefferson was the most self-consciously theological of all America's presidents. Second, he dedicated himself more deliberately and diligently to the reform of religion than any other president. Third, in partnership with James Madison, he did more to root religious liberty firmly in the American tradition than any predecessor or successor in the White House. And fourth, in succeeding centuries, no other president has been appealed to more frequently or more fervently in religious matters than Jefferson. In the entire religious dimension of human experience, therefore, he cannot be ignored.

In a letter sent to a friend in 1815, Jefferson noted, "I not only write nothing on religion, but rarely permit myself to speak on it, and never but in a reasonable society." He did, however, often write and speak about religion, both a public religion and his own private religion. With respect to the latter, Jefferson insisted that no one publish his letters, and that no one had the right to invade his private religious world. If politicians or clerics or journalists began to probe, they met with a stony silence. His religious opinions were his own, he repeatedly asserted, and no external pressures would pry them from him.

Nonetheless, Jefferson could never dismiss the subject of religion. It mesmerized him, enraged him, tantalized him, alarmed him, and sometimes inspired him. To friends and colleagues, he circulated his thoughts on religion widely, always cautioning that private letters be kept private. But from time to time he also appeared "on the record," as in his *Notes on the State of Virginia*, in his inaugural addresses, and most indelibly in his Statute for Establishing Religious Freedom. He spoke and he wrote on religion only when he chose to do so, but it is evident, especially in the surviving correspondence, that he often so chose. Religion was on his mind, on his heart, and throughout his life on both his private and his public agenda. Because this is happily the case, it is possible as well as appropriate to consider carefully the religious "side" of Thomas Jefferson.

Expressions of appreciation must first go to William B. Eerdmans Publishing Company, and especially to its Managing Editor, Charles Van Hof. No author could ask for a wiser or steadier hand. The editors of the series in which this volume appears have once again been wholly supportive. Mark A. Noll gave the manuscript a thorough and constructive reading, while Nathan O. Hatch has provided a gracious and thoughtful foreword. With his customary care and intelligent precision, Tim Straayer has guided the manuscript to its final form.

Colleagues in early American history have allowed themsevles to be exploited by agreeing to read the galleys (in one case the manuscript) and by offering their comments thereon. It is difficult to distinguish between professional courtesy and simple friendship; I have not tried to do so. One colleague, Sidney E. Mead, has not read the galleys, but only because he was not asked. With respect to Jefferson's religious ideas and their impact, nonagenarian Sidney has blazed many a trail.

Closer to home, my wife has again ("How long, O Lord, how long?") assisted all along the way. My older daughter, a development editor with another publisher, volunteered to rescue her father from numerous infelicities and/or stupidities. My debt to her is acknowledged elsewhere.

E. S. G.

1 The Anglican

> "The first settlers in this country [Virginia] were emigrants from England, of the English church, just at a point of time when it was flushed with complete victory over the religious of all other persuasions." (1787)

Jefferson's comments on Anglicanism, from his *Notes on the State of Virginia*, were penned two centuries after England's first colonial forays into the Western world and exactly 180 years after the first permanent English settlement in Jamestown. In the sixteenth century, King Henry VIII (who reigned from 1509 to 1547) led England's ecclesiastical establishment away from its organic connection with the papacy and Rome to an independent and specifically English institutional life. From an international church to a national one, the Church in England gradually became the Church of England, with Parliament supporting Henry in a series of laws that made this historic separation possible. The succeeding turbulent reigns of Edward VI (1547-53) and Mary I (1553-58) threatened this gradual evolution, but in the long rule of Elizabeth I (1558-1603) England's religious path seemed more surely and steadily laid out. Dissent was outlawed, Catholicism suppressed, papal protests ignored, and the queen installed as the earthly head of England's very own Church.

Especially after the defeat of the Spanish Armada in 1588, both England and her Church were "flushed with complete victory," a euphoria that would endure through the reign of James I (1603-25) and into the early years of Charles I. That victory fell apart in the 1640s and 1650s, not because of counterattacks by such papal powers as Spain and France, but as a result of growing political and religious unrest within England itself. The bloody English Civil War deposed Anglicanism from its throne, just as surely as it drove Charles from his. With the restoration of monarchy in 1660, however, the Anglican Church resumed its acccustomed place as the nation's official and favored religion. This seat of honor it maintained — in England — throughout the lifetime of Thomas Jefferson and well beyond.

THE CHURCH OF ENGLAND IN VIRGINIA

In Virginia, the Anglican Church enjoyed similar favor and legal support, though the Church (like the settlers themselves) suffered from the primitiveness of a western wilderness and the fluctuations of a fragile economy. Yet everything that law could do was done to ensure that (1) Anglicanism would be the formally established religion of the colony, and (2) all other forms of religion would be discouraged or driven out. Severe legislation passed in Jamestown in 1610 provided that all the people attend morning and evening prayer and that those who "shall often and willfully absent themselves" from divine services be punished according to the law: lose a day's provisions for the first offense, be whipped for the second, and for the third be condemned to the oceangoing galleys for six months. The young colony also dictated harsh penalties for those who took the name of God in vain, who spoke "impiously or maliciously against the holy and blessed Trinity," who behaved in an inappropriate manner toward any minister, or who committed any sacrilege against sacred objects within the parish church.

But it would take more than draconian laws to make the Anglican establishment in Virginia resemble that left behind in England. Legislative assemblies, year after year, labored to shore up the establishment by laying out parishes, setting salaries for ministers, ordering that a vestry of laymen ("the most sufficient and selected men") be chosen to direct the affairs of each parish, specifying a tax (in tobacco) to be paid by all landholders for the support of the Church, and so on. But compromises had to be made. Though the governance of England's Church depended upon the presence of a bishop, no bishop ever settled in colonial Virginia. As a consequence, the leading political figure, the governor, often assumed many of the duties and prerogatives normally associated with a bishop. As a missionary outpost, the Church in Virginia was loosely under the jurisdiction of the Bishop of London, who, however, never made his way to Virginia. Near the end of the seventeenth century, he did agree to appoint a representative or commissary who could, when the local clergy went along, exercise a few quite limited powers.

By the beginning of the eighteenth century, some seventy parishes had been formally laid out by the Assembly. But many of these lacked a church building or a minister, and some covered such a great territory — perhaps forty miles long and ten miles wide — as to render regular attendance at any divine service impractical. Nonetheless, the resident clergy struggled to make their own positions more secure and the establishment of the Anglican Church more reality than dream. By the middle of the eighteenth century, when Jefferson was a boy, the clergy sought to protect Anglicanism in Virginia by maintaining, insofar as possible, a monopoly on all religious services within the colony. Presbyterians, notably Samuel Davies, who had invaded the colony by that time, naturally resented and resisted the efforts to maintain that religious monopoly. Methodists (technically still within the Church of England at this time) and Baptists soon followed with their own list of resentments and began slowly building their own campaign of resistance.

A wave of revivalism in the 1740s and 1750s, often called the Great Awakening, expanded the challenge to the Anglican establishment as it brought ever more itinerant preachers into the colony. In 1739 a young Anglican from England, George Whitefield, set the pattern in Virginia as he preached in market-places and open fields, drawing huge crowds wherever he went: male and female, rich and poor, white and black, slave and free. Though himself an Anglican, Whitefield found readier accep-tance among the dissenters than within his own Church. He also found many imitators as other traveling or itinerant preachers drew crowds and critics — in roughly equal numbers.

Jefferson did not join the enthusiastic crowds, but neither did he participate in the chorus of critics. Indeed, he looked back upon this period in Virginia's history with no great pride, lamenting that "our minds were circumscribed within narrow limits." The majority of the citizens, Jefferson noted, were still so subordinate to the mother country that they observed "a bigoted intolerance for all religions but hers." When in the 1770s and 1780s Jefferson pressed for a full religious freedom in his native land, he found reason to be grateful that by that time so many Presbyterians, Methodists, and Baptists were on hand, ready to assist. They gave him (and James Madison) the popular support necessary to direct the legislative will.

Meanwhile, in 1751, five Anglican clergymen petitioned the House of Burgesses to do something about this non-Anglican "invasion." They complained about the "numerous assem-blies," some convened by "merely lay enthusiasts," at which "sundry fanatical books" were read and extemporaneous prayers and discourses offered, "sometimes by strolling pretended ministers." Samuel Davies was criticized for not being a real Presbyterian since he had been ejected from the Synod of Philadelphia, and another "pretended minister" was damned "by his strict intimacy with the Revd Mr Whitefield." Virginia was an Anglican colony, the five petitioners pointed out, and the legislature should see to it that this was true in fact and not just in name. Laws already on the books should be vigorously enforced

> to the end that all novel notions and perplexing uncertain doctrines and speculations, which tend to the subversion of true religion . . . , may be suitably check'd and discouraged; and that this Church of which we are all members . . . by all prudent and honorable means . . . be defended and supported.

The Virginia colony, the clergymen concluded, had "hitherto been remarkably happy for uniformity of religion." That uniformity should, in their firm opinion, be maintained in the 1750s with as much rigor as had been the case a century before.

Dissenters, for their part, protested that the intervening hundred years had introduced major changes in the British Empire, the most notable of which (from their point of view) was the Act of Toleration passed by Parliament in 1689. Did not Britain's Act of Toleration extend to all Britain's colonies? The answer seemed obvious to the dissenters, less obvious to some of the royal governors, hardly obvious at all to most of the Anglican clergy. If toleration were to be granted in Virginia, it would only be given slowly, carefully, begrudgingly. William Dawson, the Anglican commissary in Virginia in 1752, complained to the Bishop of London that Samuel Davies thought he should receive a license to preach anywhere at any time, rather than being restricted to a particular locale or specific churches. "Tho' we have licensed 7 houses," Dawson wrote, Davies and others still were not satisfied, and "they now most unreasonably apply for more. I think it is high time for the Government to interpose, to give their immodesty a check and to restrain their teachers within the bounds of a parish, lest their insolence should grow to a dangerous height." Should dissenting congregations still be unsatisfied, then "let the people go to [the Anglican] Church, whither they contentedly would have gone, if Mr Davies had never come among them."

By the middle of the eighteenth century, therefore, Virginia's "happy uniformity" in religion had begun to break down. Nevertheless, Anglicanism still dominated the colony, especially in the first-settled Tidewater region. There the "First Families of Virginia," who controlled most of the colony's political life, continued to defend and protect the Anglican establishment — so much so that in 1750 Anglican churches outnumbered all others combined, by a ratio of about three to one.

Such numerical dominance alone, however, does not tell the full story. Anglican parishes did more than conduct divine services. They supervised the distribution of charity, made provision for widows and orphans, kept records of births and deaths, enforced codes of moral behavior, and — in the office of church warden — kept an eye out for any delinquency in the payment of church taxes, faithful attendance at services, and strict conformity to the doctrines of the Church of England. Beyond all this, the vestry was responsible for the erection and maintenance of the church buildings themselves, taking that responsibility with a commendable seriousness that can still be appreciated in a visit to rural Virginia, centuries after the colonial period. Finally, the legislature provided each parish with glebe lands the agricultural harvest of which could be used for the further support of the church and its ministry. After the Revolution, the disposition of these lands posed a major legal problem.

The service of worship itself followed closely the prescriptions set down in the *Book of Common Prayer*, which reached a stable form in 1662. Appropriate prayer and biblical passages were indicated for the entire year, as the ecclesiastical calendar was faithfully followed. Innovation was limited largely to the minister's sermon or homily, often delivered from a raised pulpit that enabled the congregation better to see and hear its appointed messenger. Social contacts before and after the worship hour added more in the way of innovation and interest, especially since the population was so widely scattered and the absence of major towns offered little in the way of alternative gathering places. One observer, writing just prior to the Revolution, noted that before services, members of the congregation busied themselves in "giving & receiving letters of business, reading advertisements, consulting about the price of tobacco, grain &c., & settling either the lineage, age or qualities of favorite horses." Similarly, "after Service is over three quarters of an hour [is] spent in strolling round the Church among the crowd."

At the time of Jefferson's birth in 1743, Anglicanism was therefore built into the very structure of life for most Virginians; indeed, the parish church determined much of that structure, especially at such crucial junctures as birth, puberty, marriage, and death. Because plantation homes were sometimes more accessible and often more commodious than the rural churches, services that in England would always have been held in the church were in Virginia frequently held in the home. These services — a marriage, for example — were no less religious: the line between church and home may have blurred, but not the line between sacred and secular.

THOMAS JEFFERSON AS YOUNG ANGLICAN

No record survives of Jefferson's baptism, though its occurrence, whether in church or home, may be readily assumed. Thomas Jefferson did not enter the world as a protester against the Anglican establishment; he entered it as a member of a family that assumed its appropriate social position in the colony's legally approved Church. His father, Peter Jefferson, was a vestryman in the Fredericksville parish, this having been laid out in the year before Thomas was born. Two clergymen were present at Thomas Jefferson's marriage to Martha Skelton Wayles on New Year's Day, 1772. His children were no doubt baptized in due course, for such ceremony required no public profession of faith on the part of the parents. Godparents did have to make such a formal declaration, however, which prompted Jefferson to decline the honor. As he wrote to a French friend in 1788 in response to the friend's request, "The person who becomes sponsor for a child, according to the ritual of the church in which I was educated, makes a solemn profession before God and the world, of faith in the articles, which I had never sense enough to comprehend, and it has always appeared to me that comprehension must precede assent."

This Anglican ambience that surrounded Jefferson was nowhere more evident than in his early education. He repeatedly found himself in the hands of Anglican clergymen, first at the age of nine with the Reverend William Douglas for five years and then at the age of fourteen with the Reverend James Maury for two years. And when, at seventeen, he entered college, it was to study once again with Anglican clergymen.

Jefferson's five years under the tutelage of William Douglas, 1752-57, were not especially happy ones. He was obliged to board away from home with the Douglas family, and though home at Shadwell was only twelve miles away, it was too distant to make a daily trek either by foot or on horseback. The homesickness of a nine- or ten-year-old boy was mitigated to a degree by regular returns on the weekends to a family of five sisters, a somewhat distant mother, and a father often absent in connection with his surveying responsibilities. The presence of an uninspired teacher further dimmed this joyless five-year period. Jefferson later recalled that his introduction to French began at this time, as well as some clumsy instruction in the "rudiments" of Latin and Greek. Douglas's Latin was "superficial" and his Greek even worse, Jefferson glumly reported. All this came to an end in 1757, when Jefferson lost his father and gained a new teacher.

Peter Jefferson's death, when Thomas was fourteen years

old, left the latter bewildered and desolate. Yet his path had been laid out for him by a father who was determined that his son would receive the classical education that had been denied to him. Also, as local surveyor and county magistrate as well as vestryman, the father pointed the son in the direction of social responsibility and steady development. As eldest son (a younger brother had now been born), Thomas moreover enjoyed the benefits of primogeniture — a privilege granted to the firstborn male that a mature Jefferson would argue against. Two-thirds of Peter Jefferson's seventy-five hundred acres, in and around Albemarle County, eventually passed to the eldest son. Later in life, Thomas Jefferson paid tribute to his father for having ensured to him a classical education, "a sublime luxury." "I thank on my knees," he wrote, "him who directed my early education for having put into my possession this rich source of delight."

That rich source became infinitely richer under the tutelage of James Maury, "a correct classical scholar," Jefferson reported. No more rudiments of Latin and Greek, but now the refinements and the sheer joy. Maury, a graduate of the College of William and Mary, had to return to England for his ordination, since no bishop resided in Virginia. Commissary James Blair in 1742 wrote from Virginia's capital, Williamsburg, to the Bishop of London to recommend that ordination be granted to the twenty-four-year-old Maury, whom he described as "an ingenious young man" of Huguenot parentage. At college, Maury "gave a bright example of diligence in his studies, and of good behavior as to his morals. He has made good proficiency in the study of Latin and Greek authors & has read some systems of philosophy and divinity." While Blair thought that Maury should perhaps have done more with the latter, his skills with the former won Jefferson to his side.

After his ordination in London, Maury returned first to King William parish, then in 1758 to Fredericksville, where he, like his predecessor, opened a school for young boys to help support his large and growing family. In the small school,

9

Jefferson formed lasting friendships with four other boys; and in the Maury home, he saw for the first time what a library might look like as the Anglican divine freely shared some of his four hundred volumes with the budding scholars. In a letter written soon after Jefferson and his fellows departed his care, James Maury revealed something of his own philosophy of education. The classical languages, as one would expect, rank high, but not for all white male Virginians — only for those headed for one of the professions. Greek and Latin were "necessary, absolutely necessary, for those who wish to make any reputable figure in Divinity, Medicine, or Law." Geography and history, along with "at least a general knowledge of the laws," would be essential to all those called upon to administer justice at any level or who might be asked "to bear a part in the weighty business of legislation."

Maury also had good words for developing the scholar's memory, but not in memorizing idle rules or clever puzzles. History was valuable here as well, for nothing was "better calculated at once to exercise [the young students'] memories & enrich their understandings than neat, plain, succinct, affecting narration." Besides all that, the Anglican divine asked, what intellectual exercise is better suited to "entertaining the fancy, strengthening the judgment, forming the taste, fixing the morals, & mending the heart, than the study of history?" When the more mature Jefferson would start building a library of his own — to contain far more than four hundred volumes — not surprisingly, history would constitute a significant portion of the vast collection.

The Maury years, in contrast to the Douglas years, were happy ones for the young Jefferson. His course of study included the Bible, thus laying a foundation for what became a lifelong, if highly individualistic, interest. His intellectual horizons had been stretched, his love for learning had been awakened, his thirst to know something of a wider world had been stimulated. Yet now again to an Anglican world he rather routinely turned — namely, the College of William and Mary

10

in Williamsburg. A young neighbor to whom he would later become quite close, James Madison, selected the Presbyterian College of New Jersey in Princeton. But Jefferson, experiencing no great discomfort in his all-encompassing Anglican environment, chose William and Mary.

Founded in 1693, the second oldest after Harvard, this Anglican college did not grow steadily from strength to strength as the Massachusetts school managed to do. With a faculty of only seven when Jefferson enrolled in 1760, the college, because of its Anglicanism, suffered a loss of popularity during the American Revolution. Some decades after the Revolution, it suffered further when Jefferson created the University of Virginia, destined to become the state's major educational institution. The agonies of the Civil War and its aftermath in the South kept William and Mary in a weakened, almost moribund condition, so that in the twentieth century a still small and financially weak college became part of the state system of public education.

None of this claimed the attention, of course, of the young Jefferson. What did claim his attention and that of all others enrolled in 1760 (fewer than one hundred) was the clearly Anglican character of the institution. Of the seven faculty, all but one were Anglican clergymen. The president of the college served also as the rector of the Bruton Parish Church, a block or two away. The Statutes of 1727 made the religious character of the school explicit:

> For avoiding the danger of heresy, schism, and disloyalty, let the president and masters, before they enter upon these offices, give their assent to the articles of the Christian faith, in the same manner, and in the same words, as the ministers of England by act of Parliament are obliged to sign the [Thirty-nine] Articles of the Church of England.

These Statutes also spelled out the structure of the college, divided into four schools. First, the Grammar School had the charge of preparing boys for admission to the college. Jefferson,

11

because of his earlier preparation near Charlottesville, could bypass this entity. Second, the Philosophy School, where Jefferson was enrolled for two years, offered the basic liberal arts curriculum of the time: rhetoric, logic, ethics, physics, metaphysics, and mathematics. The legislation of 1727 dared to suggest that it might even be time to move beyond the bounds of Aristotelian thought, which reigned supreme in the later Middle Ages. Third, the Divinity School had responsibility for one of the major purposes of the College — namely, that Virginia "should be supplied with good ministers after the doctrine and government of the Church of England." Fourth and finally, the Indian School represented the hope that never became a reality — that "the Indians of America should be instructed in the Christian religion, and that some of the Indian youth that are well-behaved and well-inclined, being first well prepared in the divinity school, may be sent out to preach the gospel to their countrymen in their own tongue." In general, the Philosophy School had a better record than the others in the 1750s and 1760s in approaching the high purposes spelled out a generation before.

Thomas Jefferson, though in an Anglican cocoon, was about to emerge from his chrysalis to soar freely and widely over an inviting world. The college itself enlarged his experiences and broadened his sympathies, as indeed a college education in any age or place should do. In 1763, soon after his twentieth birthday, he wrote to his boyhood friend John Page in a way that indicated that this education had begun to take hold. Anglicanism provided the initial layer of learning, but Stoicism and Epicureanism had so soon made their influence felt as well. Perfect happiness will likely always elude us, Jefferson told Page, and calamities will inevitably befall. Since one cannot avoid all of life's pitfalls, the next best step is to prepare oneself for them by "a perfect resignation to the divine will." To best "surmount the difficulties thrown in our way," one should "proceed with a pious and unshaken resignation till we arrive at our journey's end." A youthful Jefferson already reflected on questions that far older men wrestled with, especially as they approached their "journey's end."

If the college broadened its young student, so did the modest cultural center of Williamsburg. In the public times of spring and fall, the town swelled in population from about 1,500 to twice that number, and it then teemed with political activity and gossip. From the school to the capitol, a mere mile away on the Duke of Gloucester Street, Jefferson passed by the the Bruton Parish Church, the home of a favorite professor, Raleigh's Tavern, the Governor's Palace, and other centers of intellectual bustle and challenge. As will be evident in Chapter 2, the mind of Jefferson now began to scan and probe and ponder in ways hardly anticipated by family, tutors, or friends.

A PERSISTING ANGLICANISM

Yet the Anglican heritage was never totally cast off. Jefferson faithfully recorded family births, deaths, and marriages in his father's prayer book. He not only attended services near his home but also contributed regularly and generously to the support of St. Anne's Church in Charlottesville. After his marriage, his relationship with the rector of St. Anne's, Charles Clay, was more than casual; his account book in 1774 indicated that he sold two of his bookcases to Clay, but deducted forty shillings for the pastor's "performing the funeral service this day on burying my sister, Elizabeth." (Well into the nineteenth century, he carried on a candid correspondence with Clay, who ceased being an Anglican rector but never ceased being a friend.) Three years later, after the abrupt disestablishment of the Anglican Church in Virginia, Jefferson contributed six pounds, more by far than any other parishioner, to the support of St. Anne's. He was also elected vestryman, a recognition not so much of his piety as of his social position in the community. And when Jefferson died, an Anglican clergyman, Frederick Hatch, officiated at his funeral; by that time, repeating the pattern that Jefferson had known so well, Hatch had become tutor to the patriarch's grandsons.

Jefferson's loyalty to Anglicanism at the parish level did not imply any intolerant rejection of other modes of worship. On the contrary, as he noted in 1822 concerning his own town of Charlottesville, "The court house is our common temple. Here Episcopalian and Presbyterian, Methodist and Baptist, meet together, join in hymning their Maker, listen with attention and devotion to each other's preachers and all mix in society in perfect harmony." The "perfect harmony," if indeed such existed, Jefferson would unhesitatingly attribute to the fact that by the 1820s no denomination in Virginia had legal leverage over any other. And Jefferson knew that such a state of affairs had come about through neither inertia nor accident.

The ritual of the Anglican (later Episcopal) tradition kept Jefferson attuned with the familiar patterns of his family and the Virginia gentry of which he was unquestionably a part. At times, as when dealing with the haunting question of slavery, he seemed tempted to turn his back on that gentry, but in the end he failed to do so. He was a Virginian: it was his "country." He was a farmer and a slaveholder: it was his patrimony. He was an Anglican and loyal son of the community: such was his solemn duty.

Jefferson's Anglicanism related to the externals of religion: liturgy, morality, and neighborly congeniality. This created no consternation, however, for the Anglican Church itself in eighteenth-century Virginia dealt more with activity than doctrine. Proper behavior, not born-again "enthusiasm," guaranteed one's acceptability to and continued membership in the gentry. Dissenters scoffed at this Anglican preoccupation with the froth of religion rather than its substance. Presbyterian James Reid confessed he would have nothing to do with Anglican services for the following reasons:

> First, I am no merchant, planter, horse jockey, nor money-catching fellow, & consequently have nothing to sell.

Secondly, I have (unluckily) no skill in horses, hogs, cocks, dogs, or gaming; therefore, my company in a church yard before or after divine service must be extremely ridiculous. Thirdly, I have a rational aversion [to] barbecues, and therefore need not go to church to hear the news of any.

This was satire, to be sure, but it contained enough truth to exempt Jefferson and other Virginia Anglicans from being subjected to any Sunday morning testing of doctrinal orthodoxy.

For in the realm of religious ideas, he would not be restrained, nor would he be obedient to any specified intellectual tradition. He would not trouble himself to quarrel with the ceremonial function of speech or the ritual function of religion. These were part of the civility that made any society, certainly any neighborhood, livable and perhaps even enjoyable. But friends did not subject other friends to a searchlight of inquisition or interrogation. Nor did friends impose on other friends a requirement that there be conformity to one's own creed or convictions. Catechisms were for children. The mature individual, while continuing his intellectual or spiritual search, could laugh or love or weep or pray as a mere mortal, finite and fallible, conforming where appropriate, dissenting where not.

In a quite limited sense, Jefferson began life as an Anglican and ended it the same way. That limited sense meant that he could and he did avail himself of the Church's rituals as any respected member of the Virginia gentry would do. On the other hand, the doctrines of the Church of England did not intrude upon or in any way limit the operations of the mature Jeffersonian mind. Furthermore, within a decade of the adoption of the Declaration of Independence, Jefferson had taken another strong and un-Anglican step: he stripped his own Church of any lingering power, in the name of religion, to afflict the bodies or the minds of his fellow citizens.

2 Student of the Enlightenment

"Your own reason is the only oracle given you by heaven." (1787)

LOVE OF LEARNING — AND BOOKS

When he entered the College of William and Mary in 1760, "it was my great good fortune," Thomas Jefferson later wrote, "and what probably fixed the destinies of my life, that Dr. William Small of Scotland was then Professor of Mathematics." But William Small, the only faculty member who was not an Anglican clergyman, taught much more than mathematics; indeed, the whole European intellectual ferment seemed grist for his mental mill. When he was appointed temporarily to fill the philosophical chair, he offered lectures on ethics, rhetoric, and belles lettres — the first in the college, Jefferson noted, ever to do so. With a "happy talent of communication" as well as "an enlarged and liberal mind," Small struck the young Jefferson as the ideal college professor.

More than that, however, he became an ideal friend. "Most happily for me," Jefferson wrote in his autobiography, Small soon grew "attached to me, and made me his daily companion when not engaged in the school; and from his conversation I got my first views of the expansion of science, and of the system of things in which we are placed." In other words, Jefferson was introduced to the Enlightenment with all the excitement of a Baconian revolution in logic and method, a Newtonian revolution in science and mathematical calculation, and a Lockean revolution in politics, philosophy, and religion. Other personages from France and Scotland would soon, by way of books, become intellectual companions as well, companions that Jefferson would revel in and return to for the rest of his life.

Before Small returned to Scotland, he rendered two other invaluable favors to Jefferson: he introduced his young student to Virginia's royal lieutenant governor, Francis Fauquier, "the ablest man who had ever filled that office," and he persuaded another faculty member, George Wythe, to become Jefferson's tutor in his chosen profession of law. "Mr. Wythe continued to be my faithful and beloved mentor in youth, and my most affectionate friend through life," Jefferson testified. As long as Small remained at the college, these four — Fauquier, Wythe, Small, and a teenage Jefferson — constituted their own private European-style salon. In addition to the conversation, as informative as it was refreshing, the "salon" occasionally provided music, with Jefferson on the violin, or perhaps cello, and others invited in to assist with harpsichord, flute, and an extra violin. "To these habitual conversations on these occasions, I owed much instruction," Jefferson reported. At this stage of his maturing, the life of the mind had in earnest now begun.

After his two years at the college, Jefferson continued to "read" law under the direction of George Wythe, though he did much of that reading back home. When he turned twenty-one, he found it necessary to spend some time in supervising the large estate that now came fully into his possession. But he continued to read in law, this system of apprenticeship being the only means of legal education available in eighteenth-century America. The morning hours he generally reserved for working his way through the difficult *Commentaries* of Sir Edward Coke, with afternoon and evening hours kept free for a wider range of subjects. When he borrowed books, he took elaborate notes and recorded them in his journals or his Literary Commonplace Book, a record he began when fifteen years of age. When he bought books, he made elaborate annotations in the margins and at the bottom of the pages.

When he was still in his twenties, the family home, Shadwell, burned, destroying the first library that Jefferson had managed to compile — a collection that he appraised at about £200. "Would to God it had been the money" rather than the books, he wrote to a friend in 1770; "then had it never cost me a sigh." But he began rebuilding immediately, writing abroad and keeping an eye out at home for books of deceased plantation owners that might be put up for sale. When Jefferson was twenty-eight years old, he had already acquired a reputation as a bibliophile, sufficient to prompt his brother-in-law, Robert Skipwith, to ask for recommendations for an ideal library costing about £30. Jefferson could not hold himself down to that paltry sum, but suggested a beginner's library of around 150 titles. He noted, however, that one could always begin with a few volumes at a time. Meanwhile, he continued to buy, in large quantities, and to read hungrily as each packet of books was deposited at his steps.

When Jefferson went abroad as an emissary to France in 1785, the opportunities for book buying marvelously multiplied. Reading readily in French, Jefferson "devoted every afternoon I was disengaged for a summer or two in examining all the principal bookstores, turning every book with my own hand and putting by everything which related to America, and indeed whatever was rare and valuable in every science."

"Whatever was rare and valuable in every science" — so speaks the true student of the Enlightenment. Now that he had access to so many books, and at far better prices than obtained in Virginia, Jefferson even volunteered to collect books for others: for James Madison, Benjamin Franklin, the College of Philadelphia, and William and Mary.

In 1784 Jefferson informed Madison that he had already acquired a good many books for him, stimulated to do so "by the combined circumstances of their utility and cheapness." But he urged Madison to send him a catalogue of the books that he would like. Madison responded with appreciation, assuring Jefferson that "all the purchases you have made for me are such as I would have made for myself with the same opportunities." He feared that any "catalogue" he might send would trouble Jefferson beyond the bounds of friendship, but, with an intellectual appetite equivalent to Jefferson's, he could not resist requesting a thirteen-volume dictionary, Pascal's *Provincial Letters*, a travel book on China, the historians of the Roman Empire, and whatever more from the pen of Comte Buffon might be available. "Of Buffon I have his original work of 31 vol., 10 vol. of Supplement, and 16 vol. on birds. I shall be glad of the continuation as it may from time to time be published." Two years before a Constitutional Convention that he did not then know would ever come to pass, Madison also requested all treatises on the ancient or modern federal republics, "on the law of nations, and the history natural and political of the New World."

Besides haunting the bookstalls in Paris, "I had standing orders," Jefferson wrote, "during the whole time I was in Europe on its principal book-marts, particularly Amsterdam, Frankfort, Madrid, and London." By the time he sold his books to the government in 1815 to launch the Library of Congress, he estimated his collection to be between nine and ten thousand volumes, adding that "nearly the whole are well bound, abundance of them elegantly, and of the choicest editions existing."

THE NOBLE TRINITY

Jefferson was a remarkable collector but an even more remarkable and voracious reader of these thousands of volumes. He absorbed the governing ideas of the European Enlightenment with the result that he emerged as a powerful instrument in forwarding the American Enlightenment. His trinity of English heroes (whose busts can still be seen by today's visitor to Monticello) included Francis Bacon (1561-1626), John Locke (1632-1704), and Isaac Newton (1642-1727). From Bacon he learned to slough off the shackles of Aristotle's science along with its deductive methods and replace these with a new science that turned to experience and induction; not the past but the future would reveal truth. "A way must be opened," Bacon wrote in his preface to *The Great Instauration*, "for the human understanding entirely different from any hitherto known." Experience and reason had been too long separated from each other, Bacon argued, and he believed that his contribution lay in bringing them together once again. "I suppose that I have established forever a true and lawful marriage between the empirical and the rational faculty." The "ill-starred divorce" between the two had thrown "into confusion all the affairs of the human family." The time to rebuild, from the ground up, had arrived. Bacon's *Novum Organum* (1620), replacing Aristotle's obsolete system of knowledge, would make that rebuilding possible.

Jefferson turned to John Locke again and again, as did the generation of which he was a part. From Locke he learned that truths did not descend from the heavens into human affairs, nor were individuals born with the knowledge necessary to cope with or shape their changing world. Truth was not freely given; it had to be learned, and earned — won through experiment and experience. So much for Locke's theory of knowledge, but he had more to offer. In his *Treatises on Civil Government*, written in the 1680s, Locke dismissed the notion of a divine right of kings and described, in detail, the state of nature wherein liberty and equality originally prevailed. By contract one surrendered a fragment of liberty in order to secure a just and limited government. Such a government could not bestow rights already present in nature, but only respect and preserve them. And in Locke's *Letter concerning Toleration*, written in the same decade, Jefferson found sentiments he would appropriate as his own. For example, "I esteem it above all things necessary," Locke wrote, "to distinguish exactly the business of civil government from that of religion, and to settle the just bounds that lie between the one and the other." And, "Neither the right nor the art of ruling does necessarily carry along with it the certain knowledge of other things, and least of all of true religion."

Isaac Newton taught Jefferson that God's world was orderly, dependable, regular, predictable. In his *Principia* (1687), the whole Western world learned that patient observation and careful mathematical calculation could reveal previously unknown truths about the nature of the universe. Planets did not "wander," but moved according to specific laws; like all matter in motion, they proceeded not by chance but by design. England's "greatest and rarest genius" (in David Hume's words) placed science firmly in the center of the modern world; indeed, Newton helped create the modern world. With acclaim pouring upon him from all directions, Newton modestly murmured that he was no genius; he merely possessed a capacity for "industry and patient thought." So did his many American disciples, not least among them Thomas Jefferson.

From Bacon, Locke, and Newton, Jefferson learned to count, collect, explore, measure, observe, arrange, invent, and put his trust in the perceptions of the present rather than in the precedents from the distant past. Jefferson never sought to pass himself off as a scientist, but he developed the virtues of that profession — not as an onerous task but as a labor of love. Politics, he noted, was his "duty," science his "passion." Beyond the intrinsic delights that it offered, science represented

21

to Jefferson the key to the future, the means to an emancipation from myths and mysteries, from institutions that cramped and bound, from modes of living or of thinking that no longer served a modern — that is to say, a scientific — world. He cultivated the friendship of doctors, astronomers, mathematicians, and inventors. His election to the presidency of the American Philosophical Society in 1797 came not in recognition of his high office as vice president of the United States but in acknowledgment of his unquestioned stature as science's most ardent amateur.

RELIGION AND THE EUROPEAN ENLIGHTENMENT

Somewhat below the higher elevations where Bacon, Locke, and Newton dwelled, other English thinkers engaged the attention of the public — and of Thomas Jefferson. These individuals questioned what for so long had been immune to questions. If the old rules and prescriptions no longer applied, then how did one define or enforce virtue? If reason and experience alone become one's authority and guide, then what were the implications for biblical revelation? for doctrinal orthodoxy? for ecclesiastical authority? And if God spoke to humankind mainly or even exclusively through the medium of nature, what did nature tell us about that God? about his eternal truths? about the nature and destiny of women and men?

Answers to a good many of these questions Jefferson found in the voluminous writings of Henry St. John, Viscount Bolingbroke (1678-1751). In the notebooks of his reading in the 1760s, Jefferson — his opinions still being molded — copied over ten thousand of Bolingbroke's words, more than from any other single source. He also recommended to his brother-in-law that five volumes of Bolingbroke's "Philosophical Works" be purchased for that beginning collection. (Jefferson had ten volumes in his own library.) Here Jefferson read that Christianity had traditionally rested not upon reason or experience

22

but upon mystery and miracle. The Bible, moreover, portrayed a deity quite different from that revealed in nature, a deity that reason could neither explain nor defend. How rational could it possibly be for the God of the whole universe to reveal himself solely to one small nation in the eastern Mediterranean and to leave the rest of the world in utter ignorance of his existence? It seemed even more irrational to believe that the Supreme Being of the cosmos had "sent his only begotten son, who had not offended him, to be sacrificed by men, who had offended him, that he might expiate their sins, and satisfy his own anger." And in his youth, Jefferson read and copied Bolingbroke's impatient dismissal of the absurdities of religious persecution. In England, "men have been burned under one reign, for the very same doctrines they were obliged to profess in another." Much later in life, Jefferson confessed to John Adams that he had read Bolingbroke first as a young man, and no fewer than five times since.

Jefferson also read, copied, and absorbed much from Anthony Ashley Cooper, third earl of Shaftesbury (1671-1713). In the latter's *Characteristicks of Men, Manners, Opinions, Times*, first published in 1711, Shaftesbury rhapsodized about the beauty and benevolence of nature, "All loving and All-lovely, All-divine." No other deity was required. But what about creeds and catechisms, commandments and prohibitions? If the walls around institutional religion crumbled and fell, then what happened to morality and a decent social order? One need not be anxious, Shaftesbury said, because men and women had within themselves an innate moral sense. Let all persons be loyal to their good instincts, follow their good tastes, be wholly correct in their good manners. Nature's pure and simple morality would come through. That would happen, however, only if all the accumulated rubbish of superstition and dogma were cleared from the path. In order to follow where nature led, humankind would first have to be free. The royal road to virtue thus turned out to be liberty, not conformity.

Jefferson also learned from, even as in his Commonplace

23

Book he argued with, such leading English deists as John Toland (1670-1722) and Matthew Tindal (1657-1733). The explicit application of Enlightenment ideas to the realm of religion undertaken by these men and others, generally designated by the name of deism, resulted in a religion deduced not from Scripture or the theologians but from reason and nature. A disciple of John Locke, but moving well beyond him in his religious conclusions, John Toland in 1696 published *Christianity Not Mysterious*, his title bearing the thrust of his argument. Christianity had previously been defended in terms of mystery; this fact alone made it unappealing, even obnoxious, to an enlightened age. If only it could be demonstrated that Christianity was a reasonable religion — yes, even a natural religion — then it would have a chance once more to hold its own in the marketplace of new and exciting ideas. Toland did not reject revelation outright, but he would not admit anything in revelation contrary to reason. If revelation on occasion went beyond reason, that might be allowed. But this moderate position would itself soon fall before additional deist pruning and probing.

In 1730, thirteen years before Jefferson was born, Matthew Tindal published a work even more widely read than Toland's. In *Christianity as Old as Creation*, Tindal not only found revelation unnecessary and miracles unbelievable but he saw religion as functionally equivalent to morality. True religion, he asserted, consisted "in a constant disposition of mind to do all the good we can, and thereby render ourselves acceptable to God in answering the end of our creation." Benevolence was both the highest duty of man and the governing attribute of God. To suppose that God can behave in any other than a benevolent way was to dishonor him and blaspheme his name. His almighty power and wisdom would then "degenerate into cruelty and craft." Reason of itself brought us to a recognition of universal love and kindness as the highest duty of all persons, Tindal wrote; such a "religious duty" needed no revelation to tell us of it, nor did it require barking priests to frighten us into craven obedience to that divine duty.

24

Jefferson gathered many other writers of similar sentiment into his library or jotted their musings in his notebooks:
Thomas Chubb, Charles Blount, Thomas Hobbes, Bernard
Mandeville, Conyers Middleton, Pierre Bayle, Montesquieu,
and more. All of these persons wrote before Jefferson entered
the College of William and Mary, so their names were known,
respected, and recommended by William Small and others to
their eager young student. Their books stood on faculty shelves,
and perhaps on those of Lieutenant Governor Francis Fauquier
also. Other Europeans, more nearly contemporary with Jefferson, would augment and reinforce ideas with which Jefferson's
mental compartment had already been partly furnished: French
names such as Diderot, Voltaire, and Volney; English names
such as Price and Priestley; Scottish names such as Hume,
Hutcheson, Kames, and Reid. These thinkers would continue
the intellectual and theological dialogue so early and so power-
fully begun.

Jefferson would soon join their ranks as a *philosophe* —
that is, not a professional philosopher but a "free-thinker" who
moved well beyond the bounds of traditional philosophy,
politics, and religion. From any country and from any period,
he would gather ideas as a reaper gathered corn, selecting and
retaining the most delectable, ignoring or discarding what he
regarded as unsuitable to his taste. Many of Jefferson's fellow
deists found English and Scottish thinkers more congenial, less
radical, less unnerving than those of France. But Jefferson
reaped there too.

The French philosophes took the academic dialogue out
of the salons and classrooms and into the streets, where
peasants no less than nobles could hear of "liberty" and "equality" and "fraternity." To the French, liberty meant chiefly an
emancipation from the twin forces of tyranny — in religion, the
Roman Catholic Church; and in politics, the Bourbon monarchy. Considering both beyond the reach of reform, many
French intellectuals found atheism rather than deism the more
attractive alternative to orthodoxy. If religion could not be

amended, then it must be wholly rejected. Similarly, terror might be the only option remaining when confronted by a tyranny so long imposed and so deeply entrenched. Some of the French took little comfort in this uncompromising radicalism. A leading conversationalist in the fashionable French salons, Madame Du Deffand, gave expression to the pervading disillusionment: "All conditions and all circumstances seem equally unfortunate to me, from the angel to the oyster. The grievous thing is to be born."

Jefferson's response could not have been more different. It was a most exciting time to be born when, especially in America, one had the unique opportunity to liberate minds, refashion the arts, establish freedoms, delve deeply into nature, reform religion, universalize education, and defeat tyranny everywhere. Enlightenment ideas from anywhere would flow freely and fully into Jefferson, and through him — modified or magnified — they would help reshape the contours of a new land.

REASON AND THE AMERICAN ENLIGHTENMENT

In 1787, Thomas Jefferson wrote from Paris to his young nephew Peter Carr, then enrolled in the College of William and Mary. Jefferson first congratulated him on having won the attention and goodwill of George Wythe, adding: "I am sure you will find this to have been one of the most fortunate events of your life, as I have ever been sensible it was of mine." Jefferson, now the more experienced uncle, advised Peter on a course of study (subject to Wythe's approval or correction) as well as, naturally, a list of books, with the suggestion that Carr send to Paris a catalogue of books that he might need within the next year and a half. Besides giving recommendations on foreign language (Spanish was preferred over Italian because of America's proximity to New Spain), Jefferson advised young Carr mostly on the subjects of religion and moral philosophy.

With respect to religion, Jefferson's advice was far more detailed than on any other question. The young man was counseled to submit all religious matters to the rigorous test of reason: "Fix reason firmly in her seat, and call to her tribunal every fact, every opinion." Carr should question even the existence of God, Jefferson wrote, because if such a being existed, he would "certainly more approve the homage of reason than of blindfolded fear." Some opinions were popular, some unpopular, but their relative popularity should count for nothing: all should be carefully scrutinized and impartially judged before you, dear nephew, make up your mind. "Your own reason is the only oracle given you by heaven, and you are answerable not for the rightness but uprightness of the decision."

If the Enlightenment was, perhaps too readily, also called the Age of Reason, one must understand what kind of reason met the philosophe's test and what kind failed. John Adams impatiently dismissed the "age of reason" label, but it has stuck nonetheless, owing in no small part to Thomas Paine's use of the phrase for the title for his two-volume slashing attack on revealed religion. And Jefferson, as noted in the letter to his nephew, was likewise ready to acclaim and rely on noble Reason — often capitalized in the eighteenth century, as it will henceforth be here whenever the word is intended to carry all of the heavy freight that the Enlightenment imposed upon it.

As the savants of the eighteenth century employed the term, Reason carried an expansive as well as a restricted meaning. The Reason of the philosophes would not be recognizable to Plato or Augustine, to Aquinas or Calvin. For Jefferson and his peers, Reason referred only to the operation of the mind upon data, with the result sifted through the senses; it arrived at truths, or dismissed errors, based upon the clear and fully persuasive testimony of experience. Such reasoning was not *a priori*, but *a posteriori* — that is, one did not begin with assumptions or innate ideas, with abstract and speculative systems, but on the contrary one began with the hard data of experience, with that which could be measured, counted, observed, and weighed. Ordinary experience, common sense, yielded truth. Metaphysical systems and grand assumptions, such as those found in Plato, yielded only whimsies, fancies, and fog. Plato spun a whole heavenly assembly of Archetypes and Eternal Forms out of his imagination; they had no grounding in either human experience or common sense. Since he had no knowledge of the methods of Bacon or the empiricism of Locke or the "patient thought" of Newton, Plato did not, could not, arrive at truth. Therefore, he and all other web-spinning metaphysicians must be dismissed.

If Reason was thus narrowed, it was also widened to become the principal channel of truth: Reason was the "only oracle." What, then, of biblical revelation? If the philosophes were hard on those who followed metaphysics, they came down even harder on those who relied on revelation. The whole notion that God spoke to people in a human language (as opposed to his own language — i.e., nature) was absurd. But even if such a thing had once upon a time happened, the vagaries of centuries of translation and transmission had left the contemporary reader of the Bible with imperfect texts, meaningless phrases, corrupted manuscripts. If, moreover, the very idea was ridiculous, the final and tangible result was even worse: tales of superstition and magic, of a jealous and vengeful deity, of deplorable ethical standards, and of embarrassing theological notions. For the student of the Enlightenment, revelation was not an avenue to truth but a roadblock thrown across every promising pathway to new understandings and scientific discoveries. Revelation did not emancipate the mind; it cramped, starved, twisted, and eroded the mental capacities of all humankind. People arrived at truth not through the cloudy and corrupted medium of revelation but through the clear and clean oracle of Reason.

If Jefferson's advice to young Peter Carr sounded radical, it only rang one of the permeating themes of the Enlightenment and of Jefferson's adult life. He would even see this overriding

28

loyalty to Reason as a religious obligation. "For the use of reason," he noted, "everyone is responsible to the God who planted it in his breast, as a light for his guidance." In a letter to Jefferson, John Adams shared with him his high view of reason, his low view of revelation. "The human understanding," Adams wrote, was "a revelation from its Maker which can never be disputed or doubted." Moreover, this "revelation" required no miracles to support it, no prophecies to commend it. "Miracles or prophecies might frighten us out of wits, might scare us to death, might induce us to lie," but they could never convince us of an absurdity that our Reason denied.

When he drew up that library list for his brother-in-law, Jefferson at the age of twenty-eight already revealed an intimate familiarity with the major thinkers of the "new age." He strongly recommended the reading of all the works of Voltaire, all the essays (in four volumes) of Hume, and — the most expensive item on his list — the entire *Dictionnaire Historique et Critique* of Pierre Bayle in five folio volumes. These authorities likewise sang the praises and virtues of Reason, even if some of them pushed the rational faculties further than Jefferson would have wished. Voltaire, for example, saw Reason as the defining characteristic of the human condition: "God has given us a principle of universal reason, as he has given feathers to birds and fur to bears." Moreover, Reason "subsists despite all the passions [of priests and tyrants] which struggle against it." Hume applied reason, uncapitalized in his case, with such vigor as to dismiss not only Christian miracles but a great deal else. And Bayle found his chief delight in poking irreparable holes in prevailing superstitions and irrational fanaticisms.

In America, Ethan Allen of Vermont even anticipated the Jeffersonian phrase when he published *Reason the Only Oracle of Man* in 1784. It is true, Allen acknowledged, that Scripture implied that "none by searching can find out God" (Job 11:7), but "I am persuaded that if mankind would dare to exercise their reason as freely on those divine topics as they do in the common concerns of life, they would, in a great measure, rid themselves of their blindness and superstition." At the same time, such persons, employing their unhindered Reason, "would gain more exalted ideas of God and their obligations to him and one another." They would also more fully appreciate God's moral government and become more proficient in their own practice of morality, "which is the last and greatest perfection that human nature is capable of."

Those who talked about the depravity of human nature unfortunately included human Reason in that condemnation. Ethan Allen regarded this as a most tragic and costly error for the whole human race. If we ever concede Reason to be depraved or spoiled, Allen warned, we then "overturn knowledge and science, and render learning, instruction and books useless and impertinent." If Reason were depraved, how then do we distinguish between a rational being and a madman? Those who would dismiss Reason ought to consider, said Allen, whether they employ Reason in their arguments against it. If so, then "they establish the principle that they are laboring to dethrone." But if they do not employ Reason, then "they are out of the reach of rational conviction, nor do they deserve a rational argument."

Sometimes called the poet of the American Revolution, Philip Frenau, a graduate of Princeton, similarly took up his pen in defense of Reason and in opposition to all those who would speak out against it.

> What human power shall dare to bind
> The mere opinions of the mind?
> Must man at that tribunal bow
> Which will no range to thought allow,
> But his best powers would sway or sink,
> And idly tells him what to THINK.

Like Jefferson, Frenau chafed at every effort "To chain the mind, or bend it down/To some mean system of their own,/And make religion's sacred cause/Amenable to human laws." So that the oracle of Reason not be silenced, the mind must be forever free.

Similarly, Elihu Palmer, a Dartmouth graduate, acclaimed *Reason, the Glory of Our Nature* and launched a deist newspaper entitled *The Temple of Reason.* If Jefferson struck some as radical in his religious opinions, Palmer angered and inflamed with a rhetoric more uncompromising, an attack on revealed religion more infuriating. Theological systems, wrote Palmer, though they claim to be of divine origin, were "among the most destructive causes by which the life of man has been afflicted." Indeed, given the kind of theology that has dominated the Western world, men and women would have been far better off if they had been "destitute of all theological opinions." The way out of that morass was the elevation of Reason to its proper role. The true destiny of Reason was "to overturn the empire of superstition and erect upon its ruins a fabric against which the storms of despotism may beat in vain." With the mind thus unshackled, the human race would emerge as "standing evidence of the divinity of thought and the unlimited power of human reason." The most destructive of all slaveries, Palmer concluded, was the slavery of the human mind.

Of Jefferson's contemporaries who extolled Reason, none rivaled him in popular appeal with the possible exception of Thomas Paine. Paine had the journalistic gift of giving abstract principles concrete and memorable expression. He did so most effectively during the American Revolution with *Common Sense,* that title being a cliché of the Enlightenment. Then, in the period of the French Revolution, he adopted as the title of a two-volume work yet another cliché, *The Age of Reason.* Though this book never won him the admiration in America that his earlier works did, it succeeded in making his name a byword and a curse. It also succeeded in provoking a strong counterattack by institutional religion against Paine in particular but against all rationalism and deism in general. Paine saw himself as a general on the battlefield inspiring the troops on behalf of Reason, but he probably did more than any other

31

individual to turn the tide of that battle, in America, against the very ramparts he defended.

NATURE AND NATURE'S GOD

To return now to Thomas Jefferson's letter to Peter Carr, we find that other great word of Enlightenment thought: "Nature." Even more than the word "Reason," the word "Nature" proved adaptable, irresistible, and eminently useful. In the area of moral philosophy, for example, Jefferson advised his nephew, in brief, to forget formal instruction and consult Nature. "I think it lost time," Jefferson declared, "to attend lectures in this branch." If men and women needed a college education to know what morality was all about, what a calamity that would be for the human race. And what "a pitiful bungler" God would be "if he had made the rules of moral conduct a matter of science." If God created human beings as social creatures, and surely he did, then of necessity he had to endow those creatures with a sense of right and wrong. "This sense is as much a part of [human] nature as the sense of hearing, seeing, feeling; it is the true foundation of morality." God gave to all persons this "moral sense, or conscience, . . . as much a part of man as his leg or arm."

The moral sense can be strengthened through exercise, to be sure, or atrophied through disuse, just as an arm or leg can be. But that gift of conscience was not limited to an elite, to a privileged class, and certainly not to moral philosophers. "State a moral case to a ploughman and a professor. The former will decide it as well, and often better than the latter, because he had not been led astray by artificial rules." The English system of justice, built on the fundamental right of trial by jury, rested on a solid foundation, for the jury of one's peers consisted not of professors or lawyers or theologians but of ordinary people possessed of ordinary sense and blessed by their extraordinary Creator with the favor of conscience. It was part of their Nature.

The word "Nature" appeared in many contexts: natural law, natural religion, natural rights, natural philosophy, Nature's God, state of Nature, and more. In all of these contexts, the meanings were not identical; indeed, they could even be contradictory. Sometimes "natural" referred to that which was original or primitive; sometimes it meant that which was universal, not limited to a particular culture or clime; other times, it signified not that which existed everywhere — perhaps it existed nowhere — but which *ought* to exist. A word of such wondrous dexterity also received then and deserves here its own capitalization. But what, exactly, did the word mean? Exactness was neither its intent nor its effect. Usage of the term did, at the very least, create a warm and positive attitude toward whatever was being described. On the other side, to call something unnatural or artificial was to condemn it to a lesser order of worth, to suggest that it was defective and perhaps dangerous.

As Peter Carr read, he well might, said Jefferson, accept those facts of Livy or Tacitus that accord with Nature. In reading the Bible, he should follow a similar path. "But those facts in the bible which contradict laws of nature must be examined with more care." Consider, for example, the famous case of Joshua commanding the sun to stand still. This required investigation because "millions believe it." But "you are astronomer enough to know how contrary it is to the law of nature that a body revolving on its axis, as the earth does, should have stopped." And by that sudden halt in its rotation, would it not have "prostrated animals, trees, buildings?" And would not a second prostration have occurred when the earth resumed its regular revolution? So what does one do when confronted with a "fact" based on inspiration and a "fact" contrary to all the laws of Nature? Examine all the circumstances, Jefferson advised, and then ask yourself which was the more improbable: an error in reporting or "a change of the laws of nature"?

Years earlier, Jefferson had recommended the works of David Hume, including the essay on miracles. There Hume

33

made the same argument that Jefferson swiftly summarized for his nephew. We are obliged to turn to experience, not authority, for truth. What has been our own personal experience? Hume asked. That human beings sometimes give erroneous or false testimony, or that Nature makes exceptions to the operation of her laws? If one heeds only experience, rejecting innate ideas and a priori assumptions, then the answer comes through clearly. Human nature is unreliable; God's Nature is orderly, fixed, and unchanging.

The Scottish jurist and philosopher Lord Kames in 1751 published his *Essays on the Principles of Morality and Natural Religion,* a work that Jefferson read early, thoroughly annotated, excerpted substantially into his Commonplace Book, and recommended to Robert Skipwith in 1771. Jefferson would have argued with Kames on some points, but not on the preferability of a natural religion to a revealed religion. Jefferson also found confirmation of and elaboration on the notion of an innate moral sense in the writings of Kames and other figures of the Scottish Enlightenment such as Francis Hutcheson and Thomas Reid. These views, influential in Jefferson's William and Mary days, continued to dominate American education for another generation or more.

So the Scottish Enlightenment crossed the Atlantic Ocean as had the French and English Enlightenments. And natural religion had much going for it in certain circles. Again, Philip Frenau could give the mood enduring poetic expression:

> Religion, such as nature taught,
>   With all divine perfection suits;
> Had all mankind this system sought
>   Sophists would cease their vain disputes,
>   And from this source would nations know
>   All that can make their heaven below.

If Ethan Allen could extol Reason, so could he write at length of "Nature as God's Revelation." All knowledge came from Reason and experience, and this we may properly call "the revelation of God, which he has revealed to us in the constitution of our rational natures." This, which deserved the name of "natural religion, . . . could be derived from none other but God." The whole purpose of Allen's treatise, he professed, was to prune traditional religion of all its "excrescences, with which Craft on the one hand, and Ignorance on the other, have loaded it." Then, men and women everywhere would see natural religion "in its native simplicity, free from alloy." He sought to address only the Reason of humankind, never "their passions, traditions, or prejudices."

So also did Elihu Palmer, Thomas Paine, and a Frenchman briefly resident in America, Comte de Volney. Jefferson was so taken with Volney's *Les Ruines, ou meditations sur les revolutions des empires* that he undertook to translate it for the American public; this task was eventually completed by Joel Barlow, and the book was published in 1799 under the title *Ruins; or, Meditations on the Revolutions of Empires*. Having set the scene of an assemblage of representatives of various revealed religions, Volney showed how disagreement and even warfare regularly resulted from the sharp divergences among the several traditions. If, however, all could agree on the essentials of natural religion, then the world arrived at understandings worthy of human rationality and divine dignity. Blind loyalty to one's own sect led to savagery and persecution; devout understanding of those laws by which God governs the universe led, on the other hand, to a "common rule" that would guide all peoples, "without distinction of country or of sect towards perfection and happiness." Following the dictates of natural religion thus brought personal happiness and a productive society, and it had the side benefit of honoring rather than demeaning the name of God. (In his youth, Abraham Lincoln also read and was impressed by Volney's "meditations.")

One of the reasons Jefferson and other deists of the eighteenth century believed that Nature spoke the language of God so clearly was that God's hand had molded the world so recently. In an age before the rise of geology and the explosion of Darwin, the earth still seemed relatively young. Jefferson would, of course, have rejected the chronology based on the book of Genesis that, as interpreted by some, fixed the date and time of creation as sometime in October in 4004 B.C. Nonetheless, the age of the world was to be measured in thousands, not millions, of years — the earth perhaps ten to fifteen thousand years old. The planet, still warm from the creative touch of God, spoke the language of a natural religion equally accessible, equally comprehensible to all.

Jefferson, like many of those whom he read as a youth, had no trouble accepting the argument for God's existence from the magnificent design evident in his creation. It was impossible, he wrote to John Adams, "for the human mind not to perceive and feel a conviction of design, consummate skill, and indefinite power in every atom of its composition." This was the case whether one contemplated the heavens above ("the movement of the heavenly bodies, so exactly held in their course by the balance of centrifugal and centripetal forces") or the earth below ("the structure of our earth itself, with its distribution of lands, waters, and atmosphere, animal and vegetable bodies . . . insects as mere atoms of life, yet as perfectly organized as man or mammoth"). To a close observer of Nature, which Jefferson surely was, the conclusion could not be denied: we see "evident proofs of the necessity of a superintending power to maintain the universe in its course and order."

The laws of Nature were God's laws; they did not have an independent status all their own. They came into being by God's decree, and they continued to operate, as Newton demonstrated, through God's unceasing providential direction. Unlike many other deists, Jefferson did not hold that God created the world and then retired from the scene; rather, he believed that God continued to create and sustain the world moment by moment. Gravity was not a property of matter: it was God's law for the orderly operation of matter, one of the means by which he brought order out of chaos. And the restoration of order goes on, as Jefferson pointed out, to fill in gaps when stars disappear or a species of animal threatens to become extinct. "Were there no restoring power," Jefferson wrote, "all existences might extinguish successively, one by one, until all should be reduced to a shapeless chaos." New England's great philosopher/theologian Jonathan Edwards shared this Jeffersonian understanding of God's presence in the world as being continuous, creative, benevolent.

If there was imperfection in the world or in a human being, that became a goad to activity — to cooperate with the operation of natural laws to minimize the evil, to eradicate the disease. As Jefferson's friend physician Benjamin Rush of Philadelphia noted, exercise of both the mind and the body was essential to restoring a proper order. Idleness was the kinsman of vice; "to do nothing is generally to do evil." The origin of evil, John Adams noted, was perhaps known only to omniscience, but we can be sure that it did not all begin in a garden. "We poor mortals have nothing to do with it, but to fabricate all the good we can out of all inevitable evils." One way to eradicate a large class of evils, Adams added, was to employ our reason to dispose of "our own unnecessary apprehensions and imaginary fears." Original sin, if such a thing even existed, was ignorance, said Volney. It was definitely not, for the Jeffersonian, an Edenic action that forever after paralyzed humankind, corrupted one's nature, or destroyed one's moral sense. Man was not a worm, not a moral midget, but one designed by God and empowered by him to conquer the infirmities, moral or physical, of this world.

Jefferson unhesitatingly rejected the atheism of some of the French philosophes, finding it illogical and untenable. For the atheist, said Jefferson, the universe had simply always existed. It has no cause, no beginning in time. For the deist, on the other hand, the great canvas of creation cried out for "a first cause, possessing intelligence and power; power in the production, and intelligence in the design and constant preservation of the system." Though in the acrimony of political campaigns Jefferson's enemies would regularly refer to him as an atheist, they could not have been further off the mark.

Indeed, Jefferson could and did share the rhapsodies of the psalmist, recommending Psalm 148 to John Adams as an excellent portrayal of Nature's God.

> Praise the Lord!
> Praise the Lord from the heavens, praise him in the
>   heights!
> Praise him all his angels, praise him, all his host!
> Praise him, sun and moon, praise him, all you shining
>   stars!
> Praise him, you highest heavens, and you waters above
>   the heavens!
> Let them praise the name of the Lord!
> For he commanded and they were created.
> And he established them for ever and ever;
> He set a law which cannot pass away.

And on through other stanzas that have trees, beasts, birds, and kings all joining in the chorus of praise. Then Jefferson quoted, to a similar effect, verses 9 and 10 of Psalm 18, comparing the latest translations in English with some Latin "mediocres," casually observing at that point that "the Greek of [James] Duport is worthy of quotation." While rejecting the notion of revelation, Jefferson could nonetheless find in the poetry of the Psalms or in the beauty of the Anglican liturgy suitable tribute to a majestic Creator revealed through a sublime creation.

"THE SCRIPTURE CALLED THE CREATION"

In Jefferson's only book, *Notes on the State of Virginia*, one finds another kind of hymn to Nature — prosaic to be sure, but devout nonetheless. His book falls chiefly in the category of natural history; but Jefferson held that once one looks carefully at Nature, one must follow her hints into government, laws, religion, and manners, for Nature instructs all. Jefferson did not approach Nature like the later Romantics, to commune with and be inspired by the snowflake or the little flower in the crannied wall. He confronted Nature like a scientific student of the Enlightenment, to measure and weigh, to tabulate and carefully observe. When the French naturalist Comte Buffon put forward the thesis that everything in Nature was inferior in North America, Jefferson responded not with heat but with data. He presented three tables that offered "A Comparative View of the Quadrupeds of Europe and of America." Strict comparisons were not always possible, since some animals were unique to Europe and some to America, but, given the same food and care in America as in Europe, animals did not degenerate here, Jefferson insisted. Tables, weights, dimensions, and lists made his point. Prejudicial argument deserved to be answered with sober observation, and fanciful assumptions with the compelling logic of experience.

For Jefferson, then, Nature was a matter of science as much as of philosophy or religion. During his presidency he seized the opportunity to send Meriwether Lewis and William Clark to explore the newly acquired Louisiana Territory. Jefferson's detailed instructions revealed once again a person who thirsted to know Nature directly, intimately, and in as much detail as possible. (What did Emerson have to tell us about the weight or size of the snowflake, or the frequency and fury with which they fall?) So Lewis and Clark were to map, sketch, and take notes on everything they saw in that vast unspoiled laboratory of Nature. "Beginning with the mouth of the Missouri," Jefferson directed, "you will take observations of latitude & longitude at all remarkable points on the river, at islands & other places." The naturalist-president added, "Your observations are to be taken with great pains & accuracy, to be entered distinctly & intelligibly for others as well as yourself." And the two explorers brought back to the White House, or to Monticello, grains that could be planted, birds that could be observed, animal heads that could be mounted, and Indian artifacts that could be preserved. Jefferson could not get too much of Nature.

Meriwether Lewis, who well knew of his fellow Virginian's insatiable eagerness to absorb all that Nature had to offer, wrote to his president from what would become North Dakota in April 1805 to prepare him for all the empirical data about to deposited on his doorstep. "I have forwarded to you from this place," Lewis noted, "67 specimens of earth, salts, and minerals; and 60 specimens of plants; these are accompanied by their respective labels expressing the days on which obtained, places where found, and also their virtues and properties when known." When all of these parcels reached the White House, a delighted president probably passed up his regular meals in order to feast on so bountiful a banquet of Nature.

Jefferson also fed joyfully on the discovery of the bones of a mammoth in North America, and he encouraged the 1801 expedition of artist Charles Willson Peale that unearthed this skeleton in upstate New York. In the first place, the size of this awesome beast refuted the base charges of Buffon that everything in North America "degenerated." In the second place, the presence of the bones added to the probability, in Jefferson's view of God's creation, that the animal somewhere still existed. "Such is the economy of nature," he wrote, "that no instance can be produced, of her having permitted any one race of her animals to become extinct; of her having formed any link in her great work so weak as to be broken." Was the mammoth just another kind of elephant? No, Jefferson responded. The elephant had been created for the tropics, the mammoth for the arctic. "When the Creator has therefore separated their nature as far as the extent of the scale of animal life allowed to this planet would permit it, it seems perverse to declare it the same, from a partial resemblance of their tusks and bones." When Peale reconstructed the skeleton of the mammoth in his own Philadelphia museum, he placed it next to the Asiatic elephant to show that God's great "chain of being" remained unbroken. The North American mammoth testified to the wondrous works of God; it rescued the nation from absurd foreign slanders; it enormously pleased the naturalist who occupied the White House.

If Nature was so all-encompassing, what place did that leave for Reason, "the only oracle"? These two great concepts of the Enlightenment, Reason and Nature, were invoked so regularly and so widely that no one will be surprised to learn that they also overlapped. Ethan Allen's *Reason the Only Oracle of Man* carried as its subtitle *Or, a Compendious System of Natural Religion*. Elihu Palmer spoke of "righteous and immortal reason" as the "glory of our nature" — bringing Reason and Nature into the same sentence and reigning from virtually the same throne. Thomas Paine, in his *Age of Reason*, spent much time talking about Nature, about that universal language of creation with which God communicates to all. This language "cannot be forged; it cannot be counterfeited; it cannot be lost; it cannot be altered; it cannot be suppressed." If one wished to know who or what God was, one used his Reason, yes; but Reason tells us to turn to Nature. "Search not the book called the scripture, which any human hand might make, but the scripture called the Creation."

When Nature spoke, one heard the very voice of God. When Reason guided, one moved as God directed. If both Nature and Reason emanated from God, should there be any surprise when they spoke in similar tones — perhaps even in identical words? No, the surprise would come if they ever appeared to be at odds with one another. But in the faith of the philosophe, this could never happen. Reason and Nature built parallel ladders from the earth below to the heavens above. The faithful pilgrim could climb either as he chose, discovering as he neared the top that the two had become one.

So Jefferson would draw upon his two sources of inspiration as he guided his state and his nation through revolution and union, as he labored for reform in religion and education, and as he propounded, in Lincoln's words, the "axioms of a free society."

41

3 The Revolutionary

"The God who gave us life gave us liberty at the
same time; the hand of force may destroy, but
cannot disjoin them." (1774)

Admitted to the practice of law in 1767, Thomas Jefferson for
the next seven years seemed headed for the career of a Virginia
attorney. Politics, however, drew him into its net, even in these
early years, as he served in the House of Burgesses from 1769
until a royal governor shut it down in the midst of Revolutionary outcries and clamor. In 1770, he began what would become
virtually a lifetime occupation: the designing, building, and
rebuilding of Monticello. And by 1772, he had a companion to
share with him the joys and sorrows of domesticity, the young
widow Martha Skelton Wayles.

In 1774, the American colonies from Massachusetts to
South Carolina railed against the growing oppression (as they
saw it) of freedoms long taken for granted on both sides of the
Atlantic. But "English liberties" apparently meant one thing in

England, and something sharply different in Virginia or New York. In response to the Boston Tea Party late in 1773, England passed the following year the Coercive Acts, which closed the port of Boston, levied a new tax to pay for the destroyed tea, provided for British troops, again, to be quartered in the private homes of Bostonians, and greatly expanded the powers of the royal governor. The purpose of these smart slaps was to isolate Massachusetts from the other colonies; the effect was to unite them. Colonists north and south rallied to Boston's defense and — as they increasingly believed — to their own defense as well.

A SUMMARY VIEW

In August of 1774, a meeting of patriots in Williamsburg prepared to make its case against this most recent of a growing list of grievances against the Empire's ever more oppressive rule. Jefferson, like all the other burgesses, was routinely elected as a delegate to this nonofficial, non–House of Burgesses gathering. Though prevented by illness from attending, he sent ahead resolutions that he had prepared to help the irregular assembly make its case against England in general and against England's Parliament in particular. To Jefferson's surprise, his resolutions, though never formally voted on, were published under the title *A Summary View of the Rights of British Americans.* This tract of twenty or so pages found quick popularity well outside the confines of Williamsburg, where it was first printed, and it brought sudden attention to its thirty-one-year-old author.

Notice has already been taken of how much attention Jefferson, along with other Enlightenment thinkers on both sides of the ocean, paid to Nature. They revered it and elevated it to a position of great authority — above man-made laws or man-made monarchs, above man-made moral codes or sectarian doctrines. In the *Summary,* however brief, the primordial authority of Nature and of natural rights rang a recurrent

43

theme. Our common Saxon ancestors, Jefferson wrote, "possessed a right, which nature has given to all men, of departing from the country in which chance, not choice, had placed them, of going in quest of new habitations." So also did those English men and women who settled North America, under the protection of those same natural rights that could never be arbitrarily denied. Free trade, for example, was such a natural right. Making laws for one's own community was another. Therefore, suspending the legislature of New York stood as but a single example of a gross violation of rights given by Nature, not by men. "Not only the principles of common sense, but the common feelings of human nature must be surrendered up, before his majesty's subjects here can be persuaded to believe that they hold their political existence at the will of a British parliament."

If one wished to know what was "unnatural," Jefferson was happy to explain. An act passed during the reign of George II forbade an American "to make a hat for himself of the fur which he has taken perhaps on his soil." Iron was mined in America, but then had to be shipped to Britain for the manufacture of machinery; to make matters even more absurd and unnatural, Americans had "to pay the freight for it to Great Britain, and freight for it back again." This violated all laws of Reason as well as of Nature, as did our submitting to a legislative body that we have never elected, never seen, and over whom we have no power of "punishment or removal." Irrational, artificial, unnatural. Neither Nature nor Nature's God could grant any blessing to behavior like that.

In 1774 Jefferson made his appeal to the king against the presumptions and insolence of Parliament. In less than two years, he would make a similar case against the king, on the very same grounds of fundamental violations against Nature. Yet here in the *Summary*, he proclaimed that even the king's powers had limits. For example, did the king think he could send military forces to America, "not made up of the people here, nor raised by the authority of our laws"? Were we to grant King George III "such a right as this, it might swallow up all

44

our other rights whenever he should think proper." The king was not above all law, most of all not above all natural law. And Americans were not infinite in their patience, for they did and do believe that "the God who gave us life gave us liberty at the same time: the hand of force may destroy, but cannot disjoin them."

A DECLARATION OF INDEPENDENCE

The next year, 1775, saw Jefferson elected to the Second Continental Congress, which, unlike its predecessor, would stay in session not for weeks but for years. Jefferson, who arrived somewhat late, had already heard of the battles of Lexington and Concord and soon would hear of another battle at Bunker Hill — all of this having occurred in only the one colony of Massachusetts. One of the tasks before this Congress, therefore, was to demonstrate to Britain that the colonies could not be played off against each other, that on the contrary they would stand together in their resistance. But would they also stand together for independence from the mother country? Some advocated delay, some immediate action, some a moderate or equivocal course between submission and rebellion. All of these differences in position and opinion would take some time to resolve; John Adams acutely described the problem as trying to get thirteen clocks to strike at precisely the same time.

Continued debate and discussion would divide, not unite, argued the persuasive Thomas Paine. Only a resolution on behalf of independence could hold the thirteen colonies together, he declared. As Britain seemed ever more bent on total humiliation, Americans seemed ever more prone to total separation. In May of 1776, Jefferson arrived back in Philadelphia after an absence of many months in Virginia attending to private affairs in Monticello and public affairs in Williamsburg. Soon Philadelphia delegates learned that Virginia's representatives in Williamsburg had already passed their own resolution calling for independence and desired that those in Philadelphia quickly do the same. On June 7, Richard Henry Lee of Virginia offered this motion for debate: "that these United Colonies are, and of right ought to be, free and independent states." Two days later, the members took a straw vote: seven states voted for independence, five voted against, and one abstained. This did not seem too promising a beginning, but many of those voting against did so on the grounds of timing or of their desire to receive further instructions from home.

One could hardly proceed with only seven states, but delay — Paine was right — would spell disaster. So that precious time would not be lost while the six other states deliberated, a committee was appointed to draft a suitable statement with respect to independence. Five men were named: John Adams (Massachusetts), Benjamin Franklin (Pennsylvania), Robert Livingston (New York), Roger Sherman (Connecticut), and Thomas Jefferson (Virginia). As in all procedures in the Continental Congress, regional balance had to be carefully preserved: two from New England, two from the Middle States, and one from the South (there was some compensation for the smaller representation accorded the South in the fact that Jefferson was named chairman). In the actual writing of the document, Jefferson may have been prepared to defer to John Adams, eight years his senior. But Adams, as he later noted, would decline since he was "obnoxious, suspected, and unpopular," while Jefferson was "very much otherwise." Also, Adams acknowledged that Jefferson could write "ten times better" than he.

Jefferson therefore undertook the task while Congress turned its attention for many days to other matters. On July 2, however, Congress convened for an official vote on Richard Henry Lee's resolution of almost a month before. This time, the opposition had vanished. With a unanimous vote in favor of independence, the delegates could now turn their attention to the draft that Thomas Jefferson had prepared. It was debated and amended on July 2 and again on July 3, and it was given a final revision and received unanimous approval on July 4. The amended and approved Declaration of Independence was then quickly printed and dispatched to the thirteen colonies, about to become states, where it was read from balconies and pulpits, in public squares and marketplaces. John Adams wrote to his wife, Abigail, that this "Day of Deliverance" (he actually thought that the Second of July, not the Fourth, would be the honored day) should be remembered "by solemn acts of devotion to God Almighty." Adams, relieved that at last the unanimous vote had come, expressed his hope that the momentous day "would be solemnized with pomp and parade, with shows, games, sports, guns, bells, bonfires, and illuminations from one end of this continent to the other, from this time forward, forever more."

The Declaration of Independence itself, as Jefferson originally wrote it, stands among other things as an enduring witness to Jefferson's religious, moral, and political views. In its necessary compression, Jefferson had to speak for himself but he also intended to speak for a free people and a new age. He wasted no time getting to the "laws of nature and of nature's God," for the preamble declared,

> When in the course of human events it becomes necessary for one people to dissolve the political bonds which have connected them with another, and to assume among the powers of the earth the separate & equal station to which the laws of nature and of nature's God entitle them, a decent respect to the opinions of mankind requires that they should declare the causes which compel them to the separation.

The famous sentence that followed drew from those same immutable, inalienable, natural laws to declare that certain truths were "self-evident": that is, they required no argumentation, no Aristotelian syllogism, no Platonic presupposition,

47

no authority whatsoever except Reason to establish their validity. And these truths, which Jefferson first referred to as "sacred and undeniable," came, like creation itself, fresh from the hand of God. They were built into the structure of the universe as surely as Newton's law of gravity was built in: they were "inherent," as Jefferson's original draft stated. Life, liberty, and the pursuit of happiness were, therefore, beyond the reach of mere governments: these rights were decreed, sustained, and authenticated by none other than Nature's God.

The most passionate section of Jefferson's draft of the Declaration, unfortunately struck out by the Congress, dealt with slavery and the slave trade. Here the negative side of natural law and natural rights could be all too vividly seen. The king, wrote Jefferson in a righteous wrath that later cooled, "has waged a cruel war against human nature itself, violating its most sacred rights of life and liberty." What Jefferson had in mind was the notorious slave trade, this "piratical warfare," "this execrable commerce," "this assemblage of horrors." Such language, much too strong for some of the delegates in Philadelphia, did not survive, nor did all of Jefferson's indignation. In 1776, however, when patriots spoke of liberty, at least some believed that that sacred and natural right had no philosophical or moral or racial limits. Though Jefferson did not quote Scripture, in his nobler moments he shared its sentiment that God was no respecter of persons — neither Jew nor Gentile, neither slave nor free.

A Revolution, already under way in 1775, now had legitimacy and authenticity — and a diplomatic passport for seeking foreign alliances in the struggle against Europe's superpower. Such alliances came, though later than most had hoped; a Continental Army was raised, though smaller than most had wished; and casualties and military reversals followed, in far larger numbers than any would have anticipated. But the tide of battle as well as of English public opinion slowly turned, and by 1783 the final terms of peace had been sealed.

LAWS FOR A NEW REPUBLIC

Long before that date, however, Thomas Jefferson began to consider what the implications of the Revolution were for the country at large and for Virginia in particular. What should be the true nature of a republican government? Its laws? Its system of education? Its religion? On the latter point, Jefferson, hurrying back from Philadelphia to Virginia, wasted no time in trying to eradicate the "spiritual tyranny" that he saw prevailing in his own state. The "Spirit of '76" meant that much had to change, and change quickly; else, the Revolution was only a hollow mockery.

In his autobiography, Jefferson quickly reviewed the favored position of Anglicanism in colonial Virginia — its parishes and glebes and taxes and public salaries. He also reviewed the history of intolerance, the "severest penalties" imposed upon Quakers and others, the harsh restrictions on dissenters in the exercise of their ministries. But now, noted Jefferson, the dissenters were in the majority in the state, even though Anglicans still held a majority in the legislative Assembly. Those two facts meant (1) that public pressure for disestablishment of the Anglican Church would be enormous and (2) that legislative resistance to any swift alteration in the status quo would be powerful. For a decade, the struggle for a full religious freedom in Virginia would involve much jockeying, posturing, delaying, backtracking, and stubborn pressing toward the ultimate goal. In that patient plodding, Jefferson took the lead, joined now by his younger neighbor and indispensable ally James Madison.

Taking his seat in the House of Delegates in October 1776, Jefferson pressed quickly to translate republicanism from a theory of government into a functioning reality. A year or two earlier, he had already indicated his impatient rejection of the notion that Christianity was "built in" to the system of English Common Law. This wrongheaded idea had been arrived at through mistranslations by the ancient clergy and misunderstandings by the pliable judges. The latter, allowing themselves to become "accomplices in the frauds of the clergy," "have taken the whole leap, and declared at once that the whole Bible" was now part of "the common law of the land." As a consequence, laws made for the Jews alone were now being given force throughout the empire, and gospel precepts directed to the instructed conscience were now being armed with "the coercions of municipal law." "We might as well say," Jefferson continued, "that the Newtonian system of philosophy is a part of the common law, as that the Christian religion is." In this as in other respects, however, Jefferson perceived the implications of being a republic more clearly than many of his fellows, in Virginia or beyond its borders. (In 1822, for example, the Supreme Court of Pennsylvania ruled that "Christianity, general Christianity, is and always has been a part of the common law" of that state.)

In the Assembly Jefferson also took steps to abolish primogeniture and thereby remove "the feudal and unnatural distinctions which made one member of every family rich, and all the rest poor." He endeavored to overhaul the educational system of the state, for if a nation wished to be both ignorant and free, he later wrote, "it expects what never was and never will be." In conjunction with others, he labored to rewrite the state's entire code of laws to correspond with republican principles and "with a single eye to reason." One no longer had to worry about what the king and his privy council might like or not like; at last, it could be done right. But it could not be done easily. Later, in looking over Jefferson's entire career, Madison evaluated his friend's efforts in revising Virginia's laws as "perhaps the most severe of his public labors." Madison added, "It consisted of 126 Bills, comprising and recasting the whole statutory code, British and Colonial, then admitted to be in force, . . . and some of the most important articles of the unwritten law." The task, simply put but not simply achieved, was to adapt the whole conglomeration "to the Independent and Republican form of government."

In the midst of so many difficult assignments, Jefferson acknowledged that "the severest contests in which I have ever been engaged" concerned religion. In this area, he wanted to move fast; most of his colleagues preferred to move at a far slower pace, if move at all. After nearly two months of wrangle and debate, Jefferson had to settle for less than half a loaf. "We prevailed so far only," he wrote, "as to repeal the laws which rendered criminal the maintenance of any religious opinions" and those laws requiring one to attend church or follow a prescribed mode of worship. Jefferson located many similar old laws on Virginia's books that were rarely enforced but nonetheless cried out for unequivocal eradication. Denial of the doctrine of the Trinity, for example, was punishable by imprisonment, and "heresy," however defined, was a capital offense. Roman Catholics could not hold civil office, and "freethinkers" might have their children taken from them. All this had to go, and, under Jefferson's direction, eventually it did.

Dissenters, moreover, were exempted from taxes collected on behalf of Anglicanism, and the salaries for Anglican clergymen were phased out over time, until the last remaining vestige of tax support for religion was eliminated in 1779. Though a majority of the delegates were indeed "churchmen," some, Jefferson noted, were "reasonable and liberal men." This enabled the Jeffersonian faction to cobble together "feeble minorities" and secure partial victories. But the contests would continue throughout Jefferson's three years in the legislature, into his governorship (1779-82), and indeed beyond.

MOVING TOWARD RELIGIOUS FREEDOM

As early as 1777, Jefferson thought to end the contests and clear the air by drafting a Bill for Establishing Religious Freedom. He tried to insert the guarantees of a "full and free liberty" in religion into the state's constitution, adopted the previous year. He was convinced that no liberty — and certainly religious liberty — should be left hanging on the whimsy of public opinion. In the end, however, the somewhat milder language of George Mason was adopted to the effect that "all men are equally entitled to the free exercise of religion" and that it was "the mutual duty of all to practice Christian forbearance, love, and charity towards each other." While this protection was clearly superior to that offered by the constitutions of several other states at the time and even for some years thereafter, it did not meet the lofty standards of the revolutionary Jefferson. Christian charity was decidedly not enough.

He pressed for a fair consideration of his bill while still in the legislature, but he did not receive it. When he became governor in 1779, he promptly sent the bill to the Assembly for its consideration; with equal promptness, it was tabled. Not only were the Anglican "churchmen" reluctant to sever all ties between their Church and the civil order — ties that had been in place for nearly two centuries — but even some of the dissenters had begun to waver on the question of *complete* separation. While they maintained that it would clearly be inappropriate to continue to give preferential status to the Church of England, particularly in the midst of a war against England, some nonetheless held that this need not mean that every official tie between religion and society had to be broken. "Some of our dissenting allies," Jefferson sadly noted, now that they had been relieved of paying taxes for the support of Anglicanism, appeared ready to support Christianity in general, or perhaps even to accept some favoritism on behalf of their own sectarian position. James Madison was especially offended by what he regarded as duplicitous behavior on the part of Virginia's Presbyterians. Now that Anglicanism was in the process of being pushed out of its cushioned seat of privilege, some Presbyterians, said Madison, "seem as ready to get up an establishment which is to take them in as they were to pull down that which shut them out."

In general, however, the Presbyterian laity continued to lean away from any sort of establishment of religion, as did most Presbyterians in the Assembly. Baptists, growing in large numbers after the Great Awakening, urged the legislators not to rest in their push for complete religious liberty until "every grievous yoke be broken . . . that in every Act the bright beams of equal Liberty and impartial Justice may shine." German Lutherans from the backcountry pressed for the process of disestablishment to continue until it was complete, as did the Quakers, who argued that Christianity depended no more on "Pecuniary Provisions" by the state than "the Salvation of Souls depends on Human learning and knowledge." By the 1780s, the Methodists had also grown into an independent entity, weaning themselves from the Anglican mother who first nurtured but then rejected them. They, along with other dissenters watching the Jeffersonian momentum build, would add their weight to the wheel.

In 1780, the capitol moved from Williamsburg to Richmond, out of the area where Anglicanism dominated and closer to the backcountry of the dissenters. Jefferson, governor during this move, found much more than religion on his mind, however, as British troops invaded Virginia and attacked Richmond. Jefferson had to order the evacuation of the new capitol, as the invading troops led by Benedict Arnold ("the greatest of all traitors," Jefferson called him) destroyed records, a foundry, and remaining ammunition stores before retreating to Portsmouth. Military matters continued to press so much upon Jefferson that in 1782 he resigned his governorship — which had not been a happy time — in favor of a boyhood friend and now Virginia's militia general, Thomas Nelson, Jr. In that same dark year, Jefferson's wife, Martha, died shortly after the birth of a daughter.

With the end of the Revolution, effectively in 1781 and formally in 1783, Virginia legislators turned their attention once more to civilian and domestic matters — and to religion. On this latter issue, the state's religious citizenry remained bitterly divided. Those divisions, moreover, were exacerbated when in 1784 the Anglicans, having reorganized themselves into the

Protestant Episcopal Church, sought and received from the state an Act of Incorporation. No other denomination had asked for incorporation by the state, nor did any think it either wise or necessary to do so. Was this just old Anglicanism trying to pour its strong ecclesiastical wine into new bottles? Many thought so, as protests mounted and passions rose.

Madison informed Jefferson that the "mutual hatred" of the dissenters toward Episcopalians had been "much in-flamed" by the incorporation issue; he added, "I am far from being sorry for it." Jefferson replied that he was "glad that the Episcopalians have again shown their teeth and fangs. The dissenters had almost forgotten them." If the Presbyterians had wavered, this presumptive act stiffened their resolve. The Hanover Presbytery advised the legislature to recognize that it had no authority whatsoever in matters spiritual or ecclesias-tical. Baptists, who had assumed that Virginia's Declaration of Rights and 1776 constitution would have prohibited such an action, admitted their "great surprise" that the legislature "at the request of a few clergymen, would incorporate the Protes-tant Episcopal Church" and would turn over all properties of the old establishment, including the glebe lands, to the sole use of this new entity. This "incorporation issue" rankled so keenly that within two years the Assembly reversed itself and re-scinded the offensive Act. (Years later, Madison as president would confront this issue all over again at the national level.)

Meanwhile, the newly disestablished Episcopalians felt harried, mistreated, and certainly misunderstood. John Page, an old boyhood friend of Jefferson's, wrote in 1785 informing him in some pique that Episcopal clergymen were starving and that the state was in danger of being caught between utter immorality on the one hand and "Enthusiastic Bigotry" on the other. One clergyman of the former establishment reported to his brother in Scotland that the Revolution "has been fatal to the Clergy of Virginia. From a fixed salary they are reduced to depend upon a precarious subscription for bread." A state convention of Virginia's Episcopalians in the same year painted a dreary and unpromising picture. The Church now had no regular government, the convention reported, and "her ministers have received but little compensation for their services." In addition, "churches stand in need of repair, and there is no fund equal to the smallest want." The adjustment from being supported by tax monies from all the citizens to being supported by voluntary contributions from only a few was indeed a traumatic one — one that the newly organized church would require years to overcome. The Virginia counties of Essex, Amelia, and Accomac, all in the Tidewater region, formally petitioned the state's legislators, also in 1785, "to take into their legislative patronage and protection, the concerns of our holy religion, a thorough knowledge and conscientious practice of which is the best security for the permanent peace and prosperity of civil government."

GENERAL ASSESSMENT AND MADISON'S MEMORIAL

So the divisions remained, in the Assembly itself no less than in the state at large. Old Virginia families rose to the defense of some sort of religious establishment. To reject Anglicanism need not be to reject Christianity; to reject one church need not require the rejection of all churches. From 1779 to 1785, the legislature worried about the fairness and the fate of some sort of "general assessment" that would support all Christian churches, resist the rise of immorality, and defend the perilously poised state against a potential decline in religion.

The popular orator Patrick Henry, backed by such other influential Virginians as Richard Henry Lee, Edmund Randolph, and John Marshall, led in the political battle for a bill that would make Christianity the official religion of the new state of Virginia. Thomas Jefferson, of course, strongly opposed to any such measure, saw in this effort a total betrayal of the "Spirit of '76." But now, as the battle approached a climax in 1785, Jefferson was off in Paris as minister from the United

States to France. He had to rely, therefore, on his young friend James Madison and the "rich resources of his luminous and discriminating mind." More than Jefferson knew, he also had to rely on the legislative skill of this one who was only twenty-five years of age when he first joined the Assembly in 1776.

With lines clearly drawn, distinguished Virginians on both sides vigorously debated the highly emotional issue. Henry's bill, for so it ultimately became, was first put to a vote at the very end of 1784; it passed by the slimmest margin of two. At a later reading, when another vote was to be taken, the legislature agreed, at Madison's urging, to put the matter over until November of 1785. That allowed time for the expression of, and perhaps for the marshaling of, public opinion. Meanwhile, the Bill for Establishing a Provision for Teachers of the Christian Religion teetered on the point of a legislative will. This bill stipulated that "the Christian Religion shall in all times coming be deemed and held to be the established Religion of this Commonwealth; and all Denominations of Christians demeaning themselves peaceably and faithfully, shall enjoy equal privileges, civil and religious." But as the emperor Constantine discovered many centuries before, if the state is going to establish a religion, it first had to be clear precisely how that religion was defined.

So here once again, the Commonwealth of Virginia was about to engage in the business of saying what constituted religion (or a church), which religious ideas would be supported, and what legal privileges would separate the insiders from the outsiders. It was not enough for a body of worshipers to call themselves a Christian church: they had to be incorporated, and that action would follow only upon a formal assent to five articles of faith. Borrowing from South Carolina's constitution, which in 1778 established Protestant Christianity as that state's official religion, all church members were required to affirm (1) that "there is one Eternal God and a future State of rewards and punishments," (2) that God was to be honored by public worship, (3) that "the Christian Religion is the true Religion," and (4) that the Bible, both Old and New Testaments, was divinely inspired. Moreover, whenever state authorities called on any member to affirm any or all of the above, that member had the duty "to bear witness to truth." Also borrowing from South Carolina's constitution, Henry's bill provided that no church member "shall speak anything in their Religious Assemblies disrespectfully or seditiously of the Government of the State." Law, order, and official religion would prevail.

Once all these criteria had been met to the satisfaction of the state, elaborate state machinery would commence its operation, collecting taxes that would be distributed to the respective approved denominations. If a church declined to receive money from the sheriff, "the money shall remain in his hands for one year." After that period, if the church had still not appointed someone to accept these funds, then the money "shall by the County Court be equally apportioned between the several Religious Societies in the parish in which such person or persons shall reside." It was all very legal, all very proper, and, from a Jeffersonian perspective, all very wrong. Quite simply, a Revolution had not been fought so that the state could continue to issue decrees concerning religion, its orthodoxy, or its support. That long and costly war had been fought for *all* liberty, civil and ecclesiastical, these two being seen in the eighteenth century as inseparable.

And that was why, in the throes of anti-British sentiment in the early 1770s, one issue that in later centuries seems so modest, so piddling, was anything but trivial at the time. The issue of bishops for the Anglican Church irritated and alarmed dissenters and others to such an extent that no Church of England bishop ever set foot on colonial soil. Bishops represented ecclesiastical tyranny, bloody persecution, lordly living, and imperious judging — at least in the minds of those not within the national church. What guarantees existed that bishops, brought to America, would not behave as bishops in England had behaved for two hundred years? No guarantee whatsoever, argued William Livingston, a Presbyterian lawyer from New York. Importing a dangerous commodity like bishops into America, an impassioned Livingston declared, would "introduce an evil more terrible to every man who sets a proper value either on his liberty, property, or conscience than the so greatly and deservedly obnoxious Stamp Act itself." Religious liberty could not be, must not be, separated from political liberty. And a Revolution that brought political liberty to America must not now be subverted by a surrender or compromise of a full freedom in religion.

This Jeffersonian position now fortunately became, eloquently and decisively, the Madisonian position as well. But Madison did not depend on eloquence alone. He saw to it that Patrick Henry, the single most powerful voice in the legislature on behalf of a general assessment, was "promoted" to the governor's chair, an office of far less influence than his position in the Assembly. Madison also saw to it that the dissenters, roused out of any lingering lethargy, sent petitions to the legislature against this multiple establishment, this entangling alliance between the churches and the state. And when Madison was persuaded to draw up his own list of reasons why that long-discussed bill for general assessment should at last be defeated, he took care to see that a great many signatures were offered in support of his position. When in August of 1785 he dispatched a copy of his arguments to Jefferson in Paris, he told him that the document "has been sent thro' the medium of confidential persons to the upper counties, and I am told it will be pretty extensively signed."

Madison's *Memorial and Remonstrance* — a prayer and a protest — gave convincing evidence of that "luminous and discriminating mind" of which Jefferson had written. When the legislature convened in October 1785, Madison and his cohorts were ready. Some twelve hundred signatures had been gathered in favor of a general assessment, some ten thousand in opposition. Madison saw the parties lined up as follows: "The Episcopal people are generally" for the Henry bill, he wrote, "though I think the zeal of some of them has cooled." The dissenting laity, in Madison's view, were almost unanimously against the bill, while a few of the clergy equivocated. But dissenters were now in the majority, as Jefferson had observed, and, given a rallying call, they might just carry the day. The *Memorial and Remonstrance* proved to be the rallying call in 1785, as it has so many times since.

On behalf of "faithful members of a free State," Madison remonstrated at length against that "Bill establishing a provision for Teachers of the Christian Religion." He presented in all fifteen carefully reasoned arguments why this bill, or any other intrusion upon religious liberty, deserved to be resisted and, if at all possible, roundly defeated. Like his Monticello neighbor, Madison found succor and support in the appeal to Reason and to Nature. Religion can be "directed only by reason and conviction, not by force or violence." The right of every person to exercise his or her conscience in this realm "is in its nature an unalienable right." The duty that man owes to his Creator preceded any duty owed to the state; that duty existed even prior to the creation of the state. How absurd, then, to surrender this original natural right, in any degree whatsoever, to some recently created, artificial legislative body. Any legislature was subject to checks and balances, but the greatest check of all was the fundamental and natural rights of the people. Even more absurd was the pretension of any legislator or magistrate to assume prerogatives in this realm, for no such persons, as Locke pointed out, had any competence to judge religious truth.

Mr. Henry's bill was to be resisted, furthermore, because (in a phrase made famous by later Supreme Court uses of it) "it is proper to take alarm at the first experiment of our liberties." This was what the patriots in Boston did when they protested the tax on tea, in itself no great matter. But "they saw all the consequences in the principle, and they avoided the consequences by denying the principle. We revere this lesson too much, soon to forget it." So from a tea party in Boston harbor to the matter at hand in Richmond, Virginia. "Who does not see," inquired a luminous Madison, "that the same authority which can establish Christianity, in exclusion of all other Religions, may establish with the same ease any particular sect of Christians, in exclusion of all other sects?" And if that should happen, then patriots would find themselves right back where they were before Lexington and Concord, before Valley Forge and Yorktown. Virginians would be saddled once again with a persecuting and tyrannical church, be it Episcopal, Presbyterian, Roman Catholic, or whatever.

Virginia's own state constitution guaranteed, Madison pointed out, an equal exercise of religious freedom to all its citizens. To violate that freedom was, then, to offend the state. But even more to the point, such a violation offended God. "If this freedom be abused, it is an offence against God, not against man," and it was therefore to God that one must ultimately answer for infringing upon a right derived from him. Besides all this, the Christian religion did not require artificial and arbitrary support. Did believers lack confidence in the "innate excellence" of the Christian religion or in the protection and "patronage of its Author?" One might well infer from the attempts to establish special protections for Christianity that Christians so feared the fallacies of their religion that they dared not "trust it to its own merits."

Then Madison turned from logic to history to inquire whether, in all those centuries since Constantine, it could be demonstrated that official establishment of religion had been a good thing. On the contrary, in Madison's reading of those hundreds of years, the effect of the state's embrace had been nearly disastrous. Among the clergy, it produced "more or less in all places pride and indolence," and among the laity "ignorance and servility." Everywhere, among all classes of people, this cozy connection between the church and state brought in its wake "superstition, bigotry, and persecution." The gem of the Christian religion had gleamed most brightly when the faithful suffered adversity rather than patronage.

And religious leaders served most honestly when they depended not upon the state but upon "the voluntary rewards of their flocks."

Having argued that Christianity did not require the support of the state, Madison similarly asserted that the state did not need to shelter itself under the wing of an official church. Indeed, when the state had done so, it had created not a higher morality but a spiritual tyranny — and in no instance had this cruel combination resulted in greater protection of the liberties of the people. "Rulers who wished to subvert the public liberty may have found an established clergy convenient auxiliaries." The best security for any government was that it be jealous of the liberties of its citizens.

Madison, along with Jefferson, saw the Henry bill not as a step toward the new postwar age of freedom but as a backward slide toward subservience and deference. "What a melancholy mark is the Bill of sudden degeneracy?" As a country, Madison asserted, we started out offering "an asylum to the persecuted and oppressed of every Nation and Religion." This proposed general assessment might look like a simple, single step, but already it "degrades from the equal rank of citizens all those whose opinions in religion do not bend to those of the Legislative authority." More depressing even than that, this Bill, if approved, would serve as a "Beacon on our Coast," warning the persecuted and oppressed to seek their asylum in some other land where liberty was not so brief and tender a flower.

Henry's bill, Madison pointed out, had not yet passed: it was only being discussed and debated. Even so, it had already at this stage proved divisive and fractious. Its mere appearance on the legislative floor had transformed "Christian forbearance, love and charity" into "animosities and jealousies, which may not soon be appeased." If this be true of just the prospect, what would be the case were it to become actual law? Madison feared that he knew the result: it "will destroy that moderation and harmony" that had heretofore prevailed among the state's several denominations. The Old World had furnished Virginians with too many examples of "torrents of blood" spilled in the name of religious conformity. All rational human beings would be loath to risk those horrors again.

At the end of the *Memorial*, Madison returned to the theme of Nature, with which he had begun. The right to freedom in religion, he explained, shared the inalienability of all other basic rights. "If we recur to its origin, it is equally the gift of nature; if we weigh its importance, it cannot be less dear to us"; and if we consult Virginia's own Declaration of Rights, we find this freedom "enumerated with equal solemnity, or rather studied emphasis." We must not take any step, however small, back toward the rejected age of darkness, but stride boldly toward a new age of light.

With petitions heard and with the *Memorial and Remonstrance* read, Patrick Henry's bill, which had been around for six years in one form or another, never came to a vote. "The table was loaded with petitions and remonstrances from all parts," Madison reported to Jefferson, "against the interposition of the legislature in matters of religion." A General Convention of Presbyterians meeting in August 1785 denounced the bill as "impolitic," "unnecessary," and "a direct violation of the Declaration of Rights." The year before, a General Committee of the Baptists had recommended that all counties that had not yet indicated their opposition to general assessment do so as quickly as possible, for such a proposal "is believed to be repugnant to the spirit of the gospel" and "every person ought to be left entirely free in respect to matters of religion." God was sufficient refuge and strength: "the gospel wants not the feeble arm of man for its support."

So the bill was allowed to "die an easy death," as George Washington had wished. The General Assembly of the Commonwealth of Virginia, challenged to rise to new heights, had met that challenge. Madison had "won." But what, exactly, had he won? An approving sentiment, perhaps, and the blocking of a bad bill. But Virginia's laws with respect to religion were left just as they were before. So at last the time had come to consider another bill — Jefferson's, composed eight years earlier and submitted to the Assembly some six years before. Was not the Assembly now in the mood to do more than merely watch a bad bill die? Could it now consider and possibly pass a Jeffersonian bill that would give religious freedom explicit legislative force and statutory permanence? Madison's *Memorial* deserves praise on many grounds, not least of which is that it paved the way for a Jeffersonian bill to become a Virginia law.

JEFFERSON'S VIRGINIA STATUTE

Virginia, it should be remembered, was the most populous of the states in 1785. Its example carried weight on that ground, to say nothing of the influence that the Virginia delegation exercised in the Constitutional Convention of 1787, as in the earlier Continental Congresses. In addition, four of the first five presidents of the United States were Virginians, and this singularity gave to Virginia's every public action an even larger impact. Finally, on behalf of the Statute itself, Jefferson regarded it as one of the two compositions of his life for which he wished to be remembered, the other being the Declaration of Independence. Both the draft that Jefferson originally wrote and the revised form that the Assembly ultimately passed therefore merit close attention.

Many in the Assembly objected to Jefferson's basic ideas concerning a full freedom in religion, but even more — a majority as it turned out — objected to the Enlightenment context in which those ideas were framed. Jefferson's draft began with these words: "Well aware that the opinions and belief of men depend not on their own will, but follow involuntarily the evidence proposed in their minds . . ." This sounded too much like an assertion that Nature was omnipotent, that a passive humanity merely "received" through its senses what Nature through its bounty bestowed. Surely man had a more active role to play than that, and, put in those terms at least, Jefferson would certainly agree. So the Assembly struck all those words out, leaving a leaner and likely more effective opening phrase, "Whereas Almighty God hath made the mind free. . . ." This was still Enlightenment enough, and in the totality of Jefferson's life it served as a more succinct summary of his operating principle.

A few lines farther down in Jefferson's long, one-sentence preamble, he included a phrase that suggested that the propagation of religion, at least by divine intention, was through "reason alone." Anglicans knew better: one must not forget the state. Dissenters knew better: enthusiasm and passion must not be dismissed. Reason may have been sufficient for the philosophe, for the student and savant of the Enlightenment, but for the masses of mankind, to say nothing of a majority of the Assembly, Reason all by itself was clearly not enough. If man did not live by bread alone, neither did he live by ratiocination alone. And so the phrase "but to extend it [religion] by its influence on reason alone" fell by the way.

Other changes veered in the direction of determining just how "free" the free exercise of religion really was — a question that has vexed the Republic ever since it was born. For example, was restraint in religion ever appropriate? While Jefferson spoke of the absence of restraint on the intellectual level, this might lead some unreflecting citizens to conclude that this also meant no restraint on the sociological or political level. Were this conceded, then, of course, no civil society could long endure. So this language likewise disappeared: "and [God] manifested his supreme will that free [the mind] shall remain by making it altogether insusceptible of restraint."

All would agree that religious behavior needed to have some check placed upon it. No person claiming religion as a protective armor could justify his or her behavior, however antisocial, on the sole ground that the motivation was "religious." Did the same hold true for religious opinion? Or was religious opinion, unlike religious behavior, free to travel any path, however idiosyncratic, that it chose? The Assembly thought not, and therefore deleted Jefferson's language: "that the opinions of men are not the object of civil government, nor under its jurisdiction." Of all the changes that the legislators made, this one probably pained Jefferson most.

The remaining changes being minor, Jefferson could soon forget any pain in the overwhelming joy that the long-delayed bill did, under Madison's superb generalship, at last become law in January of 1786. From the point of view of later history, little had been lost. What remained was, moreover, quite enough to reshape the history of Virginia forever after and of much of the country besides. But Jefferson did not enjoy being revised, whether it was in the Continental Congress of Philadelphia (where Franklin tried to comfort him with a bit of humor) or at the General Assembly of Virginia. By letter, Madison offered his comfort by assuring Jefferson that the passing of this Statute at long last brought an end to "making laws for the human mind." (Since Madison's *Memorial* did not actually have to be voted on, but only greeted with nods of approval, his document was spared the indignity of legislative revision and "improvement.")

The Jefferson bill, as passed, still managed to speak for the Enlightenment, as it did for the Revolution, for the new nation, and — most of all — for Thomas Jefferson. "Whereas Almighty God hath created the mind free," and whereas — a series of "whereases" follow — all attempts by the state to force religion upon human beings resulted not in greater piety but only in "hypocrisy and meanness," it must be time for an appropriate legislative remedy. After another implicit "whereas," Jefferson noted that if anyone had the power to force religion down people's throats, certainly an omnipotent God did. But this "holy author of our religion, who being lord both of body and of mind, yet chose not to propagate it by coercions on either." If God so chose to restrain himself, it must be time for legislative restraint as well.

Making a point similar to Madison's in the *Memorial and Remonstrance*, Jefferson noted that it would be difficult to find worse laps in which to lay religion than those of a legislative body — any legislative body. For politicians to meddle with religion, where they have no business meddling, was "impious presumption." Whereas "fallible and uninspired men have assumed dominion over the faith of others, setting up their own opinions and modes of thinking as the only true and infallible," must it not then be time for an appropriate legislative remedy?

Whenever rulers or even legislators decide that their opinions are infallible, they then take the next logical step — namely, to compel all others to believe just as they do. Or, if the masses will not go that far, they will at least be compelled to support those clergy and those institutions that do share the correct and infallible opinions of parliaments and legislatures. To permit intrusion of this sort was, said Jefferson, both "sinful and tyrannical." It was also a violation of liberty — all liberty, civil and ecclesiastical. Therefore, it was time, past time, for some appropriate legislative remedy.

Our civil rights, wrote Jefferson, have absolutely no bearing on our religious opinions, and vice versa. Opinions in physics and geometry do not incapacitate one for any public duty or office, nor should opinions in religion. South Carolina's constitution, as well as that of Massachusetts and Delaware and Maryland and more, would separate citizen from citizen on the ground of religion. Should not Virginia be bravely and significantly different? For Virginia to say that unless one "profess or renounce this or that religious opinion," that person would lose all the privileges and rewards to which other citizens were entitled would be unworthy and, for Jefferson, unthinkable. Such action would deprive humankind of — no surprise here — "a natural right."

Religion that lusted after worldly "honors and emoluments" was, by virtue of that fact, fatally corrupted. Civil magistrates, who lusted after ever more power over the bodies and minds of humankind, aggravated an already deplorable situation, destroying every remaining shred of religious liberty. These magistrates had plenty of time to use the power of the state should religious principles "break out into overt acts against peace and good order." Until that time, however, may every governor, judge, sheriff, tax collector, and legislator keep his callused hands from inflicting even the lightest touch upon the tender soul.

Now at last to one remaining implicit "whereas" that, because of its soaring eloquence, needs to be read in Jeffersonian language unalloyed:

> And finally, [whereas] truth is great and will prevail if left to herself; that she is the proper and sufficient antagonist to error, and has nothing to fear from the conflict unless by human interposition disarmed of her natural weapons, free argument and debate; errors ceasing to be errors when it is permitted freely to contradict them,

in view of all this, did not the very stones cry out for an appropriate legislative remedy? All of the arguments noted above piled one on top of another in a single sentence, in an overpowering preamble, should move mountains no less than men. The cumulative effect of the Jeffersonian barrage mandated a legislative action that was as morally right as it was now politically unavoidable.

Thus, after years of dally and delay, quibble and retreat, the General Assembly did assert

> that no man shall be compelled to frequent or support any religious worship, place, or ministry whatsoever, nor shall be enforced, restrained, molested, or burthened in his body or goods, nor shall otherwise suffer on account of his religious opinions or belief; but that all men shall be free to profess, and by argument to maintain, their opinions in matters of religion, and that the same shall in no wise diminish, enlarge, or affect their civil capacities.

A single sentence, not as long as the preamble's, gave a Jeffersonian sentiment the force of law on 16 January 1786. For

Jefferson, a struggle of nearly a decade's duration had come to an end. For the nation, the struggle for religious liberty might be said to have truly begun.

The enabling legislation quoted above should have properly concluded the Statute for Establishing Religious Freedom. But Jefferson was too nervous to let it end there. Suppose some future General Assembly, under the sway of popular opinion or of a propagandistic press (or, in a later day, of a television preacher) should seek the repeal of this precious Statute. This profound anxiety kept Jefferson awake nights. Might it not be prudent to take just one more step, add just one more short paragraph, in an effort to forestall such an unnerving eventuality? Acknowledging that one legislature had "no power to restrain the acts of succeeding Assemblies," nonetheless, this particular law was simply too vital, too fundamental to contemplate that men in their folly would someday overturn it. And so, reaching once again into the basic faith of the Enlightenment, Jefferson proclaimed that "we are free to declare, and do declare, that the rights hereby asserted are of the natural rights of mankind." May any future legislative body be warned that if it in any way revised or amended this Statute, it was not tinkering with a mere human law. On the contrary, by so doing, it challenged the prerogative of God. Let this law, therefore, this God-given right to the liberty of the soul, remain untouched, safe and sacred forever. So powerful did the force of this law appear that Jefferson would not suffer from accompanying bills that provided for preserving glebe lands, punishing Sabbath breakers, and appointing "days of public fasting and thanksgiving." The statute on religious freedom made all these other prescriptions toothless.

During all these critical deliberations, Jefferson was far removed, still in Paris. James Madison wrote swiftly (22 January 1786) to convey the great good news, though of course it would be many weeks before the intelligence reached Jefferson's anxious eyes and ears. When he finally welcomed the word from Virginia, he was so busy spreading the glad tidings that it took him some months to respond to his good friend. At last he wrote, with ill-concealed excitement, that the Statute "has been received with infinite approbation in Europe and propagated with enthusiasm." Given the nature of monarchs, it had not won royal approval anywhere, but the citizens of several European countries had joined in a chorus of praise. The Statute "has been translated into French and Italian, has been sent to most of the courts of Europe, and has been the best evidence of the falsehood of those reports which stated us to be in anarchy." Much of Europe, surprised by America's victory in the Revolution, found some solace — certainly England did — in the confident hope that this fragile young country would quickly fall apart. But it will not, Jefferson thundered, and this enlightened law provided powerful proof.

More than that, Jefferson proudly affirmed, here was a single state in a small nation taking its stand with the major nations of Europe on behalf of Enlightenment ideals. Virginia — not France, not England — had first seen "the standard of reason at length erected." For centuries, the human mind had *not* been free; on the contrary, it "has been held in vassalage by kings, priests and nobles" — Jefferson's contemptible trinity — but no more. With his pride of authorship showing, Jefferson concluded in his congratulatory note to his fellow Virginian that "it is honorable for us to have produced the first legislature who has had the courage to declare that the reason of man may be trusted with the formation of his own opinions."

From the perspective of 1786, that was certainly as much as Jefferson could say. From the perspective of more than two centuries later, it is possible to add that the Jeffersonian law set Western civilization and democratic republics everywhere upon a dramatically different path. Again and again, democratic governments would recognize that toleration was not enough, that religious freedom was not a privilege to be condescendingly bestowed but a natural right to be zealously preserved.

INFLUENCES ON JEFFERSON

Regarding both the Declaration of Independence and the Statute for Establishing Religious Freedom, Jefferson was proud to claim authorship but not necessarily originality. Concerning the Declaration, he explicitly stated that he aimed at originality of neither "principle [nor] sentiment"; the document "was intended to be an expression of the American mind, and to give to that expression the proper tone and spirit called for by the occasion." Of course, it not only expressed the American mind but helped to shape that mind for generations to come. The Statute, on the other hand, reflected only certain aspects of the American mind, but it managed to combine Enlightenment ideals with the deepest convictions of voluntary religion.

John Locke's *Letter concerning Toleration,* written a hundred years before, enunciated many of the principles that Jefferson early appropriated as his own. Locke wrote of settling the "just bounds that lie between" the civil and the ecclesiastical estate, and Jefferson's Statute can certainly and profitably be read as the American gloss on Locke's basic proposition. Those who argued that the persecutor only sought the good of the one being persecuted brought this rich sarcasm from Locke: "For it will be difficult to persuade men of sense that he, who with dry eyes and satisfaction of mind can deliver his brother to the executioner to be burnt alive, does sincerely and heartily concern himself to save that brother from the flames of hell in the world to come." Like Locke, Jefferson restricted the duties of the civil government to this world and was willing to grant to ecclesiastics and theologians the right to whatever pronouncements they might choose to make concerning the world to come.

Sometimes, Jefferson's debt to Locke was more than merely one of sentiment. The echoes in the Statute ring out in Locke's notion that "the truth certainly would do well enough if she were once left to shift for herself." In other respects, however, Jefferson clearly moved beyond Locke, who balked at granting toleration to those "who deny the being of a God." Locke, like Americans in courtrooms for centuries after, expressed grave concern that "promises, covenants, and oaths, which are the bonds of human society, can have no hold upon an atheist." Jefferson, on the other hand, was prepared to extend the liberties in and of religion to believer and nonbeliever alike. "Liberty of conscience is every man's natural right," said Locke. Exactly, said Jefferson.

Jefferson's enlightened sentiments found strong support among those for whom "liberty of conscience" was not an invention of Voltaire or Diderot but a principle of pure gold, mined from the New Testament and refined in the fires of religious persecution. Baptists in Virginia were among Madison's and Jefferson's most ardent supporters, just as Baptists in Massachusetts were among the most outspoken opponents to the firm alliance between church and state in place there. Baptist leader Isaac Backus, for example, thought that Bostonians demonstrated a lack of proper balance in being so considerably alarmed over a small tax on tea and failing to be alarmed at all over a similar tax on the conscience of all dissenters in the state. Of course citizens of Massachusetts were properly alarmed by the tea tax, "but they can avoid it by not buying the tea." Dissenters, however, had no such liberty: they must either violate conscience or pay the tax. But, explained Backus in 1774, we refuse to pay "not only on your principle of not being taxed where we are not represented, but also because we dare not render that homage to any earthly power which I, and many of my brethren, are fully convinced belongs only to God."

Backus also served the Baptist cause in the eighteenth century by reviving the reputation and writings of a sometime Baptist of the seventeenth century, Roger Williams. In his *Memorial and Remonstrance*, Madison had spoken of the "Torrents of blood [that] have been spilt in the old world, by vain attempts of the secular arm to extinguish religious discord by proscribing all difference in religious opinion." This line, and certainly this sentiment, could easily have come out of Williams's *Bloudy Tenet of Persecution,* published in London in 1644. There Williams likened the violation of one's conscience to the violation of the chaste maiden; the former was as much of a rape, a spiritual rape, as the latter. "Who can but run with zeal inflamed," Williams asked, "to prevent the deflowering of chaste souls, and spilling the blood of the innocent?" It was time — indeed, long past time — to consider the cosmic tragedy of the "whole earth, made drunk with the blood of its inhabitants."

No evidence survives of Jefferson's or Madison's having read Roger Williams, though John Locke almost certainly did. Locke also succeeded in putting his predecessor's cumbersome prose into succinct and pungent lines. But eighteenth-century Baptists, thanks in part to Isaac Backus, certainly did know of Williams and were therefore more than willing to support remonstrances, memorials, bills, and statutes that, in Williams's words, placed a "hedge or wall of separation between the garden of the church and the wilderness of the world."

JEFFERSON'S NOTES AND VIRGINIA'S INTOLERANCE

In his letter to Madison regarding the 1786 Statute, Jefferson also noted that the Virginia law was "inserted in the new Encyclopedia and is appearing in most of the publications respecting America." One of those publications "respecting America" was Jefferson's own *Notes on the State of Virginia,* formally published in 1787. In addition to the attention he gave to Nature, already noted in Chapter 2, Jefferson here turned his wary eye once more toward religion. That eye was particularly wary, as one might expect, of Anglicanism. Jefferson had no problem with institutional religion until it sought or accepted any alliance with political power. When that happened, he maintained, then the denomination — whatever denomination — invariably came to exercise that power in cruel and inhumane ways. The whole history of the Western world demonstrated the reality of that hard, sad fact. But denominations without such power, or rejecting such power, posed no threat.

So in the *Notes* he came to the defense of the Quakers, who in the seventeenth century suffered at the hands of nearly everyone, including the Anglicans. "The poor Quakers," fleeing from persecution in England, looked to the English colonies "as asylums of civil and religious freedom, but they found them free only for the reigning sect." In New England, that meant the Puritans; in Virginia, it meant the Anglicans.

In the 1650s and beyond, the House of Burgesses had passed laws that took specific aim at this radical new sect that had just burst forth in England in 1652. Laws prohibited Quakers from assembling, Quaker parents from refusing to have their children baptized according to the Anglican rite, and neighbors from showing hospitality to Quakers or distributing any of their literature. If a ship's captain brought any Quakers to Virginia, that captain would be fined or imprisoned. If Quakers were apprehended, they were jailed until exiled. The prescribed punishment for a first or second return to Virginia was relatively mild, but a third return meant death. "If no capital execution took place here, as did in New England," Jefferson observed, "it was not owing to the moderation of the church, or the spirit of the legislature."

"Anglicans retained full possession of the country for about a century," but in the aftermath of the Great Awakening and, even more, of the Revolution, that monopoly soon collapsed. Jefferson quickly reviewed the century or more of "religious slavery" and then the sequence of laws — in the passage of which he had played a major part — that from 1776 on gradually broke those ecclesiastical bonds. With us now, wrote Jefferson, it was axiomatic that "our rulers can have authority over such natural rights only as we have submitted to them." Freedom of the mind and freedom of religion had not been so submitted to such authorities, nor would they ever be. Government could legislate concerning acts, never opinions. For, said Jefferson in words that would live to haunt him, "it does me no injury for my neighbour to say there are twenty gods, or no god. It neither picks my pocket nor breaks my leg."

As witness to the wisdom of Virginia's actions, Jefferson turned to history to show the folly of coercion: the treatment of Galileo was known throughout the world, and only much later did his "error" become truth. In France, the government in its superior wisdom even outlawed the potato as a proper food. "The Newtonian principle of gravitation is now more firmly established, on the basis of reason, than it would be if the government were to step in . . . to make it an article of faith." Truth, not the sword, was the appropriate adversary of falsehood. "Reason and experiment have been indulged, and error has fled before them." This unshakable confidence in Reason was, to be sure, itself an article of faith for Jefferson, but his trust in that doctrine never wavered.

Conformity in religion, Jefferson argued, made no more sense than conformity "of face and stature." Unfortunately, nations continued to believe that uniformity of opinion was a highly desirable circumstance. Not so, said Jefferson, for uniformity produced only stagnation and decay. The effort to achieve uniformity, moreover, had resulted in the burning and torturing of millions of men, women, and children; "yet we have not advanced one inch toward uniformity." The only discernible effect of coercion in religion was "to make one half of the world fools, and the other half hypocrites." The effect of freedom of religion, on the other hand, was an unparalleled harmony, as in Pennsylvania and New York (and he might well have mentioned Rhode Island also). Citizens in these states "have made the happy discovery that the way to silence religious disputes is to take no notice of them."

Since we have been united in the Revolution and now victorious therein, Jefferson stated, no better time than the present could be found to affirm and to ensure the inalienable rights of all human beings. True, just now no one in America would tolerate an execution for heresy or a three-year prison term "for not comprehending the mysteries of the Trinity." But what about next year, next decade, next century? "A single zealot" could launch a persecution "and better men be his victims." We must move now to safeguard human freedoms not just for today but for all the days after. When Jefferson's *Notes* was first privately printed in 1785, the Bill for Establishing Religious Freedom had not been passed, so Jefferson's urgent plea is understandable. When the public edition was published in 1787, Jefferson quickly and joyfully inserted the newly adopted Statute in an appendix.

JEFFERSON'S NOTES AND THE PERPLEXITY OF RACE

When Jefferson composed the Declaration of Independence, he was faithful to the Enlightenment vision that all persons were of a "single creation," as his original draft stated. And when in 1783 he persuaded Virginians to free all children born of slaves after 1800, that vision remained clear. As noted below, he likewise in 1784 proposed in the Northwest Ordinance that slavery be abolished in all western lands covered by that document. But in his *Notes*, the vision with respect both to slavery and race grew blurry.

While admitting that his observations of the African-Americans had been limited, that he had never been to Africa, and that opportunities in Virginia for blacks to develop "their genius were not favorable, and those of exercising it less so," Jefferson nonetheless voiced his "suspicion only" that blacks did not have the same natural endowments as whites. "To justify a general conclusion," Jefferson wrote, "requires many observations." So though he was not quite ready to say that African-Americans were a distinct race, he did believe that they had at least "been made distinct by time and circumstances." More than twenty years later, in a letter written in 1809, he did point out that "whatever be their degree of talent, it is no measure of their rights."

But slavery, of course, compromised those rights or, better, violated them. And in the *Notes* Jefferson deplored the effects of slavery on both master and subject — its promotion of "the most unremitting despotism on the one part, and degrading submissions on the other." With respect to the Indians, Jefferson saw intermarriage as the ultimate solution to the divisions and suspicions. But he held no such optimistic view for the country's enslaved population. "Deep-rooted prejudices entertained by the whites; ten thousand recollections, by the blacks, of the injuries they have sustained; new provocations; the real distinctions which nature has made; and many other circumstances will divide us into parties, and produce convulsions, which will probably never end but in the extermination of one or the other race." Here, Enlightenment optimism faltered, with national consequences that were tragic.

Jefferson remained in France as the nation's minister until 1789, when he returned to find a country under a new Constitution, with another Virginian soon to be elected as the first president of the United States. And Thomas Jefferson likewise quickly entered upon that national political stage. Before turning to that epoch of Jefferson's life, however, one other appeal from the *Notes* deserves quotation: "Let us," Jefferson wrote concerning religious freedom, "give this experiment fair play." More than two centuries later, it still proves necessary from time to time to echo that fervent plea: let us give this experiment fair play.

4   The Statesman

"And may that Infinite Power, which rules the
destinies of the universe, lead our councils to
what is best." (1801)

Thomas Jefferson was still serving in Paris during the summer
of 1787 when fifty-five delegates (more or less) drafted a new
frame of government; they then submitted it to a vote of the
people, state by state, for their ratification or rejection. Since
James Madison is generally given the honorary title of "father
of the Constitution," one may assume that a Jeffersonian aura
could now and then be detected in the Philadelphia State House
— later Independence Hall. For Madison and Jefferson had
during the previous dozen years shared their hopes, vented
their mutual frustrations, and sharpened their wits against the
whetstones of each other's minds. Nonetheless, Jefferson, who
saw nothing as more important than the fixed foundation on
which a government rested, played no direct part in the drafting of the United States Constitution.

THE NORTHWEST ORDINANCE

Another document framed in 1787 by another assembly — namely, the Confederation Congress — could claim a more immediate linkage to Jefferson. The Northwest Ordinance of 1787 had its origins in the Jeffersonian Ordinance of 1784. Here the Virginian drew up the basic principles by which new states would be admitted to the Union, for following the 1783 Peace of Paris the young United States suddenly extended all the way to the Mississippi River. How would this land be governed? Would the status of the original thirteen states set them apart from newer states? Would inhabitants of those frontier lands be free to establish any sort of government that they chose? These and other questions had to be addressed, and addressed quickly, in the postwar years when everything was new, untested, uncertain.

In his Ordinance, Jefferson established the principle that only republican forms of government would be acknowledged and that new states would be admitted on terms of full equality with the older thirteen. He tried to establish the principle that slavery would not be allowed, either north or south of the Ohio River, after 1800. He did not mention religion. Having endured the revising of the Declaration of Independence as well as the Statute for Establishing Religious Freedom, Jefferson no doubt braced himself for the rewriting of his Ordinance — and, indeed, it began in due course. Nevertheless, the document that emerged in 1787, which stands as one of the pivotal official statements in America's entire history, still bore a Jeffersonian stamp. And it did mention religion.

The Northwest Ordinance also prohibited slavery, but only in the territory north of the Ohio River. In addition, it specified that no fewer than three states would be created from this land north of the Ohio and east of the Mississippi, and no more than five. (Jefferson had even suggested names for the new states, but the Congress fortunately dropped Cherronesus, Assenisipia, and Pelisipia, though it retained Illinois and

Michigan.) Whenever the population of a given region reached sixty thousand, the process of drawing up a state constitution and applying for admission to the Union could begin.

Well before a Bill of Rights had been drafted for the nation as a whole, the Northwest Ordinance specified that religious freedom would be guaranteed to all. That provision caused no controversy in the Confederation Congress, for the Jeffersonian principle enunciated so clearly in Virginia the year before quickly became a prevailing, if not universal, sentiment. But another question proved far thornier: should religion be somehow *supported* in this vast sprawling and fearsomely barbaric frontier? In April of 1785, a congressional committee proposed the following language. "There shall be reserved the central Section [640 acres] of every Township [six square miles] for the maintenance of public Schools; and the Section immediately adjoining the same to the northward, for the support of religion." Profits from these lands, like the glebe lands in colonial Virginia, would apply to their respective causes. Someone thought that the word "religion" should be replaced by the phrase "religion and charitable uses." Someone else thought that religion should be struck altogether, leaving only "charitable uses" in place. And still other members thought the whole idea of a second "northward" section set aside for special purposes ought to be dropped.

After more than two years of tortured debate, the much-mangled clause of the Northwest Ordinance revealed a kind of national schizophrenia that persisted for generations after. All members of the Congress agreed that religion was necessary to the well-being and good order of the Old Northwest. Did that not mean, therefore, that government needed to support this necessary religion? Some members of Congress said yes; the Jeffersonians said no. In this instance, after long deliberation, the Jeffersonians won. The final form of the Third Article read as follows: "Religion, Morality and knowledge being necessary to good government and the happiness of mankind . . ." — thus far unanimity, but then the Jeffersonians took over —

"Schools and the means of education shall forever be encouraged." No similar "encouragement," much less 640 acres of support, was granted to religion or to the churches. "No man," said Jefferson's Statute of the previous year, "shall be compelled to frequent or support any religious worship, place, or ministry whatsoever."

THE CONSTITUTION AND RELIGION

Three months after the adoption of the Northwest Ordinance, the weary delegates in the Constitutional Convention sent out their plan for a stronger, more centralized national government. In little over a month later, on 24 October 1787, an even wearier James Madison sent a copy to Jefferson in Paris, along with a very long letter calling his friend's attention to the principles preserved, the problems encountered, and the hopes for its adoption entertained. The "great objects" achieved, Madison wrote, were these:

1. To unite a proper energy in the Executive and a proper stability in the Legislative departments, with the essential characters of Republican Government.
2. To draw a line of demarcation which would give to the General Government every power requisite for general purposes, and leave to the States every power which might be most beneficially administered by them.
3. To provide for the different interests of different parts of the Union.
4. To adjust the clashing pretensions of the large and small States.

"Each of these objects," Madison acknowledged, "was pregnant with difficulties." That some agreement, by no means unanimous, was finally reached could be regarded as "nothing less than a miracle."

If Madison held his breath waiting for Jefferson's reply,

he held it for a very long time indeed. The slowness of the mails across the Atlantic, together with Jefferson's other duties in France, prevented him from responding until 20 December 1787 — and then it was another month or two before Madison in Montpelier could hold the letter in his hand. Jefferson offered restrained congratulations for the achievement (he did not use the word "miracle") of the delegates' difficult labors in Philadelphia. Jefferson liked the division of government into executive, judicial, and legislative branches. He thought the compromise between the large states and the small excellent, giving the small states equal representation in the Senate and the large states a more proportionate share in the House. And he strongly agreed that the House, whose members were chosen immediately by the people (senators at that time being selected by the states), was the proper repository for the power to levy taxes. The praise was less than lavish, however, for Madison's close friend also found things in the Constitution that he did not like.

He objected that the Constitution provided for no "rotation in office" — what a later age would designate "term limits." He thought this especially obnoxious in the case of the chief executive, who, as matters stood, could be reelected for life and thus be rendered, as Jefferson told John Adams, "a bad edition of a Polish king." Jefferson also confessed, "I own I am not a friend to a very energetic government. It is always oppressive." His first and most basic objection, however, was to "the omission of a bill of rights providing clearly and without the aid of sophisms for freedom of religion, freedom of the press, protections against standing armies," and several more fundamental liberties. Madison had pointed out that some thought such a bill unnecessary since the federal government held only those powers clearly specified. Jefferson demurred. "Let me add," he wrote, "that a bill of rights is what the people are entitled to against every government on earth, general or particular, and what no just government should refuse, or rest on inference." Rights must be spelled out, carved as it were in stone, and fixed beyond any fainthearted doubt or bureaucratic gibberish. And at the top of his list of rights stood freedom of religion.

By the time that Madison received Jefferson's not altogether reassuring reply, the younger man was already deeply embattled in the fight for ratification of the Constitution. Along with two New Yorkers, Alexander Hamilton and John Jay, he hurriedly helped write the now famous *Federalist Papers,* cogent arguments designed primarily to persuade the voting population of New York to support the Constitution. Madison recognized that the opposition was formidable, and in truth Jefferson's lukewarm endorsement did not help. For a few months, their long and profound friendship wavered. Madison wanted to make the new government work; Jefferson wanted to make the new government safe. One could not do everything at once. As Madison confessed in 1788 to a former neighbor of Jefferson's, Philip Mazzei, now also in Paris, "You asked me why I agreed to the constitution proposed" in Philadelphia. "I answer because I thought it safe to the liberties of the people, and the best that could be obtained from the jarring interests of the States, and the miscellaneous opinions of politicians." A more thorough reply to Mazzei and all other interested parties could be found in the *Federalist Papers,* the majority of which — and the most memorable of which — Madison composed.

From the perspective of later centuries, one can hardly imagine the Constitution *not* being ratified. The fact is, however, that ratification was a near thing. Nine states, the minimum number specified by the document itself, had ratified by 21 June 1788, when New Hampshire voted narrowly (57 to 47) in support. But none of the three authors of the *Federalist Papers* could relax, nor could Jefferson in France, for neither New York nor Virginia was among the nine, and who could imagine a viable United States without those giants?

The debate in Virginia, Madison's and Jefferson's own state, grew ever more intense, with such respected leaders as George Mason, Richard Henry Lee, and Patrick Henry lining up the opposition. When the vote finally came at the end of June, Madison could breathe a sigh of relief, but just barely: 89 votes for, 79 votes against. Then the ball passed into New York's court, the home state for both Hamilton and Jay, where many called for amendments before approval, not after. By the end of July, the vote was taken and the Constitution was approved by the closest margin of any of the states: 27 against, and 30 — with hope stuck in their throats — in favor.

Why so much opposition to a document now regarded as an icon? Many reasons erupted in the several ratification congresses, but chief among them was the omission that Jefferson had so readily identified: no Bill of Rights. Those English liberties that had been underlined in 1776, that had been fought for throughout the Revolution, and that had been secured by many of the states could be found nowhere in the Constitution of the United States. And the absence of any reference to religion, as in the case of the Northwest Ordinance, protruded like a sore thumb. Not only did the free exercise of religion receive no mention whatsoever, but the very subject of religion seemed to have been regarded as a great embarrassment. Nobody wanted to talk about it; nobody acknowledged it, even to the minimal extent of recognizing, in the vaguest language possible, an overarching Providence or an Author of creation. With respect to any hints of this nature, the Constitution stood mute before the bar of public opinion.

At one point, it did speak, and — in the minds of many — silence would have been better. Article VI included this sentence: "No religious test shall ever be required as a qualification to any office or public trust under the United States." Did that mean even the president of the country? Assured that it did, one citizen of New Hampshire exploded that "we may have a Papist, a Mohomatan, a Deist, yea an Atheist at the helm of government." A well-known Marylander, Luther Martin, contended that "in a Christian country, it would be at least decent to hold out some distinction between the professors of Christianity and downright infidelity or paganism." And in the following century, a National Reform Association lobbied for decades to rewrite the preamble of the Constitution to make explicit a Christian profession of faith on behalf of the newly organized government. The Madisonians and the Jeffersonians prevailed, however, defining the Constitution as a civil document, insulated from concerns proper to the ecclesiastical estate.

THE BILL OF RIGHTS

While such insulation could be inferred from the Constitutional silences, Thomas Jefferson, along with multitudes more, knew that mere inference was not enough. Madison, participating in face-to-face ratification discussions and quarrels, recognized that his own state was determined never to vote for the Constitution unless he personally guaranteed that a Bill of Rights would be the first order of business in the First Congress under the new frame of government. So when he was elected to the House of Representatives in 1789, he set about to fulfill that promise. While he needed no encouragement from his friend abroad, he received it nonetheless. In March of that year, Jefferson wrote to answer all the arguments raised against such a bill and to make a pitch, once more, for its swift passage. "The inconveniences" of a Bill of Rights, he told Madison, "are that it may cramp government in its useful exertions. But the evil of this is short-lived, moderate, and reparable." On the other hand, the absence of any such assurances "are permanent, afflicting, and irreparable: they are in constant progression from bad to worse." Jefferson at the moment worried more about the "tyranny of the legislatures," but he predicted that at some point in the future "the executive will come in its turn." Not now, however, Jefferson added, for "the rising race are all republicans."

The very first clause of the very First Amendment took up the subject of religion, and that subject proved as troublesome in New York (the temporary capital) as it had in Philadelphia — and as it had in Richmond. On 7 June 1789, Madison submitted his proposal for assuring freedom of religion. "The Civil Rights of none shall be abridged on account of religious belief or worship," he wrote, "nor shall any national religion be established, nor shall the full and equal rights of conscience be in any manner, nor on any pretext, infringed." Now Madison's turn had arrived to endure the indignity of being revised, amended, excluded, and abbreviated. By the end of July, a small committee of the House had condensed Madison's language to "No religion shall be established by law, nor shall the equal rights of conscience be infringed."

In August, Samuel Livermore of New Hampshire offered his version: "Congress shall make no laws touching religion, or infringing the rights of conscience." Then Fisher Ames of Massachusetts amended that to read: "Congress shall make no law establishing religion, or to prevent the free exercise thereof, or to infringe the rights of conscience." This version was then sent to the Senate, which during the first week of September subjected the religion clause to its own process of revising and amending. By 9 September, the Senate had arrived at its approved wording: "Congress shall make no law establishing articles of faith or a mode of worship, or prohibiting the free exercise of religion." The wording of the two chambers differed sufficiently to require a conference committee, which managed in less than three weeks to agree on the final language: "Congress shall make no law respecting the establishment of religion, or prohibiting the free exercise thereof."

Madison's "conscience" had been dropped, though many state constitutions held on to the word. His prohibition against "any national religion" also disappeared, but was clearly implied in what remained. On the whole, the ultimate product of sixteen words no doubt improved the verbosity of Madison's forty words, and a current Supreme Court must be grateful for the introduction of that simplicity or, at least, brevity. The First Amendment with respect to religion stands, therefore, as the product of committees, not to be claimed by any author as part of his epitaph.

The two religion clauses, the "free exercise" clause and the "establishment" clause, to use the familiar shorthand, are not just different ways of saying the same thing. "Free exercise" restrains the government from doing anything to interfere with or infringe upon a full liberty in religion. "Establishment" enjoins the government against doing anything to subsidize religion. Rather than being merely redundant, they move in opposite directions: do nothing to help, do nothing to hinder. The ground that this leaves for federal action is therefore severely limited, and that is only one of the reasons why America's courts, especially in the second half of the twentieth century, have found themselves sharply divided on exactly where the "true" legal line is to be drawn.

The first ten amendments to the Constitution (initially twelve) were sent out to the states for approval in 1789; they won ratification in 1791. North Carolina, concerned about approving any constitution that had no such enumerated rights, tardily voted 194 to 77 in favor of the Constitution on 21 November 1789. The last state to lend its approval, Rhode Island, also concerned about its rights and liberties, did not give its approval (34 to 22) until 29 May 1790. By that time, George Washington had already been in office as president for more than a year, and Thomas Jefferson as secretary of state for four months.

SERVING WITH GEORGE WASHINGTON AND JOHN ADAMS

Jefferson returned from his long mission to France in November of 1789, to be welcomed by the Assembly meeting in Richmond in December. He made his way to his beloved Monticello, where he pondered the president's offer, received en route, to become the nation's first secretary of state. Monticello beckoned, but public duty did as well. And the country stood poised at a moment in history that could thrust it forward to its rightful place among the world of true nations or pull it back into a dependency on England (a terrible fate, in Jefferson's view) or on Europe in general. Jefferson accepted the invitation also on more personal grounds: his great admiration for George Washington, the one person who could hold the nation together, the one person who could be named president without quarrel or controversy.

As Jefferson had written some years before in his *Notes on the State of Virginia*, "In war we have produced a Washington, whose memory shall be adorned while liberty shall have votaries, whose name will triumph over time, and will in future ages assume its just station among the most celebrated worthies of the world." When he took office in April of 1790, Jefferson's chief anxiety was that Washington might not live long enough to serve out his term. In fact, Washington fell seriously ill the following month, and Jefferson fretted that the fragile ship of state would crash against the rocks. But in a few weeks, the two men sallied forth on a three-day fishing trip.

Jefferson's deep sense of obligation, almost a religious obligation, to the nation is best seen in a letter written to friends and neighbors who, twenty years before, had elected him to the House of Burgesses. "We have been fellow-labourers & fellow-sufferers," he wrote in late 1789, "& heaven has rewarded us with a happy issue from our struggles." Now the time had come, he added, "to enjoy in peace & concord the blessings of self-government so long denied to mankind." His faith in the ideals of the Enlightenment undiminished, Jefferson pledged to demonstrate "the sufficiency of human reason for the care of human affairs." And majority rule, he reminded his friends, "the natural law of every society, is the only sure guardian of the rights of man."

In Washington's cabinet (a term not yet in vogue) Jefferson as secretary of state stood next to Alexander Hamilton as secretary of the treasury. Washington boasted of having two such brilliant advisers and confidants, but he fervently wished that they could find some common ground. They could not. Jefferson, sympathetic to France, envisioned a nation of small and independent farmers, "the chosen people of God." Hamilton, warmly disposed toward England, envisioned a nation built on manufacturing and financial interests, the only road to greatness. After years of feuding with Hamilton, Jefferson had had enough and retired early in Washington's second term to return to Monticello — permanently, he believed. There he wrote to Philip Mazzei, in indignation and disappointment, that "an Anglican monarchical aristocratical party has sprung up, whose avowed object is to draw over us the substance, as they have already done the forms, of the British government." Those three adjectives in front of "party" pointed to just about everything Jefferson found wrong in the contemporary world: Anglicanism still smelling of church-state union, monarchy still oppressing liberties everywhere, and aristocracy still betraying the spirit of the Revolution and majority rule. In exasperation, Jefferson reached for a biblical analogy of the American patriots who once were Samsons but who now "have had their heads shorn by the harlot England."

While he was still in Washington's cabinet, Jefferson advised his president regarding the recognition of France. The same natural law of morality that applied to human beings applied as well to nations. France must be guided by its God-given conscience, with Reason and instinct working together to spread the message of liberty and equality around the world. Jefferson, believing that France would be obedient to moral law, urged that the Republic be recognized and that its minister be officially received. That minister, Edmond Genêt, turned out to be an embarrassment to Jefferson as he foolishly violated the terms of strict neutrality that America had adopted in the war then raging between England and France. Despite Genêt's inexcusable folly, the pro-French sentiment of the Jeffersonians inspired the growth of "Democratic" and "Republican" societies across the country.

From Monticello, Jefferson, though now ostensibly keeping himself out of politics, gradually assumed the leadership of a competing political party that took the name of Republican. This faction stood over against the Federalist party, heavily favored in New England and now led by Washington's vice president, John Adams. The Constitution had not anticipated the presence of political parties, and George Washington both resented and resisted the rise of a "party spirit." By 1796, when it was clear that John Adams, a two-term vice president, would lead the Federalist party's drive for the presidency, friends persuaded a reluctant Jefferson to head the Republican "ticket" — except that there was no ticket. Prior to the Twelfth Amendment to the Constitution, added in 1804, candidates ran on a single slate, with the person receiving the highest number of votes becoming president, the one with the next highest being named vice president. One did not run for the vice presidency; one lost the race for president and thereby took second place to his bitter competitor — a political nightmare that haunted the nation during its first fifteen years under the Constitution.

If Jefferson was concerned about an Adams presidency, he grew even more concerned about the advisory role of Alexander Hamilton, leader of those sometimes designated "High Federalists." Hamilton, who represented what Jefferson most abhorred, continued to press for his "monarchical" program, working with John Adams when possible and against him when necessary. "The mass of the people," said Hamilton, "are turbulent and changing — they seldom judge or determine right." The mass of the people, argued Jefferson, constituted the only solid defenders of liberty. "The further the departure from direct and constant control by the citizens," Jefferson informed John Taylor, "the less has the government of the ingredient of republicanism." By 1795, Jefferson had concluded that parties were inevitable and "party spirit" was not necessarily a great evil. "Were parties here divided merely by a greediness for office, as in England," he observed, "to take a part with either would be unworthy of a reasonable or moral man." But when a choice was as clear-cut as between the Republicans on the one hand and the "Monocrats" on the other, then, Jefferson concluded, "I hold it as honorable to take a firm & decided part, and as immoral to pursue a middle line."

John Adams won the election of 1796, but by the narrowest of margins: 71 electoral votes to Jefferson's 68. It was not a promising beginning, and the news grew worse for Adams: he was besieged by persons still loyal to Washington or newly loyal to Hamilton, and he was saddled with the leader of the opposition as his vice president. If Adams became a bit paranoid, one can surely understand. The Alien and Sedition Acts, passed in 1798, made the whole country seem paranoid, and their illiberal spirit infuriated Jefferson. The Sedition Act in particular struck him as so wide-sweeping as to prevent any criticism of or check on the federal government. Next, said Jefferson, Congress will soon declare "that the President shall continue in office during life," and perhaps all senators too. When Jefferson and Madison encouraged states to "nullify" or declare federal acts void in their own regions, a threat to the unity of the country, to say nothing of the Adams administration, loomed menacingly. Adams called for a national day of fasting during which all citizens might entreat the Almighty to "withhold from us unreasonable discontent, from disunion, faction, sedition, and insurrection."

THE CAMPAIGN OF 1800

Faction and disunion did not disappear, however; in the wide-open presidential campaign of 1800, the bitterness only deepened. Jefferson's religion, or lack of it, emerged as a central issue in that campaign, perhaps religion's greatest visibility in a presidential race until the 1928 effort of Alfred E. Smith. Adams had hoped that Washington's two-term precedent would hold for him, but it did not. It did hold, however, for Thomas Jefferson as it did for his successors in the Virginia dynasty, James Madison and James Monroe. Adams's defeat in 1800 likewise spelled defeat for a demoralized, discredited Federalist party.

In the bruising campaign itself, however, the Federalists dedicated one more great effort, their last hurrah, to the defeat of Thomas Jefferson. Yale's president Timothy Dwight gave the campaign a head start in 1798, when he warned against any and all traffic with the Republicans. Should one be so misguided as to vote Republican, "is it that our churches may become temples of reason, our Sabbath a decade, and our psalms of praise Marseilles hymns?" What Dwight had in mind were the many reforms, including those of the calendar, that the French Revolution had introduced. Shall we too "see the Bible cast into a bonfire, the vessels of the sacramental supper borne by an ass in public profession, and our children . . . united in chanting mockeries against God . . . [to] the ruin of their religion and the loss of their souls?" Jefferson's friendship with France made him automatically liable for all the excesses, religious and otherwise, of that country's strongly anticlerical Revolution.

By 1800, the Federalists no longer shrouded their attacks in language aimed more obviously at France. Now Jefferson himself stood exposed as the target. The Reverend William Linn, Dutch Reformed minister of New York, joined in the frenzy. In the *Notes on the State of Virginia*, Linn found evidence that Jefferson rejected biblical revelation; this man who would be president even questioned the universal deluge in the days of Noah and failed utterly to hold up the Bible as the book "most ancient, the most authentic, the most interesting, and the most useful in the world." On this ground alone, Linn declared, "he ought to be rejected from the Presidency." Some would argue, said Linn, that Jefferson was a man of superb talents and remarkable abilities; so much the worse, for "the greater will be his power and the more extensive his influence in poisoning mankind."

Linn was willing to refer to Jefferson as a deist — but for anyone with a pretext to orthodoxy, the line between deism and atheism seemed hardly worth a notice. So a besieged Alexander Hamilton, fearful that his king-maker role might come to an end, demanded that New York's governor John Jay *do something*. Some "legal and constitutional step" should be taken, Hamilton urged, "to prevent an atheist in religion, and a fanatic in politics from getting possession of the helm of state."

The Federalist newspaper, the *Gazette of the United States*, in September of 1800 treated the religious issue as the crux of the campaign. Jefferson was condemned out of his own mouth — as a skeptic, a deist, "an enemy to pure morals and religion, and consequently an enemy to his country and his God." Anyone who had so little shame as to vote for Thomas Jefferson, said the *Gazette*, "insults his maker and redeemer. . . . What can screen such wretches from the just vengeance of insulted heaven!" The time for decision was at hand, shouted the newspaper, as the printer reached for larger type. Every American must lay his hand upon his heart and ask whether he will continue allegiance to "GOD — AND A RELIGIOUS PRESIDENT; or impiously declare for JEFFERSON AND NO GOD!!!" The editors admired that exclamatory summary of the campaign so much that they printed it over and over.

Jefferson's *Notes* provided even more ammunition. Whoever could write that it made no difference to him whether his neighbor believed in one God, twenty gods, or no god could not be a friend to Christianity. And whoever could say that the centuries of church-state alliance resulted only in making one-half of the world fools and the other half hypocrites could not be trusted in any position of power anywhere in the United States. Jefferson took great pride in the Virginia Statute for Establishing Religious Freedom. But, asked William Smith of South Carolina, "Does religion flourish in Virginia more than it did, or more than in the Eastern States?" All that talk about religious liberty and religious freedom has, "in my opinion," said Smith, "an immediate tendency to produce a total disregard to public worship, an absolute indifference to all religion whatsoever."

Since religion was so closely tied to morality, Federalist campaigners found it easy, even irresistible, to suggest that one who held such extreme religious views could not be trusted in moral matters either. Society would become "loose." Or, as one propagandist put it, "If Jefferson is elected," then "those morals which protect our lives from the knife of the assassin — which guard the chastity of our wives and daughters from seduction and violence" will be jeopardized or jettisoned. For a candidate who honored Reason, it must have seemed that all rationality had dropped totally out of sight.

Jefferson, clearly hurt by these attacks on his integrity and character, declined to respond in public. As he wrote to one friend, "I know that I might have filled the courts of the United States with actions for these slanders," but it would have given him no satisfaction for the grievous loss of character. So he would leave his enemies "to the reproof of their own consciences." And if they had a deficiency in that department, there would nevertheless "come a day when the false witness will meet a Judge who has not slept over his slanders."

But if Jefferson maintained a stoic silence in public, his private letters overflowed with resentment and anger — most of which was directed against the clergy of New England. That "irritable tribe of priests," those "bigots in religion and government," those "barbarians" who wanted to return the nation to the dark ages of the past — these and other candid expressions reveal the depth of an anticlericalism that can be laid directly at the door of the campaign of 1800. "If there had never been a priest," Jefferson sourly observed later, "there would never have been an infidel." Never again after this wounding campaign would Jefferson relax regarding those clergy who lusted after preferment and power or those who would cramp or shut down the minds of humankind. We can be grateful, Jefferson noted, that "the laws of the present day withhold their hands from blood; but lies and slander still remain to them."

The Jeffersonian Republicans, of course, had their pamphleteers and newspapers and boosters who spoke of their candidate in glowing terms. Jefferson was characterized as "the enlightened citizen, the patriot, the philosopher, and friend of man." Voters were called to remember who guided Virginia in its resistance to Britain, who wrote the Declaration of Independence, who served his nation with distinction all those years in France, and who with dignity and coolness directed the nation's foreign affairs as secretary of state. We give you a man, the Republicans in effect declared, who is rich in experience, proven in character, tested by the powers of Europe, and patriotic to the core. "Look up to that man," the voters in New Jersey were told, who "has not given to his enemies a single cause for reproach; who cannot be impeached of immorality nor of vice." On the contrary, he had labored tirelessly "to promote toleration in religion and freedom in politics; to cultivate the arts and virtues at home, and to shun the vices and depravities of corrupt foreign governments." Such a man clearly deserved your support, your confidence, your vote.

If the Federalists could find religious ammunition against Jefferson in his *Notes* and in his Statute, his friends, drawing on those same sources, could refute the wildest charges against him. In the *Notes*, for example, Jefferson wrote, "Can the liberties of a nation be thought secure, when we have removed their only firm basis, a conviction in the minds of the people, that these liberties are the gift of God?" Did this sound like an atheist? Or even, for that matter, did it sound like some irresponsible, anarchical, Jacobin deist? In the Statute, Jefferson wrote of "Almighty God" who created the mind free and of the "Holy Author of our Religion, . . . Lord both of body and mind." These words, one Republican concluded, were "worth a thousand commentaries." Let any fair mind put them up against the slander and calumnies oozing, day after day, out of the Federalist camp.

So the Jeffersonians defended their candidate from religious attack. But, in the name of religion, they also went on the offensive against the Federalist John Adams. After all, Adams came from the state of Massachusetts, where no statute of re-

ligious freedom had been written and where no church had
been disestablished. Indeed, the state's constitution (in the
drafting of which Adams had played a leading role) specified
that the legislature had the power to authorize "the support
and maintenance of public Protestant teachers of piety, religion,
and morality." That constitution further decreed that all men
had the duty "publicly, and at stated seasons, to worship the
SUPREME BEING, the great Creator and Preserver of the universe." So also, the governor, the legislators, and all state offi-
cials must, upon their election to office, take the following oath:
"I do declare that I believe the Christian religion, and have firm
persuasion of its truth." If John Adams could support such laws
in Massachusetts, then what dark designs might he have for
the nation?

Those who imagined the worst of Adams, or played on
the fears of those who might, found grist for their campaign
mills when in March of 1799 President Adams called for a
national day of fasting. This act in itself need not have been
alarming, but the language he used and mood he evoked
seemed to echo the sentiments of the General Assembly of the
Presbyterian Church — and that was alarming. Many, including Jefferson, believed that the Presbyterians hungered for
some special status as a National Church. If the wings of southern Episcopalians had been clipped by the Revolution, and if
the appeal of the Congregationalists had been circumscribed
by the fact that they did not range in significant numbers beyond New England, perhaps the Presbyterians could surface
as a "compromise candidate" between the North and the
South. In this way, some dared to hope, religion could still have
a powerful public presence.

All of this, more fancy than fact, made for excellent campaign material. The Presbyterians, in their call for a national
fast, warned of a "bursting storm" — French infidelity? Jeffersonian deism? — "which threatens to sweep before it the religious principles, institutions, and morals of our people." God
had a controversy "with our nation," the General Assembly

95

concluded. It was a few months later that President Adams proclaimed a day of fasting on the grounds that the "foundations of all religious, moral, and social obligations" were being steadily undermined. "I have thought proper to recommend . . . ," said the President, "that Thursday, the twenty-fifth day of April next [1799], be observed, throughout the United States of America, as a day of solemn humiliation, fasting, and prayer." Then Adams, in quite Presbyterian-sounding language, called upon the American people to repent.

It was Adams, however, who later repented, convinced that this tactical error cost him his reelection. As he wrote to his and Jefferson's friend Benjamin Rush of Philadelphia, he was held up in 1800 as a threat to the religious liberties of the American people, as a schemer designing to foist off a Presbyterian establishment upon the nation. "I had no concern" with the General Assembly, Adams assured Rush, but no one believed me. "A general suspicion prevailed that the Presbyterian Church was ambitious and aimed at an establishment of a national church." Adams's political enemies accused him of being "the head of this political and ecclesiastical project." And so the damage was done. "The secret whisper ran through all the sects," Adams informed Rush, "Let us have Jefferson, Madison, Burr, anybody . . . rather than a Presbyterian President." On both sides of the political fence, religion was a tinderbox, ready to burst into flame at the slightest spark.

PRESIDENT JEFFERSON AND THE WALL OF SEPARATION

After a deeply divisive campaign, when at last the ballots were counted, the Federalists had won 65 electoral votes, the Republicans 73. Not a smashing victory for the Jeffersonians, to be sure; but for that party, matters quickly grew worse. Thomas Jefferson and Aaron Burr had received exactly the same number of votes. Who, then, should be president and who vice president? The House of Representatives, invested with the responsibility of making the determination, went through thirty-six tedious roll calls before Jefferson finally emerged on top. Before the next election, the Constitution was amended to preclude such folly.

Thomas Jefferson's first task as president was, therefore, to heal, to bind up a nation almost as divided as the one Lincoln addressed sixty-five years later in his Second Inaugural. In Jefferson's First Inaugural, and the first to be delivered in the new federal city of Washington, D.C., a bruised and sobered president pleaded with his fellow citizens to "unite with one heart and one mind." May words be softened and wounds healed. "Let us restore to social intercourse that harmony and affection without which liberty and even life itself are but dreary things." Not every difference of opinion, he keenly observed, is "a difference of principle." In fine, "we are all republicans — we are all federalists." This irenic commitment to unity did not, however, reduce or diminish, even at this tense moment, Jefferson's clarion call to liberty. "Sometimes it is said that man cannot be trusted with the government of himself." But consider the implications. "Can he, then, be trusted with the government of others? Or have we found angels in the form of kings to govern him?" No, not in America; not in either party; not in any age.

Jefferson concluded his first presidential address with what might be called a testimony to his public religion, very different from his carefully guarded private religion. A half-century earlier, Benjamin Franklin had written of the "Necessity of a Publick Religion," a religion that spoke more to and on behalf of the social order than to the individual mind or heart. Jefferson no doubt had such essential utility in mind (as have presidents before and since) when he closed with these words: "And may that Infinite Power which rules the destinies of the universe, lead our councils to what is best, and give them a favorable issue for your peace and prosperity." In employing this kind of language, Jefferson followed a tradition that both preceding presidents had set. George Washington voiced his assurance that "there never was a people, who had more reason to acknowledge a divine interposition in their affairs, than those of the United States." And John Adams spoke of an "over-ruling Providence" that enabled a small knot of colonies to defeat a mighty empire.

Jefferson could not altogether avoid the priestly role that presidential powers thrust upon him, but he did reject the more intrusive elements which that "bully pulpit" afforded. He would not, for example, proclaim national feast days or days of "solemn humiliation, fasting, and prayer." He would not follow the example of John Adams or George Washington in this regard — not just because it had for Adams been a political mistake, but because it was for Jefferson a religious mistake as well. Giving thanks to God or repenting before God were private religious activities, pious devotions, if you will; civil officers, whether mayors, governors, or presidents, had no business in these intimate matters. The people had other representatives, persons of their own choosing, with full responsibilities in the ecclesiastical realm. Besides, did we not now have a First Amendment, and did we not understand what it meant?

Shortly after assuming his presidential office, Jefferson received a formal address from the Danbury Baptist Association in Connecticut. Having few friends in Connecticut, a largely Federalist state, he gladly read their warm words of congratulations on his election. They also requested that Jefferson set aside a day of fasting so that the nation might more quickly recover from the strident ad hominem campaign. Jefferson was not willing to accede to that request for reasons just noted, but he could not pass up the opportunity to explain his position. He drafted a reply that he forwarded to his attorney general, Levi Lincoln, for advice. The Danbury Baptists, he informed Lincoln, afforded him the occasion, "which I have long wished to find, of saying why I do not proclaim fastings and thanksgivings, as my predecessors did." This reply, Jefferson added, "will give great offence to the New England clergy, but the advocate of religious freedom is to expect neither peace nor forgiveness from them." Since Lincoln was from Massachusetts, Jefferson thought he would be sensitive to any unintentional harshness of language. Jefferson sensed that the dish he was about to serve might need to be made more palatable for Northern stomachs; "it is at present seasoned to the Southern taste only," and perhaps more suitable for a Virginia table than for any other.

The approved letter of reply to the Danbury Association, dated 1 January 1802, has acquired a juridical history all its own. A single long sentence demands, therefore, full quotation:

> Believing with you that religion is a matter which lies solely between man and his God, that he owes account to none other for his faith or his worship, that the legislative powers of government reach actions only, and not opinions, I contemplate with sovereign reverence that act of the whole American people which declared that their legislature should "make no law respecting an establishment of religion, or prohibiting the free exercise thereof," thus building a wall of separation between Church and State.

The clincher that comes at the very end offered Jefferson's own clear understanding of what the First Amendment intended to achieve. That action of "the whole American people" (for the Bill of Rights had to be ratified by special conventions of the citizens) did not draw pale lines in invisible ink between the civil and ecclesiastical estates: it built a *wall*. So Jefferson believed, and on such a belief Jefferson would act. And by a quirk of memory or rhetoric, Jefferson's "wall of separation" phrase, to be found nowhere in the Constitution, came to grow more familiar than the constitutional language itself.

Four years later, in his Second Inaugural Address, Jefferson had retreated not one inch from his position on presidential proclamations relating to religion. Making his stance explicit to the Congress and to all the American people rather than just a few Baptists huddled together in Connecticut, the president stated that "in matters of religion, I have considered that its free exercise is placed by the constitution independent of the powers of the general government." Any governmental tampering with religion was meddling; more than that, it was constitutionally prohibited meddling. "I have therefore," Jefferson continued, carefully refrained from prescribing any religious exercises for the population at large. These he would leave to the "direction and discipline" of others. From this position Jefferson, unlike both his predecessors and his successors, did not budge. The Constitution, after all, had constructed a wall.

With respect to public religion, however, Jefferson continued to invoke the blessings of a divine providence. The president had his own individual "wall": that erected between private religion, which he would not touch in any official capacity, and public religion, which he would endorse and support. Thus, in his Second Inaugural, he also called for "the favor of that Being in whose hands we are, who led our fathers, as Israel of old, from their native land and planted them in a country flowing with all the necessaries and comforts of life." Jefferson not only knew his Bible, he also knew when it seemed most appropriate to evoke its imagery.

BREACHING THE WALL?

But did Jefferson himself, in matters other than fasts and feasts, scale that wall? Some have thought so, with particular reference to the Indians. In 1789, the secretary of war in George Washington's administration, Henry Knox, recommended that missionaries "of excellent moral character" be sent to Indians on the frontier and that these persons "should be well supplied with all the instruments of husbandry, and the necessary stock for a farm." Missionaries were not to buy and sell land or engage in commerce in any way but were to be the Indians' "friends and fathers." Knox conceded that such an effort "might not fully effect the civilization of the Indians," but it should at least dispose them favorably toward the United States and its interests. To those who objected to the plan on the basis of its cost, Knox answered that, compared with the use of force, "it would be found the highest economy" to pursue this approach.

Jefferson continued the practice of providing farm tools and small grants from a fund set up by Congress in 1802 for the stated purpose of civilizing the Indians. In 1803, William Henry Harrison, then governor of the Indian Territory, signed a treaty with the Kaskaskia Indians in Illinois; he signed on behalf of the United States government and during Jefferson's first term as president. The language of the treaty indicates that the Kaskaskia had already been baptized and taken into the Catholic Church, "to which they are much attached." For its part in reaching agreement with this group, the United States pledged one hundred dollars for the next seven years in support of a Catholic missionary whose duties would include the instruction of as many children as possible "in the rudiments of literature." "And the United States will further give the sum of three hundred dollars to assist said tribe in the erection of a church."

What may one make of all this? Was the Jefferson of 1803 a different Jefferson from the one of 1776 or 1786? Some have so argued. On the other hand, correspondence in the last decades of his life demonstrates that his commitment to religious freedom had wavered in no way; in fact, it had hardened. The question, then, is whether the Indian treaty represents a major inconsistency on the part of the libertarian Thomas Jefferson.

Several points should be made. First, the explicit congressional intent in setting aside funds was to promote the civilizing, not the Christianizing, of the Kaskaskia. They had already been converted and baptized, so the purpose was not religious but political: to stabilize the relationship between the government and the Indians by means other than war and to mitigate their hostility toward the United States. Second, Jefferson, or more properly Governor William Henry Harrison, like Henry Knox before him, took advantage of the most readily available means (viz., the missionaries) for achieving these purposes at modest costs to the federal treasury. Third, here again one sees a resort to public religion — that is, to a socially useful application of the moral and educational dimensions of religion. Jefferson proudly claimed in his Second Inaugural, concerning the "aborigines," that "we have . . . liberally furnished them with the implements of husbandry and household use" and "have placed among them instructors in the arts of first necessity."

Though the religious involvement was in this instance severely limited, both in numbers and space, Jefferson's secretary of state, James Madison, rightly warned his president that some might detect in this action "a principle not according with the exemption of religion from civil power." Jefferson was willing to take that chance, partly because his general policy toward the Indians at this time took a pragmatic turn. Indian land claims would be surrendered as an agricultural life displaced a hunting one, as white settlements pressed more closely upon the tribes, and as mounting debts encouraged the Indians to sell more and more land "for money to buy stock, utensils & necessities for their farms & families." With these words, in a letter to his secretary of war, Henry Dearborn, Jefferson began laying out an Indian policy that would clearly place the interests of the United States first. A few hundred dollars for a Catholic missionary would soften that self-interest some, but not much.

The president who refused to proclaim feasts and fasts must, however, be held responsible for having done just that as a young Virginian in 1774. As Britain's hostile intentions toward Massachusetts grew more alarming, Jefferson joined others in the belief that something must be done to arouse Virginians "from the lethargy into which they had fallen, as to passing events." Therefore, as Jefferson wrote in his autobiography, "we cooked up a resolution . . . for appointing the 1st day of June . . . for a day of fasting, humiliation, and prayer." The purpose of this day, Jefferson explained, was "to implore Heaven to avert from us the evils of civil war, to inspire us with firmness in support of our rights, and to turn the hearts of the King and Parliament to moderation and justice."

One may be astonished to find Jefferson associated with such a resolution. He did not present it to the House of Burgesses himself, believing Robert Carter Nicholas, "whose grave and religious character was more in unison with the tone of our resolution," the more appropriate sponsor. The resolution was read; it passed unanimously; and then "the Governor dissolved us, as usual." Virginia in 1774 still retained a royal governor, still possessed an established Anglican Church, still stood years away from approving a bill implementing religious freedom. One's astonishment is mitigated, therefore, by recognizing that a thirty-one-year-old Jefferson, not yet even the author of *A Summary View*, casting about for some acceptable means of awakening public opinion in a lethargic Virginia, chose a time-honored technique that would meet with universal approbation. Was it a propaganda ploy? Yes. Was it using religion, at least public religion, for political purposes? Yes. Was it a blatant contradiction of the Jefferson yet to be? No. In 1774, Jefferson worked within the frame of a royal and Anglican colony in order shortly to help create a free and republican state.

The Louisiana Purchase of 1803 overshadowed all other presidential actions of Jefferson's first term. Though he had doubts that the Constitution authorized this acquisition from France, the bargain (about three cents an acre, when the U.S. was charging two dollars an acre in the Old Northwest) proved irresistible. Jefferson even considered a constitutional amendment to make his authority explicit, but such a process would take months, perhaps years; meanwhile, Napoleon could quite conceivably change his mind. Concluding that this was not the time to engage in "metaphysical subtleties," Jefferson approved the treaty, as did the Senate, by a vote of 26 to 6.

Sometimes circumstances simply required an "energetic government."

Now the nation had unimpeded access to the Mississippi River, that great "highway" for all Americans rapidly settling the West, and with the stroke of a pen the United States burst to twice its earlier size. This purchase also gave Jefferson, as previously noted, a chance to learn a good deal more about the Nature that he cherished, even as it reduced the pressure that white settlements exerted on the Indians. The latter could now cross the Mississippi and find room for the hunt, if that was still their choice, or for the farm, as Jefferson preferred.

RELIGIOUS CONCERNS

Also in 1803, while riding back from Monticello to Washington, Jefferson read a small book by Joseph Priestley, *Socrates and Jesus Compared*. Priestley (1733-1804), English chemist, discoverer of oxygen, and Unitarian clergyman, exerted a major influence upon Jefferson and the development of his religious opinions, a subject to be explored at greater length in Chapter 5. At this juncture, however, a busy but always curious president could hardly wait until he returned to the White House to write Priestley of "the pleasure I had in the perusal" of his booklet and of "the desire it excited to see you take up the subject on a more extensive scale."

Since the English scientist died the next year, that larger task could not be fully discharged; that being the case, Jefferson felt the burden of religious reform more heavily on his own shoulders. But before Priestley died, he had the opportunity to reply at least twice to this presidential note. In the first reply in May 1803, he expressed his great pleasure "that you are not so much occupied by public business, but that you are at leisure for speculations of a different and higher nature." In the second reply the following December, Priestley promised to send Jefferson more scientific and theological works and offered his congratulations on the purchase of the Louisiana Territory. Neither Priestley nor Jefferson, one may safely conclude, spent all of his time on matters of a "higher nature."

When in 1804 Jefferson was elected to a second term, the ballots told a very different story from those counted in 1800. Now seventeen states cast 162 electoral votes for the Republicans and only 14 for the Federalists (from Connecticut and Delaware). The "religious issue" of 1800 no longer dominated in 1804, though Connecticut remained unforgiving, even declaring deism a felony in 1808. As the demise of the Federalist party approached, the party's desire for intimate ties between the church and the state faded. Though the last remaining tie, that in Massachusetts, did not break until after Jefferson's death, during his presidency and afterward he saw state after state follow an increasingly republican path in religious affairs.

Throughout his two terms as president, however, Jefferson continued to feel the pressure of a limited constituency that wanted him to be more "priestly," to lead the country religiously as well as politically. A Presbyterian minister in New York (and later professor at Princeton Seminary), Samuel Miller, wrote to Jefferson on 23 January 1808 urging him to take a more favorable view of national fasts. The president did not have to order them, suggested Miller; he could merely recommend them. Real advantages obtained, Miller pointed out, when the whole country at one time turned to repentance and prayer. Jefferson, who remained unmoved, nonetheless wrote a courteous and detailed reply in one more effort to explain his position — a position, he noted, that both Reason and the Constitution confirmed.

Miller wished Jefferson only to "recommend," not prescribe, the appropriate religious exercise. But this recommendation must still carry the authority of the U.S. government behind it, Jefferson wrote, and some indirect penalty for disobedience — the penalty of public disapproval, if nothing more. (And, as Madison would later observe, "An *advisory* Government is a contradiction in terms.") More fundamentally, the president declared, "I do not believe it is for the interest of religion to invite the civil magistrate to direct its exercises, its discipline, or its doctrines." Furthermore, this responsibility and right rested squarely with the religious societies themselves, and "this right can never be safer than in their own hands, where the Constitution has deposited it."

If Presbyterians and Congregationalists continued to chafe under the leadership of a separationist president, many dissenters rejoiced in the direction in which they saw their nation move. For example, a radical New England preacher, Elias Smith, struck out with a determination to democratize everything: politics, medicine, journalism, and religion. If Jefferson had faith in the common people, Smith had even more. If Jefferson believed that religion was "a matter that lies solely between man and his God," Smith would follow that premise to its logical conclusion — and beyond. If Jefferson asserted inalienable rights to life, liberty, and the pursuit of happiness, Smith asserted an equivalent right "to follow the Scripture wherever it leads him, even an equal right with Bishops and Pastors of the churches."

In Jefferson, Elias Smith saw the fulfillment of the obscure prophecies of the book of Revelation (a book in which Jefferson had no confidence whatsoever). In Revelation 16:12, Smith pointed out, one read of the sixth angel, who "poured out his vial upon the great river Euphrates; and the water thereof was dried up, that the ways of the kings of the east might be prepared." When Smith interpreted this verse, he saw Jefferson as the sixth angel of the apocalypse, who prepared the way for God's wrathful destruction of Babylon. As Michael Kenny pointed out in his perceptive biography of Elias Smith (*The Law of Perfect Liberty*), "To the discerning it was possible to see the . . . fierceness of God's wrath in the electoral misfortunes of the Federalists and the progressive collapse of established religion, while the temporal rule of Thomas Jefferson and the Democratic-Republicans could equally well be seen as standing in very close proximity to the second coming of Christ." And

Smith, who regarded Jeffersonianism as the political equivalent of Christian salvation, thought the end of the present age was near at hand. "What people ever saw such a day as we see in this year, 1808?"

Another New Englander, John Leland, who preached in Virginia in the 1770s and 1780s, returned to Massachusetts in 1791 to continue a ministry that combined free-church Christianity with Jeffersonian democracy. In 1801, Leland gained instant notoriety when he journeyed to Washington to present President Jefferson with a mammoth head of cheese (1,450 pounds) made in his hometown of Cheshire. While in the capital, he visited the Senate, where he was dismayed to find that the chaplain actually *read* his prayers. This moved the nonliturgical Baptist to comment that the minister needed the eyes of a goose so that he could turn one eye toward heaven while keeping the other eye on his book. Leland hoped that if such chaplains or any chaplains were required for this duty, they would be paid for not by the government but by private donation.

Leland heartily endorsed Jefferson's position on fasts and feasts. He even questioned whether the Christian Sunday had the same force of command behind it that the Jewish Sabbath did. But, said Leland, if Christ did appoint Sunday to be observed, "he did it as the head of the church, and not as the king of nations." Ecclesiastical institutions supported through civil law may, added Leland, "call themselves churches of Christ, but in reality they are creatures of the state." In 1804, this "Jeffersonian itinerant" (to use Lyman Butterfield's phrase) observed that experience "has informed us that the fondness of magistrates to foster Christianity has done it more harm than all the persecutions ever did." In words that would make his president proud, he declared that "persecution, like a lion, tears the saints to death, but leaves Christianity pure; state establishment of religion, like a bear, hugs the saints, but corrupts Christianity." Leland had no less dedication than Jefferson to religious freedom, for he saw in that freedom the

107

only possibility for the pure and believing church that Christ intended.

Not all clergy, of course, even in 1804 or 1808 shared the sentiments of Leland and Smith. Nor had all Federalist clergy thrown in the towel after the election of 1800. As their grip weakened, their rhetoric strengthened. The Congregational pastor in Medford, Massachusetts, David Osgood, noted that in the Jeffersonian years, the people confronted a choice of being "the friend of Jesus Christ or Thomas Paine." Federalists in Essex County, Massachusetts, regularly invited Osgood to pray at their official meetings "because they knew he would employ the most bitter invective against the Jefferson administration." George Washington, argued Osgood, was our King David, whereas Thomas Jefferson played the part of the rebellious son Absalom, who lured the nation away from the safe path so carefully charted. By 1810, Osgood had forgiven nothing and no one. When the people chose Jefferson as their president, he exclaimed, "I did at that time, and do still, firmly believe that they sinned against Heaven in a grievous and aggravated manner."

In Wrentham, Massachusetts, the Reverend Nathanael Emmons in 1801 preached a fast-day sermon on the "strange and deplorable event" that brought about a radical and regrettable change of leadership — in Israel, or was it the United States? Though Emmons never named Jefferson, he drew the analogy not to Absalom but to King Jeroboam, who replaced his two wise and righteous predecessors, David and Solomon (Adams and Washington). Jeroboam employed "every artifice to prejudice the people against the former administration," causing this disaffection "by basely misrepresenting the wise measures of that wise and excellent ruler." "Artful and designing politicians" have brought their nation to its present sorry state, Emmons declaimed, this being a direct result of their "depravity of the heart" more than their "weakness of the understanding." What had happened in the election of 1800 resulted not from honest choice but from crafty deception.

Emmons, Osgood, and others would labor throughout Jefferson's two terms to remove the scales from men's eyes. In 1808, with the election of Jefferson's ally James Madison, those scales had apparently not fallen.

From the American Revolution through the turn of the next century, Americans generally saw the future as bright with promise. As deist Thomas Paine said in the Revolutionary years, "The birthday of a new world is at hand." As Congregationalist David Tappan said in those same years, the Revolution was "a chain which is gradually drawing after it the most glorious consequences to mankind," ultimately fulfilling scriptural prophecies concerning the millennium to come. Both secularist and saint envisioned a future in which liberty, peace, virtue, knowledge, and happiness would cover the earth. Enlightenment thought complemented millennial thought in the confident push toward the final triumph of Reason and freedom. As Princeton's Samuel Stanhope Smith declared in 1790, the people needed no "other millennium than the general progress of science & civilization."

Jefferson, the congenital optimist, accepted and endorsed that sort of apocalyptic prophecy. The French Revolution together with the Jeffersonian revolution of 1800 caused Federalist optimism to falter, however, though some clung to the hope that France would turn Protestant and Jefferson would fall. Republicans managed to take up much of the slack, turning gloom into hope. As Ruth Bloch noted in her *Visionary Republic*, Republicans had less difficulty in adapting the millennialism of the American Revolution to their own grand visions of America's destiny. At the time of his inauguration in 1801, Jefferson informed Joseph Priestley that the nation had now learned to look forward, not backward; America would prepare itself for a great future rather than accept the tragic fate of being bound to a degrading past. "The great extent of our Republic is new," Jefferson announced. "Its sparse habitation is new. The mighty wave of public opinion which has rolled over it is new." And for the years that lay ahead, this watchword would inspire and embolden the nation: "We can no longer say there is nothing new under the sun."

Even in religion, or especially in religion, one should prepare for the new.

5 The Religious Reformer

"I separate, therefore, the gold from the dross."
(1820)

After Thomas Jefferson left the White House in March of 1809, he rarely left his Virginia hilltop home, and then only to spend a few weeks in his summer home, Poplar Forest, some ninety miles — a three-day journey — southwest of Monticello. The retirement from public life that he thought might come when he left George Washington's cabinet at the end of 1793 was at last his. The restless mind now had freedom to turn to any number of subjects — beyond politics — that continued to challenge and intrigue. Among those subjects, none stood higher than religion.

JOSEPH PRIESTLEY AND A CORRUPTED RELIGION

Of course, Jefferson did not wait for his retirement from public life to begin the reform of his own religious opinions or to consider the reform of religion, especially Christianity, itself. His first personal contact with Joseph Priestley occurred in 1797 in Philadelphia, where the latter delivered a series of lectures. Priestley, having been besieged by mobs in Birmingham, England, and having lost both his home and his laboratory to their fury, had retreated in 1791 to London. Even there his radicalism in religion and his embrace of France magnified his unpopularity and aggravated the danger he faced. So in 1794, at the urging of Jefferson and others, he migrated to America, settling in Pennsylvania for the last decade of his turbulent life.

Jefferson learned much from Priestley's lectures, but he gained even greater intellectual satisfaction from reading Priestley's *History of the Corruptions of Christianity*, originally published in 1782. Since Jefferson owned the 1793 edition of this work, he probably read it about the time that Priestley migrated to America, or shortly after. In any case, this one book influenced Jefferson's religious views profoundly — in all likelihood more profoundly than any other single volume. And in reading it, often, Jefferson made a critical discovery for and about himself. He thought that he had utterly rejected Christianity; now he found to his relief, and perhaps to his delight as well, that he had only rejected a hopelessly corrupted form of Christianity. Somewhere underneath all that dross, pure gold could yet be found.

Priestley argued, for example, that the real "mystery" of the Trinity was that so many Christians believed it. For Jesus did not teach it, the Bible did not proclaim it, and Reason could not honor it. Jesus lived as a human being, claimed to be nothing more than the "son of man," whose mission was to show all humankind how they should live and what God expected of them. The Old Testament honored monotheism, as did the New Testament, rightly read. Priestley added (and here Jefferson did not follow him) that God rewarded Jesus' perfect obedience by raising him from the dead, and he will do the same for all others who follow the example that Jesus set. The resurrection of Jesus did not, however, signify his divinity; he remained after death as in life fully human, never fully or even partly divine.

Centuries of Christian thinkers had argued interminably about the effect of Christ's sacrifice on the cross — the nature of the atonement by which he assured salvation to the obedient and faithful segments of humanity. Priestley settled those long arguments, at least to his own satisfaction, by simply scuttling them. There was no "atonement," no "sacrifice," no transfer of Christ's own righteousness to appease an otherwise vengeful and merciless God. The Creator of the universe did not need to be convinced that he should be a God of love and benevolence: he already was. The death of Jesus was simply another action of selfless devotion, demonstrating an all-embracing charity superior to that of even the great moral instructors of antiquity.

Almost all of this Jefferson found congenial and even comforting. He would not now have to turn his back on the religion that the majority of his fellow citizens continued to embrace. He could join with them in its essentials, its true substance, and assist them in scraping off the heavy barnacles that impeded Christianity's smooth passage around the globe. The oneness of God: how rational, how natural, how biblically correct! Jesus as a moral teacher, quite likely the greatest of all moral teachers: how inspiring, how simple, how socially necessary! The dogmas of Anglicanism or Calvinism or Catholicism: how burdensome, how contrary to both Reason and Nature, how dispensable! Jefferson thought less highly of miracles than did Priestley, he had no interest in or concern about a bodily resurrection, and he found it easier to dismiss the writings of the apostle Paul than Priestley did. Despite these and other points of difference, Jefferson's reading of Priestley was like Immanuel Kant's reading of David Hume: it awakened him from dogmatic slumber and pointed him toward a new reformulation or reformation of the Christian religion.

BENJAMIN RUSH AND THE SYLLABUS

Benjamin Rush (1745-1813), member of the Continental Congress in 1776 and signer of the Declaration of Independence, enjoyed a warm friendship with both John Adams and Thomas Jefferson in those politically heady days. At that time, Rush had already completed his medical education at the University of Edinburgh, returning to Philadelphia to practice medicine and teach chemistry at the recently opened College of Philadelphia. Like Jefferson, however, Rush had a mind that roamed freely across many fields of human endeavor: politics, social reform, psychiatry — and religion. As Jefferson sought to make religion more rational, Rush undertook a similar task with respect to medicine. "It would seem," he wrote Jefferson in 1803, "as if a certain portion of superstition belonged necessarily to the human mind, and that that part of it which has been banished from religion had taken sanctuary in medicine."

When President Jefferson read Priestley's *Socrates and Jesus Compared* in 1803, the exact nature of that reformulation began to take clearer shape. In the letter that he wrote to Priestley immediately after his return to the White House, he recalled that conversations with Benjamin Rush years before had assisted him along the way to a personal reconstruction of religion, and he had even promised "some day" to send Rush a more detailed view of a revised "Christian system." "I have reflected on it often since," Jefferson told Priestley, "and even sketched the outlines in my own mind." And so he now sketched, ever so briefly for his correspondent, the approach he would take. He planned to begin with the ancients, those much-loved classical writers whom he had read and continued to read in their original Greek and Latin: "Pythagoras, Epicurus, Epictetus, Socrates, Cicero, Seneca, Antoninus." He would do justice to their insights, he assured Priestley, but would also clarify their limitations. He would then turn to the Jews, as understood through their own ancient scriptures, giving them full credit for their affirmation of the unity of God but pointing out some deficiencies in their conception of the divine attributes.

Then, "I should proceed to a view of the life, character, and doctrines of Jesus," whom he would describe as having improved on both the morality and the theology of what he had inherited. Jesus, revising some of the older and limited notions, "endeavored to bring them to the principles of a pure deism . . . [and] to reform their moral doctrines to the standard of reason, justice, and philanthropy." Jesus taught "the belief in a future state," and Jefferson endorsed the teaching, for it constituted a central element in his notion of a moral universe. But all questions of divinity and of inspiration Jefferson would leave aside, he informed Priestley, along with all those arcane dogmas that have provoked "the unthinking part of mankind to throw off the whole system in disgust." When that whole system was thoroughly reformed, the masses would see that Jesus' "system of morality was the most benevolent and sublime probably that has ever been taught." Even more, the character of Jesus, shorn of all the hobbling burdens thrust upon it, would shine forth as "the most innocent" and "the most eloquent . . . that has ever been exhibited to man." President Jefferson apologized that at this moment in his life he had time for only an "outline," but he would continue to reflect.

Three weeks after completing this letter to Priestley, Jefferson wrote to his Philadelphia friend Benjamin Rush. This communication revealed what an extraordinary amount of reflection ("while on the road and otherwise unoccupied") the president had engaged in — and in so brief a compass of time. The outline had now been expanded to the point where Jefferson referred to it as a "Syllabus," though he did not drop "outline" altogether. The basic structure remained, but Jefferson had fleshed out some of the starkly stated points. He suggested, for example, that the ancient moralists had done well in teaching a control of the passions but taught poorly about "our duties to others." They drew their circle of concern much too narrowly, wrote Jefferson. Similarly, the ancient Jews followed the dictates of Reason and sound morality within their own nation, but they were harsh and repressive toward all others.

Jesus came into just this parochial world, a person whose "parentage was obscure, his condition poor, [and] his education null." On the other hand, he made the most of great "natural endowments" and pursued a life both "correct and innocent." But Jesus, like Socrates, suffered the fate that befalls those who never leave a line of text from their own hand. His teachings were recorded by "the most unlettered and ignorant of men." And his sadly premature death soon resulted in a fateful "combination of the altar and the throne." Such a combination conspired then, as it has always done since, against any effort "to enlighten and reform mankind." As a result, what Jesus actually did teach comes to us down through the centuries "mutilated, misstated, and often unintelligible." It was this "history of corruption" that demanded correction and reform in order that the original simplicity and sublimity of the religion of Jesus could be clearly seen.

Jefferson sent the Syllabus to his close friend, knowing that Rush would never expose it "to the malignant perversions of those who make every word from me a text for new mispresentations and calumnies." He also sent a copy to trusted cabinet members such as Secretary of War Henry Dearborn and Attorney General Levi Lincoln. Jefferson asked Dearborn and Lincoln, when they had finished reading the Syllabus, to please return it along with his cover letter. But three days later, in response to a request from Lincoln, Jefferson told him that he could keep a copy, confident that this good man would never let it get into print. For if that should happen, then your president "would become the butt of every set of disquisitions which every priest would undertake to write on every tenet it expresses."

116

Benjamin Rush read the Syllabus "with great attention," he informed Jefferson in May 1803, and "was much pleased to find you are by no means so heterodox as you have been supposed by your enemies." Rush did indicate, however, that his own view of the nature and mission of Christ differed from that of his old friend, now president. But, Rush added, "we will agree to disagree," as he expressed a skepticism akin to Jefferson's that religious dogma had little to do with moral behavior. Doctrine determined little so far as conduct was concerned, and even "less of our future acceptance at the bar of the Supreme Judge of the World."

To Rush, Jefferson commented regarding Priestley's theology that some differences of opinion between those two friends also existed, "but in the main object of my syllabus we go perfectly together." After Priestley read through his copy of the Syllabus, which Jefferson forwarded on 24 April 1803, he thought the congruence less than perfect. And in fact Jefferson acknowledged that "there is a point or two in which you and I probably differ." But Jefferson did not want to push the disagreements because Priestley, who had moved from Philadelphia to Northumberland, Pennsylvania, suffered from deteriorating health. Jefferson, always the Virginian, thought that he should move farther south, where a more temperate climate would improve one's health, happiness, and even moral condition. He noted that he could not help but agree with the astronomer David Rittenhouse, who wondered "that men should ever settle in a Northern climate, as long as there is room for them in a Southern one."

Priestley responded to the Syllabus the following May in some amazement that Jefferson should deny that Jesus claimed to be on a divine mission. That opinion, Priestley commented somewhat sharply, was one "that I do not remember ever to have heard before." Priestley found in the New Testament and in the testimony of the early Christians quite enough evidence to convince him that Jesus did, in fact, assert his mission to be divine. Were this not the case, Priestley added, the whole ex-

117

pansion of Christianity became inexplicable. To believe that the Christian religion could otherwise rise and spread — now that would really be a miracle, and Jefferson rejected miracles. With Jesus on a divine mission, Priestley concluded, "the whole of subsequent history" becomes "consistent and natural," and of no other hypothesis whatsoever can this be said.

Six months later Priestley informed Jefferson that he had begun the undertaking that the latter had encouraged him to complete — namely, pursuing the comparison between Jesus and Socrates "on a more extensive scale." Jefferson replied with gratitude, since "you are so much in possession of the whole subject that you will do it better and easier than any other person living." But as Priestley's health continued to fail, the firstfruits of his efforts disappointed Jefferson, and by February of 1804, the Unitarian scientist was dead. Now, no one remained who could undertake the task that Jefferson had outlined and for whose completion he devoutly hoped. No one, that is, except Jefferson himself.

"THE PHILOSOPHY OF JESUS OF NAZARETH"

When the news of Priestley's death reached Jefferson on 16 February 1804, he set to work immediately to somehow distill the moral teachings of Jesus in a form that would allow their simple "sublime and benevolent" character to shine through; it was what the president later described as the work of one or two evenings only, while at the White House "overwhelmed with other business." By March, the forty-six-page volume had been bound — not for publication, to be sure, but to be shared with a small circle of friends and to be used by Jefferson for his own study and devotion. Though the original of this compilation, "The Philosophy of Jesus of Nazareth," has been lost, an editor of the *Jefferson Papers*, Dickinson Adams, has, in a remarkable feat of literary skill, essentially reconstructed the text as well as the process of its compilation.

Jefferson took two copies of the New Testament in the King James Version and cut out those verses from the Gospels of Matthew, Mark, Luke, and John that — in his view — best conveyed the "pure and unsophisticated doctrines" of Jesus. Having undertaken the task of separating the authentic and original Jesus from the later Platonized and ecclesiasticized Jesus, Jefferson told John Adams that he found the true sayings "as easily distinguishable as diamonds in a dunghill." Jefferson worked without a knowledge of manuscript transmission or oral traditions or any of the biblical apparatus that later centuries would introduce. Rather, taking Reason and Nature as his trusted guides, he determined by sense and sound what had fallen from the lips of Jesus himself. And the result was pure gold, gold separated from the dross, as he told William Short much later. In examining the Gospels carefully, Jefferson found on the one hand "many passages of fine imagination, correct morality, and of the most lovely benevolence." But all that beauty sat trapped in "so much ignorance, so much absurdity, so much untruth, charlatanism, and imposture." Something had to be done to extract the gold, and "I found the work obvious and easy."

The result, as Dickinson Adams has demonstrated, highlighted the parables and ethical teachings even as it minimized the miraculous and the theological. Jefferson operated on the principle that the genuine teachings had to be simple and clear enough for unlettered fishermen to understand and remember. What was obscure or esoteric therefore fell fruitless by the wayside, like the seed cast on stony ground. Jefferson declared that this compilation would be used chiefly for his own purposes: to reinforce his conviction that the founder of the Christian religion concerned himself primarily with the moral condition of humankind. Such a convenient booklet would enable the busy president regularly to meditate upon those teachings without being distracted or offended by the dung.

While "The Philosophy of Jesus" remained Jefferson's own private manual of devotion, he shared it with a few friends, as he had the Syllabus. In August of 1804, he wrote Benjamin Rush that "I shall some of these days ask you to read" the "little volume" on Jesus. Rush, who had responded positively to the Syllabus sent the year before, now gave a disconcerting reply. Unless Jefferson's "little volume" advanced the divinity of Jesus "and renders his *death* as well as his *life* necessary for the restoration of mankind, I shall not accord with its author." Jefferson, who had abandoned all notions of atonement and divinity, therefore declined to send his modest editing effort to his good friend.

Comrades since the American Revolution, Jefferson and Rush shared the conviction that the young Republic needed some religious or moral cohesion. Rush saw Christianity and Republicanism as essentially partners in a confident march toward the universal happiness of humankind. As he told Jefferson during the campaign of 1800, "It is only necessary for Republicanism to ally itself to the Christian Religion, to overturn all the corrupted political and religious institutions in the world." Jefferson, far less sure that such an alliance made sense, continued to express his fears concerning a power-hungry clergy and a theologically abstruse Christianity. But once the pure gold of Christianity emerged from the mire, then that moralized version might possibly provide the essential ethical glue for the nation.

As Jefferson wrote in 1801 to a former senator from Vermont, "The Christian religion when divested of the rags in which" it had been enveloped and "brought to the original purity and simplicity of its benevolent founder, is a religion of all others most friendly to liberty, science, and the freest expansions of the human mind." These words, written well before he composed the Syllabus or "The Philosophy of Jesus," indicate that Jefferson had a public as well as a private motive in constructing a new religious "system." But with political enemies abounding, he could not afford to go "public" yet, and would in fact refrain from doing so for the remainder of his life.

Benjamin Rush continued to support Jefferson in any battles for freedom in religion, as he had during the Revolution. "I agree with you," Rush wrote to the president in 1801, "in your wishes to keep religion and government independent of each other." Rush then imagined a returned-from-the-grave apostle Paul condemning the machinations of the New England clergy and pointing out to them that, as had been mentioned eighteen centuries before, "your kingdom is not of this World." Rush even tried to comfort his friend by putting a good face on the cruel attacks of the campaign. Slander, the Philadelphia physician assured Jefferson, "not only supplies the place of fame, but it is much more powerful in exciting our faculties into vigorous and successful exercises."

RUSH AS "HONEST BROKER"

Despite his rejection of Jefferson's less-than-orthodox views of Jesus, Rush remained on good terms with his fellow revolutionary, both during the eight years of Jefferson's presidency and afterward, until his own death in 1813. Shortly before that death, Benjamin Rush performed another valuable service on behalf of his friend: he bridged the seemingly unbridgeable chasm between Thomas Jefferson and John Adams, now both retired from the scene of political struggle. The two had been good friends earlier, but the campaign of 1800 was so strident and the defeat for Adams so galling that for a dozen years these two patriots had virtually nothing to say to each other. What a loss to future generations of Americans, thought Rush, if these two notable ex-presidents continued to avoid one another in surly silence.

Early in 1811, Rush told Jefferson that old and intimate friendships, no matter how sorely tested, should not be allowed to die. "When I consider your early attachment to Mr. Adams, and his to you," Rush wrote, and "when I consider how much the liberties and independence of the United States owe to the concert of your principles and labors; and when I reflect upon the sameness of your opinions at present upon most of the subjects of government," then it made eminent sense for the walls of silence to come tumbling down. "I have ardently wished a friendly and epistolary intercourse might be revived between you before you take a final leave of the common object of your affections." Rush believed that not much time on this earth remained to him; perhaps the same would prove to be the case of his two close friends. "Before you meet in another world," why not take a step toward each other in this one?

Whenever Rush heard an encouraging word from John Adams, he hurriedly passed it along to Jefferson. Whenever Rush wrote to Adams, he pushed him as fast and far as friendship would allow. Were he near enough to Braintree, he told Adams, he would "put a pen into your hand and guide it while it wrote the following note to Mr. Jefferson":

> My dear old friend and fellow laborer in the cause of the liberties and independence of our common country, I salute you with the most cordial good wishes for your health and happiness.
>
> John Adams

If only this magic could be performed, then, Rush told Jefferson at the end of 1811, "patriotism, liberty, science, and religion would all gain a triumph by it."

When Rush was finally able to pass along Adams's expressions of warmest feelings toward Jefferson, the latter wrote — not to Adams — but to Benjamin Rush to say that "I only needed this knowledge to revive towards him all the affections of the most cordial moments of our lives." At which point, Rush, like the good broker he was, wrote — not to Jefferson — but to Adams: "And now, my dear friend, permit me again to suggest to you to receive the olive branch which has thus been offered . . . by the hand of a man who still loves you." Rush concluded with this exuberant plea: "Fellow laborers in erect-

ing the great fabric of American independence! . . . embrace —
embrace each other!" It worked. For the next fourteen years,
the most revealing correspondence of any two former presidents in the nation's history flowed freely between the two
omnivorous minds. And Rush was absolutely on target: "patriotism, liberty, science, and religion" would and did gain
enormously from the resulting "epistolary intercourse."

"THE LIFE AND MORALS OF JESUS"

While engaged with this flow of letters between Braintree and
Monticello, Jefferson also found time to treat more extensively
the "philosophy of Jesus," to which he had given attention so
many years before. When he sent a copy of the Syllabus to John
Adams in 1813, he remarked that "this skeleton" still needed
to be supplied "with arteries, with veins, with nerves, muscles
and flesh." But, he added, that task was still "really beyond
my time and information." Six or seven years later, however,
he had prepared "The Life and Morals of Jesus," now drawing
from New Testaments in Greek, Latin, French, and English. The
resulting creation, still an editing task only, excused Jefferson
from any obligation to offer commentary on or exegesis of the
selected verses themselves. Those who, like Jefferson, had a
command of all four languages could extract nuances and ver-
bal peculiarities for themselves, but Jefferson viewed his task
as simply that of presenting the diamonds. If the gems needed
polishing, let others do it.

The text of this so-called "Jefferson Bible," unlike that of
the Syllabus, did survive — but just barely (being passed
around among the heirs for decades), until it came into the
possession of the Smithsonian in 1895. Within the next decade,
it found its way into print several times, but not until the
Princeton University Press edition of 1983 did it receive the
appropriate editorial care. If Jefferson ever considered publishing it in his own lifetime, he was forewarned in 1816 of the

likely misunderstandings that would greet it. In that year, he sent a letter to an old friend, Charles Thomson, telling him of his plans to add to his "wee little book" on the philosophy of Jesus with an expanded work drawn from the languages noted above. But on the basis of his already completed work, Jefferson informed Thomson, he was prepared to acknowledge that "I am a real Christian, that is to say, a disciple of the doctrines of Jesus, very different from the Platonists."

The aging Thomson, not as careful with this letter as Jefferson regularly warned his correspondents to be, left the communication lying about to be read and interpreted by others. Thomson himself added to the confusion by suggesting that Jefferson had become an orthodox Christian and was about to write a book on the subject. The rumors flew, to the dismay and disgust of Jefferson, who did his best to quell them. Such eagerness to find some hidden truth where none existed convinced Jefferson, all over again, to be as private as possible concerning his own views on religion. To a Dutch clergyman and close friend of Adams's, Francis Adrian Van der Kemp, Jefferson wrote in 1816 that he clearly could not be too careful. Every copy of the Syllabus, for example, was back in his own hands, except for one that John Adams still retained. And why all this caution? "I am unwilling to draw on myself a swarm of insects," Jefferson noted, "whose buz is more disquieting than their bite." Though long out of office, Jefferson had not slipped from public view. He would correspond with his friends, quietly, but keep his innermost thoughts from a public always too curious, always too ready to misinterpret and misjudge.

Few if any of his contemporaries, therefore, had the opportunity to dip into or learn from "Jefferson's Bible." He did not mention it in any surviving correspondence, and his own family appears to have been unaware of it. In a later age, however, one can examine in detail what Jefferson honored in the Gospel accounts as well as what he silently omitted, the omissions being even more revealing than the inclusions. Roughly twice the size of his earlier "wee little book," "The

Life and Morals of Jesus" nonetheless remains more booklet than book. The compiling of it no doubt gave Jefferson much satisfaction, and the — perhaps daily — reading of it in the evenings gave him "something moral, whereon to ruminate in the intervals of sleep."

Proceeding in roughly chronological order, Jefferson began with the birth of Jesus, drawing chiefly on Luke's Gospel. But he plunged immediately into Luke's second chapter, where Mary and Joseph make their way to Bethlehem, omitting all of the first chapter's recounting of conversations with and announcements by the angels. Gabriel's explanation to Mary of her surprising conception — namely, that "the Holy Ghost shall come upon thee, and the power of the Highest shall overshadow thee" — also found no place in this deist's version. (Similarly, Matthew's story of the three wise men and King Herod's ordering the slaying of all of Bethlehem's male children under the age of two were passed by.) Staying with Luke's account, then, one read of the babe born "in swaddling-clothes, and laid in a manger." Jefferson again revealed his dislike of the angels and of anything that reeked of the supernatural when he skipped the appearance of the angel to the shepherds watching over their flocks by night, as well as the heavenly host singing "Glory to God in the highest."

On a far more mundane level, Jefferson's version moved quickly from the swaddling clothes to a circumcision on the eighth day, soon followed by Jesus' visit to the Jerusalem Temple at the age of twelve years. When his parents missed him after a day's journey out from town, they returned to rebuke him for making them anxious about his whereabouts. According to Luke, Jesus replied, "Wist ye not that I must be about my Father's business?" Then Luke adds, "And they did not understand the saying which he spake unto them." Neither did Jefferson, so he dropped the exchange. Luke 2 concludes, "And Jesus grew in wisdom and stature, and in favor with God and man." Jefferson concludes more succinctly: "And Jesus grew in wisdom and stature."

With the beginning of Jesus' public ministry in Matthew 3, Mark 1, and Luke 3, Jefferson moved among these three "synoptic" Gospels (he had received a "harmony" of the Gospels from Joseph Priestley's son in 1804), with occasional selections from the Gospel according to John. He began again with Luke (3:1-2), but passed over the reference to Jesus' preaching a baptism of repentance for the forgiveness of sins. Jefferson included the baptism of Jesus, but naturally did not include anything about the heavens opening up or the Spirit of God "descending like a dove" or a voice from heaven saying, "Thou art my beloved Son; in thee I am well pleased." On literary if not philosophical grounds, Jefferson also omitted Luke's genealogy of some fifteen verses. Rather, in Jefferson's version, Jesus moved quickly to Capernaum with his family and his disciples. All three synoptic Gospels tell of Jesus' "temptation in the wilderness" for forty days and forty nights (Matthew 4:1-11; Mark 1:12-13; Luke 4:1-13), but since this story did not enhance Jefferson's portrait of Jesus as moral teacher and reformer, he deleted it. On the other hand, the account in John's Gospel of Jesus' driving the money changers from the Temple (John 2:12-16) received ample attention. John's account in the same chapter of the miracle at Cana, where Jesus changed water into wine, however, won no notice. Miracles, like angels, suffered from a low priority.

And so Jefferson cut and clipped, pasted and shifted among the four languages and the four brief biographies, choosing that which gave the "sublime code of morals" every prominence and rejecting that which made of Jesus some sort of supernatural miracle worker or street-theater healer. Jefferson also revealed no taste for arcane prophecies and dark apocalyptic sayings. On these grounds, one would expect the Sermon on the Mount to fill many pages in the Jeffersonian "Bible," and so it does. Since that "sermon" was reported only by Matthew and Luke, Jefferson needed now to choose from only two biographical accounts.

Jefferson presented the beatitudes in Matthew's version

(5:1-12), then switched abruptly to Luke's "woes" (6:24-26), then returned to the fifth chapter of Matthew, which he followed almost to the end. He deleted the counsel "be ye perfect, even as your Father in heaven is perfect," preferring Luke's lines about loving your enemies and doing good, as well as "Be ye, therefore, merciful, as your Father in heaven also is merciful." Jefferson at that point took up Matthew's account (chapter 6) of almsgiving, the Lord's Prayer, treasures in heaven, and the lilies of the field homily that concludes, "Take therefore no thought for the morrow: for the morrow shall take thought for the things of itself. Sufficient unto the day is the evil thereof." Those words must have more than once brought comfort to a beleaguered president and vilified reformer.

Matthew 7 also began with the kind of moral instruction that Jefferson found so congenial: do not judge the mote in your brother's eye while neglecting the beam in your own; do not cast pearls before swine or be so cruel as to give a son who asks for bread a stone instead. And then the most memorable moral command of all: "Therefore all things whatsoever ye would that men should do to you, do ye even so to them: for this is the law and the prophets." Jefferson happily included the command "Beware of false prophets," for he had encountered so many of them. And he even more happily took to himself the words that one could know men by their fruits, for the Monticello reformer liked nothing more than to emphasize that works, not faith, separated the true prophets from the false ones, the gentle sheep from the "ravening wolves." Thus, how simple the eternal moral truth: "A good tree cannot bring forth evil fruit, neither can a corrupt tree bring forth good fruit." So if men were to be judged at all, it would be not by their words, which were so cheap, but by their deeds, which were so dear.

But then Matthew's account veered off into a discussion of heavenly things, of salvation and damnation (7:21-23), so Jefferson veered off too, in order to substitute a passage from a much later chapter (Matthew 12:35-37). He then returned to the final verses of chapter 7 concerning the wise man who built his house not upon the sand but upon a rock: "And the rain descended, and the floods came, and the winds blew, and beat upon the house; and it fell not: for it was founded upon a rock." And so ended the Sermon on the Mount, where Jesus impressed the multitudes, "for he taught them as one having authority, and not as the scribes."

Jefferson now jumped more frequently among the several accounts, still relying chiefly on Matthew and Luke, where most of the moral teachings are found, less on John, and least of all on Mark. Matthew, however, included narratives of miraculous cures and a raising from the dead (8:2–9:34) that Jefferson passed over. He turned rather to Luke, where the Pharisees condemned Jesus for associating with a woman of unsavory reputation, but Jesus, who found in her so much to forgive, treated her with honor (7:36-46). But when Luke included the words of Jesus concerning the forgiveness of sins, Jefferson's interests quickly faded.

Jesus warned his disciples (Luke 12:3) with words to which Jefferson would have given vigorous assent as he read: "Therefore whatsoever ye have spoken in darkness, shall be heard in the light; and that which ye have spoken in the ear in closets, shall be proclaimed upon the house-tops." Jefferson, who carefully refrained from adding any marginalia, may have wished to note that this was particularly true if a suspected deist/atheist in America who was so presumptive as to run for president said anything about religion.

After omitting a few verses that spoke of angels, Jefferson included the remainder of Luke 12, for it conveyed solid moral instruction. One should beware of covetousness and greed, "for a man's life consisteth not in the abundance of the things which he possesseth." And only the fool built bigger and better barns for his material possessions while he ignored all of life's richer dimensions. There's more to life, Jesus pointed out here, than what one shall eat or drink or even how long one shall live. Once again, consider the lilies of the field who neither toil nor spin, yet "Solomon, in all his glory, was not arrayed like one of these." So sell your goods and give alms, "for where your treasure is, there will your heart be also." And be a good steward of what had been so abundantly granted to you. Jefferson had little difficulty applying that last moral lesson to America as well as to his own life.

If a moral lesson was embedded in a miracle, the lesson survived in Jeffersonian scripture, but the miracle did not. Even when this took some rather careful cutting with scissors or razor, Jefferson managed to maintain Jesus' role as a great moral teacher, not as a shaman or faith healer. With the Pharisees taking it on the chin, Jesus explained that inner cleanliness was far more important than well-washed dishes. And "woe" to those who kept the minutiae of religious ritual while ignoring the "judgment and love of God." Lawyer Jefferson, demonstrating his magnanimity, even reproduced this verse: "Woe unto you, lawyers! for ye have lade men with burdens grievous to be borne, and ye yourselves touch not the burdens with one of your fingers" (Luke 11:52).

When on the Sabbath day Jesus was approached by a man with a withered hand for healing (Matthew 12:9-10), the Pharisees queried Jesus about the lawfulness of healing on that sacred day. Jesus turned the question aside with more of his own. At that point, Jefferson lost interest in the withered hand and the miracle by which it was healed to reach into the rarely used Mark for a single verse to make a moral point: "And he said unto them, The sabbath was made for man, and not man for the sabbath" (2:27). In this Virginian's Bible, the man's hand never got healed, although man's spirit may have been.

In the canonized Gospels, Jesus distinguished between what was central and what was peripheral in the moral life. A man was defiled not because of what he ate but because of what he said and, even more, what he did. Jefferson merely carried the principle of the essential versus redundant further, as he eliminated any homiletic reflection that obscured the precious moral truth. Too much dross concealed the gold; too much dung buried the diamonds. This sometimes resulted in questions left hanging in the air, in stories that appear to have lost their point. The story of the man blind from birth (John 9) was introduced by the disciples' raising the question about the cause of the blindness: the man's own sin or that of his parents. Neither, Jesus replied, and there Jefferson stopped. In the full story, Jesus proceeded to mix clay with saliva, apply the poultice, and heal the lifelong blindness, thereby permitting him to make the heavy theological point "I am the light of the world." Jefferson settled for the more modest practical point that any direct connection between disease and sin was a questionable one.

In the Gospel according to John, where Jesus makes the most unambiguous claims to divinity ("the Father is in me, and I in him"; "I am the way, the truth, and the life: no man cometh unto the Father but by me"; "I am in the Father, and the Father in me"; etc.), Jefferson repeatedly turned away from all such claims. One of the most striking examples of this occurs in chapter 13, where Jefferson included the verses (21-26) relating to the Last Supper. Then verse 31 begins, "Therefore, when he was gone out, Jesus said . . ." What Jesus said at that point was, "Now is the Son of man glorified, and God is glorified in him." But Jefferson dropped that and the two following verses to jump abruptly to the moral message, "A new commandment I give unto you, That ye love one another; as I have loved you, that ye also love one another" (v. 34). When quoting from John, Jefferson kept his blade busy.

Finally, in passages treating the last days of Jesus, Jefferson stayed with the mortal man who died on the cross and was buried. After the soldiers pierced Jesus' side with a sword, "Joseph of Arimathea . . . besought Pilate that he might take away the body of Jesus: and Pilate gave him leave" (John 19:38). After preparing the body for burial, disciples transported it to a new tomb in the crucifixion garden. At that point, taking fragments from John and from Matthew, Jefferson's scriptures concluded, "There laid they Jesus and rolled a great stone to the door of the sepulchre, and departed." No resurrection, no appearances of a risen Lord, no ascension into heaven. A great teacher, the greatest of all moral teachers, had died and was buried.

If after reading "Jefferson's Bible" one is left primarily with the impression of slashing razors and editorial severity, it may be instructive to compare Jefferson's treatment of Scripture with that of Thomas Paine. As he prepared to write his *Age of Reason,* Paine said, "I have now gone through the Bible as a man would go through a wood with an axe on his shoulder and fell trees." It was an apt figure. Paine wanted to see how much he could destroy; Jefferson wanted to see how much he could preserve. The earlier labors of Jefferson in Washington and his more extensive labors at Monticello were labors of reverence and awe before an ethic that exceeded all that the Greeks, Romans, and Jews had managed to teach. The retired president did not produce his small book to shock or offend a somnolent world; he composed it for himself, for his devotion, for his assurance, for a more restful sleep at nights and a more confident greeting of the mornings. He cherished the diamonds.

Religion Reformed

Jefferson the religious reformer led no reformation movement, published no book on religion, founded no new sect. Though often urged to take a more public stand, he strongly, even impatiently, resisted such entreaties. When a sympathetic correspondent asked permission to publish one of Jefferson's letters on religion, the reply was "No, my dear Sir, not for the world." Jefferson added that he held little hope of changing the minds of the orthodox. "I should as soon undertake to bring the crazy skulls of Bedlam to sound understanding." And to yet another friend, he wrote in 1815, "Of publishing a book on religion, my dear Sir, I never had an idea." To try to straighten out all the different sects in America would be like trying to cut down all the nation's trees all by oneself. In his old age, Jefferson noted, he sought tranquillity, not sectarian warfare.

Nonetheless, in his voluminous correspondence, Jefferson defended his own religious view at some length and in some heat; he also gently proselytized where possible, seeking to bring others around to his positions. And what were those positions? As a reformer, even if a private one, Jefferson wished most to substitute "morals for mysteries," Unity for Trinity with respect to the godhead, and cosmic justice for chaos or parochial self-interest. We will consider each of these in turn.

"MORALS FOR MYSTERIES"

The Jeffersonian Bible made this reformer's preference for morality crystal clear. His letters reveal with equal clarity his repugnance for mystery. Again and again he condemned the theologizing, scholasticizing process that turned a simple way of life into a complex and noxious metaphysic. Jefferson held Plato (and Neo-Platonism) responsible for a great deal of this, along with the fourth-century theologian Athanasius and the sixteenth-century theologian John Calvin. They and others came in for repeated condemnations, together with their co-conspirators — the priests and professional clergy who would be out of business except for their remarkable talent for per-petuating mystery.

To John Adams in 1813, Jefferson vented his fury over the way in which the religion of Jesus had become the religion of "Platonists and Plotinists, the Stagyrites and Gamalielites, the Eclectics the Gnostics and Scholastics." Jefferson's list went on, and then he added his own numerous et ceteras. The only appropriate reply to this whole catalogue, Jefferson noted, was "Nonsense." He told Adams that he hoped that his Syllabus would encourage others to prepare a "euthanasia for Platonic Christianity." The next year revealed a Jefferson not yet finished with Plato, as he wrote Adams of "the whimsies, the puerilities, and unintelligible jargon" he found in the Greek philosopher. To be sure that he was doing Plato no injustice, he "amused" himself with a careful rereading of the *Republic*. "I am wrong, however, in calling it amusement, for it was the heaviest task-work I ever went through." And Jefferson asked in amazement how the world could "have so long consented to give reputation to such nonsense as this." If one subtracted from Plato "his sophisms, futilities, and incomprehensibilities," nothing worth talking about remained.

Jefferson thought that his own generation, to say nothing of those before, had been victims of fashion and authority, had been indoctrinated in the belief that Plato deservedly enjoyed a great reputation. The time had come to submit Plato to the test of Reason. "His foggy mind is forever presenting the semblances of objects which, half seen thro' a mist, can be defined neither in form or dimension." This mistiness, which should have consigned him to oblivion, on the contrary — and quite incredibly — brought "him immortality of fame and reverence." Plato by himself could be simply dismissed. What he had done to Christianity, however, with the help of the priests, could not.

When the Christian clergy, said Jefferson, discovered that the simple message of Jesus could be understood by everyone, that it was "too plain to need explanation," they got busy building an artificial system, as misty as Plato's, that would require constant explanation, cause endless controversy, and — most important of all — give the priests steady employment into perpetuity. A child could understand Jesus. Thousands of ponderous volumes have not yet clarified Plato. Jefferson could only be grateful that Platonic Republicanism had not become as popular as Platonic Christianity, for had that happened, we should all be living "pell mell together, like the beasts of the field or forest."

In John Adams, Jefferson found a sympathetic ear. For Adams agreed that slogging through Plato once more amounted to nothing more than "tedious toil." When he had finished, Adams told Jefferson, "my disappointment was very great, my astonishment was greater and my disgust was shocking." Just about the most valuable jewel that he culled out of Platonic dung, Adams reported, was that sneezing could cure hiccups. "Accordingly, I have cured myself and all my friends of that provoking disorder, for thirty years, with a pinch of snuff." Plato found no allies either in Braintree or at Monticello.

Others manufactured mystery as well, and Calvin rated almost as "highly" as Plato. "Calvinism has introduced into the Christian religion more new absurdities," Jefferson wrote in 1818, "than its leader had purged it of old ones." Simple morality had been transformed into "Hierophantic mysteries and Scholastic subtleties." This resulting concoction has been "nicknamed Christianity," but, Jefferson assured New Hampshire newspaperman Salma Hale, only by "getting back to the plain and unsophisticated precepts of Christ" do "we become *real* Christians."

When Thomas B. Parker, a Unitarian minister, sent Jefferson a pamphlet that he had written on Calvin and Samuel Hopkins (New England's contemporary Calvinist) showing that the positions of both men conflicted with the Bible and with common sense, Jefferson spoke in his 1819 response of their theological "insanities." Reasoning would have been wasted on either man, he commented; "the strait jacket alone was their proper remedy." If he were to found a new sect, he added, "my fundamental principle would be the reverse of Calvin's, that we are saved by our good works which are within our power, and not by our faith which is not within our power." Mystery messed up religion; in addition, by putting all its emphases in the wrong places, it subverted morality.

Sometimes, for Jefferson, "faith" functioned as a synonym for "mystery" but always as an antonym to "Reason." The person who gave up Reason "has no remaining guard against absurdities the most monstrous, and like a ship without rudder is the sport of every wind." In human beings of this ilk, "gullibility which they call faith," wrote Jefferson in 1822, "takes the helm from the hand of reason and the mind becomes a wreck." Reason and common sense remained the tests by which to judge all things, including the propaganda coming from all the denominations and sects. And Reason tells us, as does Jesus, that we are to look at deeds more than words, at morals more than mysteries. Hear the sum of all religion "as expressed by its best preacher," Jefferson urged: "fear God and love thy neighbor." This creed contained no mystery and required no explanation — "but this won't do. It gives no scope to make dupes; priests could not live by it."

What relationship existed, for Jefferson, between religion and morality? The connection at times seemed so close as to make the two virtually identical, but not quite. Jefferson still retained a reverence toward the universe and the God who created it. But religion apart from morality appalled him. He saw the quarrels in religion as confined to the dogmas "which are totally unconnected with morality." Humankind should therefore forget the divisive and meaningless quarrels and concentrate on the unifying and significant moral substance. Those issues "on which we schismatise" were essentially pointless or "innocent," Jefferson wrote in 1809, and for that reason he would avoid "disturbing the tranquility of others" in such matters.

In this same 1809 letter to James Fishback, a Kentucky Presbyterian layman and doctor who became a Baptist minister, Jefferson recognized the social necessity of religion's moral dimension. "Reading, reflection, and time have convinced me that the interests of society require the observation of those moral precepts only in which all religions agree." In a long footnote that he ultimately did not include in the letter, he spelled out the grounds of agreement: "All forbid us to murder, steal, plunder, bear false witness, &c.," and these prohibitions every society required. What society did not require, however, was uniformity with respect to "vestments, ceremonies, physical opinions, and metaphysical speculations totally unconnected with morality." From these latter questions have flowed factions, separations, and oceans of blood.

How many human lives have been lost, Jefferson asked, in contests with the sword over those simple words attributed to Jesus: "Do this in remembrance of me"? While we can agree on Christ's morals, we "lose ourselves in subtleties about his nature, his conception maculate or immaculate, whether he was a god or not a god." Likewise, we divide over whether Christians "are to be initiated by simple aspersion, by immersion, or without water; whether [their] priests must be robed in white, in black, or not robed at all." The time had come, Jefferson wearily concluded, for all these "unimportant" and "mischievous" questions to be consigned "to the sleep of death, never to be awakened from it." The concern of society and of all rational human beings must focus on religion's moral dimension.

If, therefore, men and women must be moral, it inescapably followed that they must be free. What meaning can "good" and "evil" have if one were not free to choose the first and reject the second? So the doctrine of predestination and its Calvinist twin, the doctrine of original sin, had to be jettisoned from the mental furniture of all enlightened and liberated Americans. Natural man has a disposition to do good, not evil, to live a moral, not a sinful life. These "reveries, not to say insanities," of the likes of Calvin and Hopkins blocked that freedom without which neither a moral life nor a moral order made any sense at all.

Jefferson's partner in such radical ruminations, John Adams, agreed in condemning these pernicious doctrines. The notion of original sin, Adams noted, permitted a cheap and easy evasion of all moral responsibility. "I am answerable for my own sins," he wrote in 1815, "because I know they were my own faults; and that is enough for me to know." Adams also supported Jefferson in his emphasis upon deeds, not words, and morality, not mystery. "Be good fathers, sons, brothers, neighbors, friends, patriots . . . ," Adams wrote to

Benjamin Rush in 1812, and let an omniscient wisdom take care of the rest: "trust the ruler with his skies."

Men and women must be free; beyond that, of course, they must will to do good. What assurance can any society have that the latter truly obtains? Jefferson's optimism rested on just such an assurance — indeed, a religious conviction — with respect to "the care of the Creator in making the moral principle so much a part of our constitution as that no errors of reasoning or speculation might lead us astray from its observance in practice." In a long and important letter written in 1814 to Thomas Law, an Anglican layman who emigrated to the United States in 1793, Jefferson elaborated his moral philosophy. Some have placed the foundation of morality in the love of God, Jefferson noted, but such atheists as Diderot, d'Holbach, and Condorcet "have been among the most virtuous of men." Others say that morality is only self-love, thinly disguised. If we "feed the hungry, clothe the naked, [and] bind up the wounds of the man beaten by thieves," we do so, said Helvetius, only because these acts give us pleasure. But that begs the real question, Jefferson pointed out — namely, "How happens it that they give us pleasure?"

Having raised the question, Jefferson had his answer ready. "Because nature hath implanted in our breasts a love of others, a sense of duty to them, a moral instinct in short, which prompts us irresistibly to feel and to succour their distresses." But do all human beings have such a moral instinct? Yes, said Jefferson, in the same sense that all human beings are fashioned to see, hear, taste, smell, and touch. "The want or imperfection of the moral sense in some men, like the want or imperfection of the senses of sight and hearing in others, is no proof that it is not a general characteristic of the species." And where an imperfection does exist, we still have recourse to education, to Reason, to peer pressure, to the punishments of the law, and even to "the prospects of a future state of retribution for the evil as well as the good done while here." For the vast majority of humanity, though, Jefferson devoutly believed the moral instinct to be a God-given reality. "I think it," he asserted, "the brightest gem with which the human character is studded."

Eradicate mystery and elevate morality; dispose of any and all doctrine that would imply that men and women were not free to be moral; and recognize or, if necessary, unearth that bright gem of moral instinct. If the instinct required guidance or substance, the moral code of Jesus stood ready to fill that need. Jefferson, who thought this element of religious reform to be the most significant, both socially and personally, gave it every possible emphasis. And when his private letters as well as his private writings at last became known, he would even have had reason to hope that it might be an enduring legacy.

UNITY VERSUS TRINITY

One mystery (though Jefferson rarely used that nice a word to describe it) deserved special attention: the mysterious doctrine of the Trinity. Such particular notice was merited because in the antithesis to this doctrine one found fidelity both to Reason and to history. In attacking the doctrine of the Trinity, first, on rational grounds, Jefferson pointed out what seemed to him all too obvious — that it was "too late in the day for men of sincerity to pretend they believe in the Platonic mysticisms that three are one, and one is three; and yet the one is not three, and the three are not one." Writing here to John Adams in 1813, Jefferson, who believed so fervently in the power of Reason, could not fathom the possibility that all "thinking men" would not acclaim the new doctrine: the Unity of God. "I remember to have heard Dr. Priestley say," he told Adams, "that if all England would candidly examine themselves, and confess, they would find that Unitarianism was really the religion of all."

It certainly was the religion of John Adams, who had considered himself a Unitarian for sixty years. "Had you and I been forty days with Moses on Mount Sinai," Adams wrote to Jefferson soon after he received the letter quoted above, and were we told that "one was three and three, one, we might not have had the courage to deny it, but we could never have believed it." For truths come from Nature and from Reason, and no revelation, no miracle, no prophecy could ever convince us to "believe that 2 and 2 make 5." If forced to assert something so flagrantly contrary to Reason, "we should be more likely to say in our hearts . . . There is no God! no Truth."

Whether Jefferson needed this confirmation or not, his own language of condemnation grew ever stronger. "Ideas must be distinct before reason can act upon them," he wrote in 1816, "and no man ever had a distinct idea of the trinity. It is the mere Abracadabra of the mountebanks calling themselves priests of Jesus." Such priests specialize in "shedding darkness, like the scuttle fish, thro' the element in which they move, and making it impenetrable to the eye of a pursuing enemy." Only Reason could counteract the darkness with which so much of the world had thus been inked.

"When shall we have done away with the incomprehensible jargon of the Trinitarian arithmetic?" Jefferson impatiently asked a Unitarian correspondent in 1821. System builders and theological scholastics "have so distorted and deformed the doctrines of Jesus," he wrote, "so muffled them in mysticisms, fancies, and falsehoods, have caricatured them into forms so monstrous and inconceivable, as to shock reasonable thinkers." Having previously asserted that there would never have been an infidel if there had never been a priest, Jefferson now widened his net to include many others: "Had there never been a commentator, there never would have been an infidel." He remained hopeful, however, in these last years of his life: "I have little doubt that the whole of our country will soon be rallied to the Unity of the Creator, and, I hope, to the pure doctrines of Jesus also."

If trinitarian arithmetic was irrational, it was also, in Jefferson's view, ahistorical. The great improvement that Judaism had made upon all its surrounding religions was its repeated emphasis on the oneness of God. "Hear, O Israel, the Lord thy God is one God." And Jesus did nothing, Jefferson vigorously argued, to minimize or detract from that divine oneness. "The religion of Jesus," Jefferson assured Jared Sparks in 1820, "is founded on the Unity of God, and this principle, chiefly, gave it triumph over the rabble of heathen gods then acknowledged." Such was and such remained, in Jefferson's conviction, the thinking man's religion. But then those commentators! "The metaphysical insanities of Athanasius, of Loyola, and of Calvin, are to my understanding, mere relapses into polytheism, differing from paganism only by being more unintelligible."

Priestley's *History of the Corruptions of Christianity* helped convince Jefferson, as previously noted, that he was on solid historical ground concerning the unity of God. Another English Unitarian and strong friend of America during its Revolution, Richard Price, reinforced Jefferson in this stand. And Jefferson, who while in Paris sent books to so many, when back in America happily welcomed books from Price on rational religion. In fact, Price had the honor of introducing Jefferson to Priestley's works. With Adams and many other Unitarian correspondents at home, along with English Unitarians abroad, Jefferson did not stand alone in grounding his rejection of the doctrine of the Trinity in history no less than in Reason. And he believed, erroneously it turned out, that with a nudge here and there thousands would soon join him in affirming the unity of God. In this case, if not in many others, the religious reformer thought that all he had to do was wait.

COSMIC JUSTICE VERSUS SELF-INTEREST

Finally, Jefferson did not so much reform as emphatically assert the view that, this being a moral universe, cosmic justice would ultimately prevail. The orthodox majority held to the concept of divine "rewards and punishments" — in the language of the eighteenth century, used so tenaciously that many insisted it be placed in their state constitutions for all officeholders to affirm. The Pennsylvania constitution of 1790, for example, declared that "no person, who acknowledges the being of a God, and a future state of rewards and punishments," would be disqualified from holding public office. Tennessee in that same year put the matter negatively: "No person who denies the being of God, or a future state of rewards and punishments" would be eligible for any office "in the civil department of this State."

Here, orthodoxy held no monopoly. Calvinists and deists could agree (1) that officeholders had to swear an oath by Almighty God and (2) that this God held sway as the only ultimate enforcer of moral duties. Jesus taught "the doctrine of a future state," Jefferson reported to Benjamin Rush in 1803, "and wielded it with efficacy, as an important incentive, supplementary to other motives for moral conduct." That moral instinct in the breast of every man and woman demanded, simply *demanded*, that the good prosper and the wicked suffer. Since this was so manifestly not the case in life on earth, then in the life to come God's moral accounting must fall into correct balance. The Creator who firmly planted a moral structure in humanity could not fail to plant a similar structure in the universe itself. Otherwise, cosmic justice was a farce and the moral demands placed upon our natures a cruel joke.

Once again, John Adams leaped at the opportunity to reinforce and strongly second the Jeffersonian position. "A future state will set all right," Adams asserted; "without the supposition of a future state I can make nothing of this Universe, but a Chaos." And in a letter to Jefferson in 1818, he went even further: "If I did not believe in a future state, I should believe in no God." The universe, in such a case, "with all its swelling pomp," would be nothing but "a boyish fire work." The sacrificial strivings of humankind toward more liberty, more equality, more happiness required heavenly authentication.

The moral argument, the social necessity, dictated the truth of immortality. Indeed, said Jefferson, never one to miss the chance for another swipe at Plato, if the only arguments for the immortality of the soul were those offered by Plato, "not a man in the world would believe it." One of the great improvements that Jesus made in the religion of his birth was to emphasize "the doctrine of a future state, which was either doubted or disbelieved by the Jews." So why did Jefferson, as he cut and pasted, decline to include those verses reporting the resurrection of Jesus?

Comfortable with the general notion of immortality, Jefferson had no interest in a bodily resurrection — his own or that of anyone else. The precise nature of one's existence after death remained unclear, even dark. And in that darkness Jefferson affirmed that he was content "to trust for the future to him who has been so good for the past." If there was ever a subject in which persons peered through a glass darkly, that subject was the exact shape or nature that life takes after death. As Jefferson told Adams in 1820, "Ignorance, in these cases, is truly the softest pillow on which I can lay my head." But it was enough to affirm the pervasively held creed of deism: God, freedom, and immortality.

Thus far the deist Jefferson on immortality. Jefferson as husband, father, and friend offered to himself and others the comforting and familiar assurances of the New Testament and Christian concern. In an 1804 letter to a boyhood friend, John Page, Jefferson observed how "few stragglers remain to count the fallen." On the other hand, he added (showing a familiarity with the writings of Paul even if he did not generally care for them), "We sorrow not then as others who have no hope." When John Adams lost his beloved Abigail, Jefferson wrote in the most tender of terms to comfort him and bid him to look forward to that "ecstatic meeting with the friends we have loved and lost and whom we shall still love and never lose again. God bless you," Jefferson concluded, "and support you under your heavy affliction." In a poem written for his surviv-

142

ing daughter shortly before his death, Jefferson found similar assurance for himself. There he spoke of the "welcoming shore" and of the "two seraphs," his deceased wife and daughter, who would greet him upon his arrival. Like many another person who saw this life slipping away (one foot in the grave, and the other "uplifted," he said), the hope for some sort of life to come grew steadily stronger. Yet he, like John Adams, choked at the thought of heaven as some kind of cosmic lottery that required one to join the right church, say the right words, bow before the right altar in order to secure that greedily coveted ticket to heaven.

THE THEOLOGY OF JESUS — AND OF JEFFERSON

In professing the oneness of God, Jefferson hoped to bring about reform. In professing the existence of God, on the other hand, he mainly conformed. He accepted, for example, the popular cosmological argument as sufficient proof of a divine being. In examining "all this design, cause and effect" evident in Nature, he wrote, one could not fail to detect "a fabricator of things from matter and motion." The Creator also regulates and preserves, and even regenerates some of the motion and matter into new forms. For as we noted earlier, Jefferson did not believe his Creator retired from the scene once the original act of creation had passed. One might well describe him as a "warm deist," or perhaps a Newtonian deist, affirming that God's molding genius was ever active, ever present. He was not in any sense an aloof, passionless deist. As Jefferson wrote in detail and even in exultation to John Adams in 1823, "it is impossible for the human mind," when contemplating the vast universe, "not to perceive and feel a conviction of design, consummate skill, and infinite power in every atom of its composition."

Of the reality of this God, Jefferson entertained no doubt. Of that Divine Being's exact nature, however, he was less sure.

Jesus told us, Jefferson reminded the Philadelphia Calvinist Ezra Stiles Ely, that God is a spirit, but he did not trouble to define the word. Nor do I, said Jefferson. "I am therefore of his theology, believing that we have neither words nor ideas adequate" to define God's true nature. One of the reasons for this reticence rested on his philosophical materialism. Jefferson — and at this point he and Adams parted company — found materialism far more appealing than its opposite. Adams thought materialism to be fixed, mechanical, without life or feeling. Jefferson, on the contrary, argued that any refuge in idealism or "spirit-ism" approached those Platonic fogs and mists.

Employing a kind of Cartesian reductionism, Jefferson explained that he could sense his own existence and the existence of bodies other than himself. This he called *matter*. Then, "I feel them changing place. This gives me *motion*." What is left over after matter and motion? Nothing; and this "nothing" had no independent status: it was simply the absence of matter. Even as God gave us our Reason, which deserved to be trusted, so he gave us our senses, on which we may also depend. "When once we quit the basis of sensation, all is in the wind." To speak of God or angels or souls as immaterial existences was "to talk of *nothings*." And what could be more absurd than to assert that "nothing made something"?

Medieval man came up with the persisting distinction between spirit and matter, Jefferson pointed out. But Jesus made no such distinction, nor does Reason. The Creator can endow matter with strange and invisible qualities, such as Newton's law of gravity, or the compass needle's magnetism, or the brain's power to influence gross matter through its ideas. Can even the soul be matter? Yes, said Jefferson, pointing to John Locke, who "openly maintained the materialism of the soul, and charged with blasphemy those who deny that Omnipotence could give the faculty of thinking to certain combinations of matter." Materialism need not be crass or mechanical, and for Jefferson it was neither.

144

If Priestley found Christian history to be mainly an account of corruptions, and if Jefferson found Christianity to be purest in the teachings of Jesus, then one of the paths to reform and to a right theology was a return to the original, "the pure and primitive gospel." Jefferson noted in 1822 that he found happiness "in the prospect of a restoration of primitive Christianity." Approaching his eightieth year, however, he gladly left "to younger athletes to encounter and lop off the false branches which have been engrafted into it by the mythologists of the middle and modern ages." Though a forward-looking optimist in political matters, Jefferson saw the religious golden age as lying in the past, "getting back to the plain and unsophisticated precepts of Christ . . . towards a restoration of his genuine doctrines." This language sounded remarkably like that of Alexander Campbell, who in the last two decades of Jefferson's life preached on the frontier a message of restoration and return. No evidence of any contact or correspondence, however, between this founder of the Disciples of Christ and the former president of the United States has survived.

Thomas Jefferson — rationalist, moralist, primitivist, monotheist. Was he also a Unitarian? He corresponded frequently with Unitarians; he read with appreciation a discourse of William Ellery Channing's sent to him by a friend; he even attended one of Priestley's Unitarian churches when he stayed in Philadelphia. But in writing to Timothy Pickering in 1821, Jefferson acknowledged that Unitarians did not all think alike, "as between Doctors Price and Priestley, for example." Nor would he and Pickering always agree, he added. "As the Creator has made no two faces alike, so no two minds, and probably no two creeds." Neither an Arian, believing that God created Jesus before the world, nor a Socinian, believing that God elevated Jesus to divinity and raised him from the dead, Jefferson did not fit neatly into any category. Recognizing this, he confessed to Ezra Stiles Ely in 1819: "I am of a sect by myself, as far as I know."

Nonetheless, he had great confidence that Unitarianism,

as representative of a rational religion, would take over America. And the older he grew, the more confident he became. "No one sees with greater pleasure than myself," he wrote in 1822, "the progress of reason in its advance towards rational Christianity." And the next year, he affirmed his "trust that there is not a young man now living in the U.S. who will not die a Unitarian." To a former Methodist, now turned Unitarian, he added later that same year, "I confidently expect that the present generation will see Unitarianism become the general religion of the United States." He saw Unitarianism already prevailing in the East, "dawning in the West, and advancing toward the South." Priestley's learned writings will soon "be in every hand," and the "Athanasian paradox" will crumble. In all of these predictions, Jefferson was magnificently wrong. Yet if one had supreme confidence in Reason and supreme confidence in America, what could be more logical than the ultimate triumph of the religion he embraced in the land that he loved?

Still another label may be applied to Jefferson, the one utilized in the heading for this chapter: religious reformer. In his own estimation, he brought peace, not a sword. He would purify, not destroy. But a wider public has always had difficulty perceiving such distinctions clearly or accepting them generously. In writing of Jesus' reform of Judaism, Jefferson observed that "the office of reformer of the superstitions of a nation is ever dangerous." By 1820, when he wrote those words, he knew that they applied well beyond the first century of the Christian era, well beyond the land of Judea.

6 The Educator

"Whereas Almighty God hath created the mind
free . . ." (1786)

The quotation above, as was noted in Chapter 3, introduced
the preamble to Jefferson's Statute for Establishing Religious
Freedom. Those words, however, stood for more than that,
since the sentiment they embodied undergirded Jefferson's
whole approach to education at every level. Indeed, they may
be fairly taken as the preamble to his entire adult life.

From the time that Jefferson entered the College of William and Mary in 1760, he never stopped thinking about education: his own, that of his friends and neighbors, that of his
state and the nation as a whole. He thought about it as legislator
and governor, as minister to France and as president; and in
his old age at Monticello, the thoughts turned into obsessions.
In all of this reflection and active pursuit, he also carefully
considered the proper relationship between religion and education: not what had been, but what ought to be.

THE BILL FOR THE MORE GENERAL DIFFUSION
OF KNOWLEDGE

Jefferson's first and most ambitious educational plan for his state came in 1778 as part of the general revision of Virginia's laws to reflect the new independence from England. As a member of the new legislature that supplanted the old House of Burgesses, Jefferson drew up a Bill for the More General Diffusion of Knowledge, the essentials of which he repeated later in his *Notes on the State of Virginia*. The details recorded here reveal how elaborate and concrete his reflections on education had already become. Virginia, which possessed hardly anything that could be called a *system* of education, now needed precisely that; and America, which had embarked upon a bold democratic experiment, likewise needed a model for the education of its citizens — all of its citizens.

If Jefferson saw the people as the ultimate foundation upon which democracy rested, he also saw the education of those people not as an option but as a necessity. "No other sure foundation," he told George Wythe, could be devised. And to Madison he indicated his sense of urgency regarding "the education of the common people." We must, he wrote, rely "on their good sense" for the preservation of "a due degree of liberty." Jefferson also had to rely, once more, on the legislative diligence of Madison to try to guide his expansive, and necessarily expensive, bill through a skeptical aggregate of legislators.

Jefferson proposed dividing the whole state into "hundreds" or "wards" of a size large enough to build and maintain an elementary school but small enough that children would not have to travel more than a few miles from home. Some five or six square miles in size, these wards, as Jefferson later told John Adams, would resemble the New England townships and, he hoped, be similarly successful in raising the level of literacy throughout his state. Furthermore, these wards, or "little republics," might also work something like the effective town meetings of Massachusetts and elsewhere, reaching the grass roots quickly and hearing the voice of the people sympathetically.

At these primary schools, "all the free children, male and female," living within the bounds of the ward would be eligible to attend for three years at no cost to themselves or their parents. If parents or guardians so chose, the children could remain in the primary school beyond the three years at their own expense. Here, in addition to instruction in reading, writing, and arithmetic, young pupils would receive lessons in moral improvement, primarily through the vehicle of literature and history, and they would study the evils of tyranny along with the benefits of freedom.

Primary schools, to the extent that such could be found in colonial Virginia, had operated under the influence of the Anglican Church and the Anglican clergy. Sometimes they even gathered on unused glebe lands. Jefferson envisioned a state-sponsored and state-supported educational system in which the influence of any single denomination, or of all together for that matter, would be minimized. He also recommended that the Bible not be used as a basic book of instruction in these tender years, since children were "at an age when their judgments are not sufficiently matured for religious enquiries." Instead, their minds should be turned toward the "most useful facts from Grecian, Roman, European and American history." Such "useful facts" would provide their own kind of moral lessons — and instruction in such virtues could not begin too early.

Jefferson's plan also allowed for twenty middle-tier or grammar schools, more selective institutions where the wealthier families could send those apt pupils from roughly the age of eight to fifteen or sixteen. That elitism was balanced, however, by selecting annually from among the poor "the best genius" from each of the wards to go on to grammar school at the state's expense. "By this means," Jefferson wrote in the *Notes*, "twenty of the best geniuses will be raked from the rubbish annually, and be instructed, at the public expense, as far as the grammar schools go." Those not measuring up to the demands of grammar school education could be dropped at the end of any year, but those who did well could remain for the full six years of instruction.

Instruction would build upon the subjects offered in the primary school, but more would be added in the way of geography, history, elementary science, literature, and mathematics. The learning of language received great emphasis in this plan, for the memory during these years "is then most susceptible and tenacious of impressions; and the learning of languages being chiefly a work of memory, it seems precisely fitted to the powers of this period." Jefferson gladly included Latin, Greek, and Hebrew in his curriculum, since these would be essential for persons going into the professions, not excluding clergy, and the college years came too late for such skills to be acquired. The grammar schools were designed to prepare an even higher order of geniuses for college, but Jefferson also purposed to keep the minds busy. If these years were "to pass in idleness, the mind becomes lethargic and impotent, as would the body it inhabits if unexercised during the same time."

At the end of the six years of grammar school instruction, Jefferson specified that another winnowing take place. About half of those graduating, "chosen for the superiority of their parts and disposition," should proceed to college, where for three years their room, board, and educational expenses would be covered by the state. The lower half of the graduating classes, "of still superior parts," could then be suitably employed as grammar school instructors. At the College of William and Mary, the curriculum and governance of which Jefferson likewise planned to revise, students "would be exposed to all the useful sciences." They would also dedicate themselves to the good of the whole civil community, the commonweal, and not be allowed to pursue narrow private interests. This broader public spirit, which the eighteenth century often called "virtue," played a large part in the educational vision not only of Jefferson but of all the other founders who gave significant attention to pedagogy. The goal of education, in their view, was to produce free moral agents whose will to do good was matched by a knowledge of how and where to do the most good.

When Jefferson thought of his third tier of higher education, he had in 1778 no other entity to embrace than the College of William and Mary. That institution, therefore, rose to the top of his educational plan, with authority to supervise the curriculum of both the primary and the grammar schools. Under the aegis of the college, the State of Virginia, which lagged well behind Massachusetts in provisions for its young citizens, would acquire a uniform system of education for all of its youth. But for this plan to be acceptable to Jefferson, to say nothing of many other citizens, the College of William and Mary had to cease being an Anglican school and become a public one. Jefferson therefore included recommendations that the Anglican governing board be replaced by a secular board chosen by the General Assembly and that the number of professorships be increased from six to eight in order to accommodate the growth in knowledge, especially within the sciences.

Jefferson not only had great confidence in the merits of his plan but also thought this bill the most important single element in the revised code of laws. The fate of Virginia and of the Republic depended on some arrangement for universal education, an arrangement that recognized the right of all to a minimum level of instruction and gave the truly meritorious student, whether rich or poor, the opportunity to proceed to the very top. Jefferson passionately believed that a great deal depended on the swift passage of his Bill for the More General Diffusion of Knowledge, but it had taken nine years for his religious freedom legislation ultimately to succeed, and it would take far longer to taste victory here. In fact, he never tasted it; nothing resembling his grand plan for public education arrived until long after his death.

Jefferson worked hard as a legislator to secure approval
of the bill, and even harder as governor, but to no avail. When
he departed for France, he had to leave this hope for his state,
as others, in the capable hands of James Madison. Feeling some
desperation when, after eight long years, nothing had happened to the education bill, Jefferson in 1786 wrote to his old
friend and mentor in Williamsburg, George Wythe. Stressing
the importance of making learning available to all, he begged,
"Preach, my dear Sir, a crusade against ignorance; establish
and improve the law for educating the common people." Many
had objected to the bill on the grounds of its cost, Jefferson
noted, but they should count the cost of the alternative. "Let
our countrymen know," he added, "that the tax which will be
paid for this purpose is not more than the thousandth part of
what will be paid to kings, priests and nobles who will rise up
among us if we leave the people in ignorance." Writing from
France before its own revolution, Jefferson knew more than he
wished to about the unholy trinity of kings, priests, and nobles.
"If any body thinks that" these oppressors "are good conser-
vators of the public happiness," Jefferson told Wythe, "send
him here. It is the best school in the universe to cure him of
that folly."

By the end of 1786, Madison sensed that the legislative
sentiment for passing Jefferson's bill was scarcely more
favorable than before. In the previous year, he told Jefferson,
it had made no sense even to risk a vote. This year, some had
proposed passage with the proviso that its operation be "sus-
pended for three or four years. Even in this form, however,
there would be hazard in pushing it to a final question." Perhaps, Madison suggested, it would be best to wait for another
round of revision until objections to the expense, either for the
counties or for the state, diminished. Early in 1787, Madison
wrote again with no better news. The bill had passed two
readings "by a small majority," but no one pushed for another
reading. In addition to the question of cost, two other objections
were raised: first, "the difficulty of executing it in the present

sparse settlement of the Country," and second, "the inequality of the districts as represented by the Western members." Later that year, as Madison busied himself in a Constitutional Convention in Philadelphia, his absence from Richmond further dimmed the prospects for this Jeffersonian dream.

For nearly two hundred years, the "sparse settlement" of Virginia had haunted Anglican efforts at an effective establishment. Now that predominantly rural character (again, unlike Massachusetts) would threaten, if not doom, hopes for a genuine educational establishment. Anglicanism, moreover, had not altogether lost its ability to alarm the non-Anglican population, even though disestablishment had been achieved and even though a Statute for Establishing Religious Freedom would soon pass. There stood the Anglican College of William and Mary at the very head of the entire educational proposal. True, Jefferson had advanced major reforms for the college, but they had not yet taken place, and perhaps they never would.

As governor of the state in 1779, and hence a member of the college's Board of Visitors, Jefferson did manage to abolish the two professorships in divinity, substituting one professorship in law and another in science. But for the non-Anglican citizenry, this was not enough; and for the Anglican citizenry, it was too much. While the college remained a private and religious school, Jefferson argued that, "being founded and endowed with the lands and revenues of the public, and intended for their sole use and improvement," it now really belonged to the state and not to a wholly Anglican governing board. However sound the reasoning, tradition stood fast. Jefferson tried desperately to work with the only college he had available to him, but he found his actions blocked or misunderstood at every turn. So religion, which had given him trouble locally and would give him more trouble nationally, helped delay and ultimately defeat a heroic effort to give Virginia a full-blown system of secular education.

For Jefferson, the urgency for passing some educational plan could be defended on both a personal and a political level.

He made the political case eloquently in his *Notes*, where he said, as he so often did, that the people themselves were the "only safe depositories" of governmental power. "And to render even them safe their minds must be improved to a certain degree." Every form of government, Jefferson wrote, has within it "some trace of human weakness, some germ of corruption and degeneracy." If the people trusted wholly in their rulers, kept no watch over or check on their use of power, then sooner or later those cunning rulers would find that small germ and, through their wickedness, bring disease to a whole country. "Every government degenerates when trusted to the rulers of the people alone." If, therefore, the burden of governing rested in the last analysis upon the people, an inescapable burden then rested upon the leaders of a durable republic to equip and prepare citizens for their essential tasks. "Whenever the people are well-informed," Jefferson told Richard Price in 1789, "they can be trusted with their own government." Furthermore, only education can render "the people the safe, as they are the ultimate, guardians of their own liberty."

Freedom of the press necessarily followed as an ingredient essential to a democratic order, but only a literate public could avail itself of that free press. Similarly, the best protection against corruption lay not in confining the franchise to a wealthy and aristocratic elite, as in England, where only one man in ten could vote for members of Parliament, but in making adult suffrage universal. Then, if a wicked ruler wished to buy the people's votes, he would have to buy a whole country. Bribery on such a scale would defy this "means of corruption." But if voting be granted this broadly, education must manifest an equal breadth. And so Jefferson concluded, perhaps plaintively, in the *Notes*, "An amendment to our constitution [i.e., Virginia's] must here come in aid of the public education. The influence over government must be shared among all the people."

Jefferson later confided to John Adams how he saw the education bill as the capstone of reform in his state. He proposed the abolition of primogeniture, and that was approved. He proposed a law doing away with entails that limited the inheritance of property to a specified line of succession, and that was approved. These changes "laid the axe to the root of pseudo-aristocracy." Then, after a long wait, the law for religious freedom passed, and that "put down the aristocracy of the clergy, and restored to the citizen the freedom of the mind." All that remained for a democratic egalitarianism to prevail, then, was the reform of education. If only the bill had passed, he told Adams in 1813, that "would have raised the mass of the people to the high ground of moral respectability necessary to their own safety, and to orderly government." Then Virginia would have had a true or natural aristocracy, not a false or artificial one.

Back in the 1780s, when Jefferson was still fighting for the passage of his bill, some argued that the country as a whole was too weak, too poor, to invest that heavily in education. Perhaps the best course of action would be to send promising young men abroad for their education. Being himself abroad, Jefferson did not find such advice persuasive. Writing in 1785 to a young Virginian in France, John Banister Jr., Jefferson spoke chiefly of the disadvantages of sending any young American to Europe for his education. "If he goes to England, he learns drinking, horse racing, and boxing." If he goes to the Continent, his morals no less than his mind are endangered. "He acquires a fondness for European luxury and dissipation, and a contempt for the simplicity of his own country. . . . He is led, by the strongest of all the human passions, into a spirit for female intrigue . . . [and] learns to consider fidelity to the marriage bed as an ungentlemanly practice, and inconsistent with happiness." Indeed, Jefferson thought that no young man should go to Europe without a chaperone until he had reached the age of thirty or more. In any case, America needed to educate its own in the manners and morals that a republic required as well as in the arts and sciences appropriate to a new and enlightened age. Only in the field of medicine did

Jefferson concede in the 1780s that one might need to venture abroad for the necessary professional training.

On a personal no less than a political level, Jefferson could conceive of no possible alternative to education. Ignorance remained the root of all evil, the cause of poverty, superstition, and general misery. Without education, one's path led only backward, and the rest of the world slipped silently ahead of all those who turned their backs on learning. Some people feared education because they feared innovation; or they pretended to favor education, but it turned out to be of a type that allowed only a worship of the ancestors. Every advance in science had been decried and denounced as "innovation." But such innovation was the law of life, no less than of education. As Jefferson wrote to another physician friend, Benjamin Waterhouse, "When I contemplate the immense advances in science and discoveries in the arts which have been made within the period of my life, I look forward with confidence to equal advances by the present generation." Only in that manner could today's youth become wiser than their fathers, as the fathers grew wiser "than the burners of witches."

Jefferson had proclaimed the inalienable rights to life, liberty, and the pursuit of happiness, but to pursue happiness meant to pursue education. And that process of education, preferably a lifelong one, could be relied upon, said Jefferson, more than any other, "for ameliorating the condition, promoting the virtue, and advancing the happiness of man." In writing to John Adams in 1813, Jefferson reminded his old colleague that the two parties differed on the capacity of education to improve the human condition. Those who believed in the "improvability of the human mind, in science, in ethics, in government, etc.," argued that "no definite limits could be assigned to that progress." The opponents of reform, on the other hand, "denied improvement, and advocated steady adherence to the principles, practices and institutions of our fathers, which they represented as the consummation of wisdom, and acme of excellence, beyond which the human mind could never advance." Jefferson could never be content with "received wisdom," weary clichés, well-worn ruts, and the "tried and true." If so often and for so long tried, it just may no longer be true.

When Jefferson hinted that Adams might still be counseling young men to look backward rather than forward, Adams took offense. Jefferson had quoted an address of Adams to the young men of Philadelphia in which he declared that they would find no principles or systems of education more suitable "to be transferred to your posterity, than those you have received from your ancestors." But, asked Adams in a piqued response to his Monticello pen pal, just "who were these ancestors? Among them were Thomas Jefferson and John Adams. And I very coolly believed that no two men among those ancestors did more towards [liberty and independence] than those two." Beyond that, said Adams, he appealed only to the "general principles of Christianity, and the general principles of English and American liberty." Here stood a heritage not to be set brusquely aside; Adams added that even your much esteemed Newton and Locke, Rousseau and Bolingbroke, would agree. So please, he entreated Jefferson, do not charge me with "narrow thoughts . . . bigoted, enthusiastic, or superstitious principles." That argument firmly settled, the two patriarchs continued to exchange mutually reinforcing ideas on the inestimable value of education.

Religion and Education

If Jefferson felt so strongly about education and if he had major concerns about religion, how did he see the relationship, if any, between these two vital entities? Since the answer is complex, it will be offered under three headings: first, education and morality; second, instruction in the essentials of religion; and third, the rejection of all sectarian instruction and control.

EDUCATION AND MORALITY

Just as Jefferson closely linked religion with morality, so he considered morality to be an essential element of all education, from the primary grades through the university. Indeed, morality could not be divorced from the American experiment itself: "I have ever cherished" the conviction, Jefferson wrote in 1813, "that peace, prosperity, liberty, and morals have an intimate connection." All citizens bore a moral responsibility, but especially so the leaders of a democracy, who must serve as public examples of a dedication to virtue.

One cannot begin too early to develop the attention to moral improvement and the habits of moral choices. Reason has its limits here, Jefferson acknowledged, telling Maria Cosway in his famous "Heart and Head" letter of 1786 that while science belonged to the head, "morals were too essential to the happiness of man to be risked on the uncertain combinations of the head." Jefferson believed that Reason had misled him on occasion in the past, as he represented a personified Heart saying to a personified Head, "I do not know that I ever did a good thing on your suggestion, or a dirty thing without it." England and France enjoyed some reputation in science, but little in virtue. "And if science produces no better fruits than tyranny, murder, rapine, and destitution of national morality," Jefferson confided to Adams in 1813, "I would rather wish our country to be ignorant, honest, and estimable, as our neighboring savages are."

One should not, however, have to make the cruel choice between head and heart, or between science on the one hand and morality on the other. A proper education would steer the malleable young person in a direction that encouraged the development of both. As we have seen, Jefferson maintained that God gives a moral instinct to all, thus taking the first vital step on our behalf. Humankind is not depraved; God did not condemn a great proportion of the human race to damnation long before they had been born. On the contrary, he carefully placed the young child in the path to be trod. Education must keep the children there, widening this path into ever greater ethical understanding and practical application. Without moral illumination, one cannot govern oneself; without moral illumination, a republic cannot stand. As John Adams put it so succinctly in 1776, "The only foundation of a free constitution is pure virtue." Without a moral foundation, people may dissolve governments as often as they wish, but they only manage to exchange one tyranny for another.

In Jefferson's three-tier plan of education, he intended that primary education, through reading, would improve "the morals and faculties" of young pupils. They should come to understand, moreover, their duties to their neighbors and to their country. Like his boyhood Anglican tutor, James Maury, Jefferson found the reading of history to be effective in instilling an appreciation for the sorts of moral dilemmas that require resolute choices in order to save either a life or a country. "History by apprising [the young pupils] of the past will enable them to judge of the future," Jefferson wrote in the *Notes;* "it will avail them of the experience of other times and nations; it will qualify them as judges of the actions and designs of men." Such judgments would not, of course, spring full blown into the mind of the six-year-old, but the lessons of history would be repeated for the benefit of the eight-year-old, the twelve-year-old, and so on. Education in morality was not a lesson of the day, but of every day and of every year. Education then became a process of making right choices, a technique for allowing the moral instinct of the heart ever more steadily to direct the knowledge stored in the head.

The moral faculty required exercise and training every bit as much as the physical body did. "Lose no occasion," Jefferson told the young Peter Carr in 1787, "of exercising your dispositions to be grateful, to be generous, to be charitable, to be humane, to be true, just, firm, orderly, courageous, &c." Those dispositions had already been planted in your breast by a benevolent Creator as surely as small muscles have been given

159

to a newborn babe. Without exercise, however, all would atrophy and die. Every act of doing good was a practice drill, Jefferson told Carr, "which will strengthen your moral faculties and increase your worth." Virtue should eventually become not so much a conscious or agonizing choice as a reflex, a deeply ingrained habit. And having reached that point, one could speak not of calculation but of character.

Jefferson's older contemporary Benjamin Franklin (1706-90) argued in similar fashion that only by degrees did one at last achieve a virtuous character. Continued, steady, repeated moral choices, "long habits of virtue," resulted in a deep-seated morality that at last became "natural." Or, in more modern parlance, the properly educated man or woman made the right choice so often and so regularly that such a choice simply became "second nature." One may as a youth do right rather than wrong for fear of punishment or hope of reward, parental or divine, but that was acceptable to Franklin, for such behavior helped to establish the essential *habit*. It has become popular to ridicule Franklin for his "moral accounting," for his daily record of how well he managed to live up to his own expectations regarding any specific virtue. But how else did right behavior become second nature? How else, except through carefully scrutinized habit, did one become virtuous?

Of course, moral training began in the home even before the school, and continued in the home parallel with the school. In that connection, Jefferson worried about the lessons that slavery "taught" to the observant child. The slave-owning parent, more often than not, behaved like a tyrant toward his or her slave. "The parent storms, the child looks on, catches the lineaments of wrath, puts on the same airs in the circles of smaller slaves, gives a loose to the worst of passions," Jefferson wrote in the *Notes*. The child "thus nursed, educated, and daily exercised in tyranny, cannot but be stamped by it with odious peculiarities." Slavery had a lot to answer for, but one of its insurmountable burdens was that no amount of schooling could eradicate the indelible moral lessons that it silently taught.

In his own home, Jefferson took seriously the moral training of his two daughters. They needed a solid education not only for their own sakes but also also for the sake of their children, since it was likely that "they would be placed in a country situation" and hence have to undertake the task of educating both sons and daughters. Of his own daughters, Jefferson wished for "moral rectitude" above all other attainments or skills. And that habit, like the habits of "industry, resolution, independence, and ingenuity," needed to be developed early and practiced constantly. Jefferson's expectations were high, he wrote to his fifteen-year-old Martha, "yet not higher than you may attain. Industry and resolution are all that are wanting." Good habits did not come easily, but it was part of the American character, Jefferson assured Martha, "to consider nothing as desperate — to surmount every difficulty by resolution and contrivance." Good could conquer evil, and virtue could defeat vice, but not without resolve — and regular exercise.

Scholars have given appropriate attention to the Puritan ethic in the Revolutionary age of America's history. So far as Jefferson's own moral code was concerned, he shared much with the Puritans. Like the English Whigs (who learned from the Puritans), Jefferson abhorred luxury and cultivated frugality. In the White House, he astounded all and dismayed many by dismissing the niceties of English protocol, by dispensing with the wig and aristocratic dress, by ignoring rank and station, by riding around Washington on horseback alone or with only a single servant. England in the eighteenth century had set the pattern for luxurious indulgence, for idleness instead of industry, and for private rather than public well-being. America should set an example of the contrary, turning forthrightly away from a soft self-indulgence toward a muscular fortitude and resolve. If the American Revolution required us to sacrifice and do without, John Adams told his wife Abigail, so much the better. Adversities and distresses "will have this good effect, at least: it will inspire us with many virtues, which we have not, and correct many errors, follies, and vices, which threaten to disturb, dishonor, and destroy us." On this point, the New Englander and the Virginian wholly agreed.

They also agreed in eschewing vice as destructive of the body personal no less than the body politic. Jefferson labored so long over "The Life and Morals of Jesus" because they constituted a school for virtue, both for himself and for others. He advised young men against a European education because of the effect it might have on their morals and private behavior. And the advice he gave so freely to others, he took to himself. A man of Stoic restraint ("Murmur not at the ways of Providence") and an Epicurean ("the most rational system" of the ancients) who prized intellectual pleasures above all others, Jefferson endeavored to provide a steady public example of habitual right choice. Even on slavery he began as an abolitionist, though the clarity of his vision in this troubled realm steadily dimmed over the years. The Puritans had an advantage over him in the confrontation and compromise with slavery, but in the classic virtues of honesty, industry, temperance, courage, chastity, and more, he could not be "out-Puritaned" by those whose dogmas he did so readily reject.

TEACHING THE ESSENTIALS OF RELIGION

In the age of Enlightenment, Jefferson shared with others the view that natural religion dealt largely, though not wholly, with morality. Voltaire commented, "I understand by natural religion the principles of morality common to the human race." In writing to John Adams, Jefferson vigorously rejected all sectarian dogmas, but just as vigorously argued for those moral precepts "innate in man" that "constitute true religion." Jefferson agreed with Adams that if by religion one meant sectarianism, "this would be the best of all possible worlds, if there were no religion in it." But if one looked to the essence of religion — namely, morality and its Author — then without it, as he quoted Adams once again, "this would be something not fit to be named, even indeed a Hell."

If one proceeded to disestablish the Anglican Church, which bore a major responsibility in the realm of moral instruction and disciplined behavior, then the resulting vacuum must be quickly filled. So Jefferson found yet another reason to feel a keen sense of frustration in the long legislative delay concerning his education bill. The demand for moral education had not changed; the institutions responsible for that education had changed. As the Anglican Church found itself being displaced, the secular school needed to step into the breach, and to do so with all dispatch.

When dealing with religion in public education, the trick was to include those matters on which Reason and common sense could agree and then to exclude all else. Reason and common sense agreed on the basic elements of morality, and any religion that did not inculcate such a morality was unworthy of the name and deserved no following. Beyond that, however, it was obvious to common sense and to every rational being that a Creator, Preserver, and Supreme Ruler of the universe existed, "the author of all the relations of morality, and of the obligations these [imply]." To teach students that the world just happened, or that it had simply always existed, was to betray their education. The God revealed in Nature and to Reason deserved a place in the classroom, as in life. For Jefferson, such teaching was "neutral," not the exclusive possession of this denomination or that. Its presumed neutrality derived, of course, from the fact that it coincided perfectly with Jefferson's own religious point of view.

He could concede more to himself than to others in this matter of the essentials. He attacked John Adams for advocating adherence to "the *general principles* of Christianity" — Adams's emphasis. To Jefferson, this sounded like sectarianism. To Adams that sounded like nonsense. He delivered these remarks, Adams responded, to an audience of young men in Philadelphia that included "Roman Catholics, English Episcopalians, Scotch and American Presbyterians, Methodists, Moravians, Anabaptists, German Lutherans, German Calvinists, Universalists, Arians, Priestleyans, Socinians, Independents, Congregationalists, . . . Deists and Atheists, and 'Protestants quie ne croyent rien' [who believe in nothing]." Could anyone seriously believe that he, Adams, advocated holding on to all of that? Of course not. He spoke only of "general principles." Perhaps he deserved as much leniency with his "neutrality" as Jefferson claimed for his.

In any case, Jefferson did not fear to include religious "truths" in his curriculum, just as long as these truths were rational, universal, and "neutral." At the end of the twentieth century, a list of such truths would be difficult to formulate. Even at the end of the eighteenth century such a list would have been extremely short and not even then beyond all controversy. To most of the orthodox, the God of Nature or of Reason paled in comparison with the God of Revelation. And freedom (to pursue briefly the deist creed for the moment) might be a matter of agreement politically but certainly not theologically or philosophically. Then, with respect to personal immortality, if Jefferson's views on this subject had been known in any detail, no schoolmaster in Virginia or elsewhere would have cared to inject that largely agnostic outlook into the classroom.

It is much easier, therefore, to locate the essentials of Jefferson's own religion than it is to discover a doctrinal consensus suitable for public education. Jefferson probably did find agreement on teaching Hebrew, Greek, and Latin in the grammar schools, for these languages, he noted, were the "depositories of the originals, and of the earliest and most respected authorities of the faith of every sect." But such linguistic equipment only made it possible for the mature student, using those tools, to arrive at religious truths on an individual basis. Or the cynic might say, and Jefferson in some moods would agree, that these tools only equipped the scholar with sharper swords for rebuking, disputing, and promoting further schism.

By studiously eliminating all sectarian dogmas and all teaching about religion on which denominations disagreed, Jefferson honestly did not think he had eliminated religion from his curriculum. But until "every young man now living" did in fact become a Unitarian, along with his family and their descendants, he had virtually done just that.

NO SECTARIAN INSTRUCTION; NO SECTARIAN CONTROL

On these points, Jefferson was both clearer and more consistent. In the 1770s, he tried to free the College of William and Mary from its Anglican control. In the 1780s, he expressed his dismay over the "religious frenzy" that erupted in the recently founded Presbyterian Hampden-Sydney College. In the 1790s, he supported the idea of a denominationally free national university proposed by both Washington and Adams; in his own administration, Jefferson too recommended that an eminent federal institution of learning be established. All colonial colleges had religious sponsorship, and new church colleges sprang up in abundance in the 1780s and 1790s — Episcopal, Congregational, Presbyterian, Methodist, and German Reformed. Jefferson, joined by his secretary of state, James Madison, believed the time had come, even if a constitutional amendment was required, to create a potentially great university forever free of sectarian control.

Madison continued the campaign for a national university as president, urging Congress in 1810 to consider the advantages of such a "seminary of learning." Rising above local prejudices and jealousies, a university of this sort would help create a national character and give greater impetus toward "social harmony." Above all, such a university "in the center of the nation . . . would contribute not less to strengthen the foundations than to adorn the structure of our free and happy system of government." A House committee, later reporting favorably on Madison's recommendation, spoke of the scientific and literary renown that would come to the nation, as this university presented "the interesting spectacle of a young nation, bending its whole strength to the pursuit of true greatness." Yet nothing came of this or later proposals (e.g., those of President John Quincy Adams), so Jefferson and Madison, after their respective presidencies, turned their attention toward the creation of such a university at the state rather than the federal level.

In 1816 Jefferson even involved himself, though at some distance, in the famous Dartmouth Case, an attempt to change the college from a private Congregational institution to a public, nonsectarian one. No one disputed the fact that Dartmouth College had been founded in 1769 as a sectarian school with a private board of trustees and with a charter granted by the English crown. Now, however, after the Revolution and under a new national government, and with the state of New Hampshire possessing no other institution of higher learning, should not some change be made in the charter so that Dartmouth might belong to all the citizens of the state and not just the members of a single sect? Jefferson felt strongly that the answer should be yes. Many others, including ultimately the U.S. Supreme Court, thought otherwise.

New Hampshire's governor, William Plumer, was — amazingly enough — a Jeffersonian Republican, not a Federalist. Wholly sympathetic to Jefferson's position, Plumer even persuaded the state legislature to assert its control over the school. In 1816, Jefferson voiced his strong support in a letter to the governor, arguing against the idea that "institutions established for the use of the nation cannot be touched or modified" in any way. "Our lawyers and priests," Jefferson added, "suppose that preceding generations held the earth more freely than we do" and that they "had a right to impose laws unalterable by ourselves." In short, they believe that "the earth belongs to the dead, and not to the living." Any sober reflection on that proposition would, Jefferson firmly believed, expose its intrinsic absurdity.

If the Jefferson-Plumer position was a strong one, it did not go unanswered. The oratorical wonder Daniel Webster, an 1801 alumnus of Dartmouth, appeared before the Supreme Court to plead his school's case. The charter gave to the original twelve trustees, he pointed out, sole right and authority over the college, and any "forcible intrusion of others violates those rights" and had no precedent in either English or American law. Then, according to an unofficial observer, Webster concluded his appeal with great emotion and power: "It is, Sir, as I have said, a small College. And yet there are those who love it." And when "I see my alma mater surrounded, like Caesar in the senate house," receiving wounding stab after stab, Webster could not bear to have his dear school turn to him and say, "Et tu quoque mi fili! And thou too, my son!"

Whether the logic or the emotion was the more persuasive, the Court agreed with Webster. John Marshall, who though a Virginian was a Federalist, overturned both the state legislature and the state's highest court to affirm the legitimacy of the contract originally made. What New Hampshire had attempted to do, said Marshall, was "repugnant to the Constitution of the United States." What Marshall did was repugnant to Jefferson, but this significant judicial decision of 1819 gave great encouragement to other church-related colleges, both existing and contemplated, assuring them that the state could not wrest from them their sectarian and contractual control.

It so happened that neither could Jefferson wrest the Anglican control away from the College of William and Mary. He proposed that the college move to a more central location in the state, probably Richmond, and that could be considered. But his desire to sever all ties with Anglicanism fell outside the realm of possibility. Madison, who shared his colleague's dismay with respect to Dartmouth, wrote that "the time surely cannot be distant when it must be seen by all that what is granted by the public authority for the public good, not for that of individuals, may be withdrawn and otherwise applied, when the public good so requires." When in Virginia that time seemed ever more "distant," Jefferson concluded that he must make educational plans that moved around, rather than through, his alma mater. By 1819, he feared that the College of William and Mary, being passed over in this fashion, would spread "sour grapes" against any scheme to create a truly public university elsewhere in the state. But the enlightened members of the Virginia establishment would not be misled, Jefferson told Madison. Besides, the weakness and the remoteness of his old school ("long kept in a state of languor and inefficiency," he informed Adams) made its objections increasingly irrelevant. In 1824, he even boldly proposed to discontinue his old college altogether, using its endowment to create ten intermediate institutions, something like community colleges, between the grammar schools and the newly approved university. Nothing, however, came of this idea.

Jefferson did not win every battle, but neither did he relax in his campaign against the encroachment of stifling dogma into the classroom. Sectarian instruction would first cramp the mind, then destroy it. He sent his daughters to a Roman Catholic nunnery in France, but only after being assured that "not a word is ever spoken to them on the subject of religion." "The atmosphere of our country," he wrote in 1822, "is unquestionably charged with a threatening cloud of fanaticism, lighter in some parts, denser in others, but too heavy in all." And while one might not be able to clean out that fanaticism from every corner of the land, the schools at least must be protected from it. Some sects, he noted, would have nothing at all to do with education unless they exercised complete control over it. Concerning the quality or worth of that education, Jefferson had little doubt.

In his *Age of Reason*, Thomas Paine included a brief chapter on the effects of Christianity on education. Those effects, as one might suspect, Paine portrayed in darkest hue. When science advanced to the point that some aspects of the Christian faith came into question (e.g., with Galileo), the ecclesiastical authorities responded, said Paine, by cutting "learning down to a size less dangerous to their project." Learning could safely concentrate on the dead languages, so energies were poured in that direction. If one wondered why the period between the ancient philosophers and the moderns like Descartes and Newton was "a vast sandy desert," Paine's answer was direct: "The Christian system laid all waste." Had Benjamin Franklin dared in the Middle Ages to draw lightning from the heavens, he probably would have been set afire in his own flames.

Jefferson, who never painted with quite so broad a brush as Paine, would nonetheless have agreed that a dogmatic education was a contradiction in terms, an oxymoron of momentous and calamitous proportion. The whole Western world was committed to progress; more critically, a new nation would die without it. Education must be the catalyst, not the halter or blinder or brake. Jefferson fervently believed that only by means of a universal secular system of education could the United States join the modern world and fully participate in the new age now at hand. Dogmatism and sectarianism must go, for Almighty God had made the mind free.

THE UNIVERSITY OF VIRGINIA

By the time he reached seventy years of age, Jefferson — despite his general optimism — occasionally grew glum, not only about an invigorated sectarianism but also about a younger generation's indifference to a life of the mind. "Our post-revolutionary youth," he wrote Adams in 1814, "are born under happier stars than you and I were. They acquire all learning in their mothers' womb, and bring it into the world ready-made." The notion that education must be worked at, laboriously earned, agonizingly sweated over may have vanished from the face of the earth. "The information of books is no longer necessary," he added, and all knowledge not innate

169

was held in contempt, "or neglect at least." But, with an almost audible sigh, Jefferson supposed that this fad too would pass and genuine learning someday return to favor.

The problem was aggravated, Jefferson noted, by the growth in every neighborhood of "petty academies" that gave their pupils just enough taste of learning to inoculate them against the real thing. Such schools hired a couple of men who knew a little Latin and perhaps some Greek, could display a globe of the earth, possessed "the first six books of Euclid, [and] imagine and communicate this as the sum of science." Optimism quavered. Perhaps before too long, Jefferson allowed himself to hope, we will at length see the necessity "of establishing institutions, here as in Europe, where every branch of science, useful at this day, may be taught in its highest degrees." Not for the first time did it cross Jefferson's mind to create just such an institution, not in Washington, certainly not in New Hampshire, and sadly not in Williamsburg, but close to his own "little mountain" in Virginia. And it would not be a petty academy.

As early as 1800, well before the presidential election of that year, Jefferson wrote to his confidant in both science and religion, Joseph Priestley, to lay out the plan, just beginning to form in his mind, of creating a university that was "broad & liberal & *modern*." Instead of sending Virginians to Northern schools, where they might be infected by Federalism and who knows what sectarian persuasions, Jefferson would erect a school of such distinction as "to be a temptation to the youth of other states to come, and drink of the cup of knowledge & fraternize with us." Jefferson proposed a heavy emphasis on science, but called on Priestley for advice on how the field should be divided and how much could be expected of a single professor. Priestley responded "concisely" and helpfully, fortunately giving Jefferson the benefit of his counsel before his death in 1804 and long before the plans for a university began to take concrete form.

Another Jeffersonian friend, Benjamin Rush, anticipated

even the 1800 letter to Priestley. For in 1788 and again in 1798, Rush set down his hopes for and plans of a national university. These provided no useful model for Jefferson, however, since the more conservative Rush resolved to make religion — indeed, the Christian religion — central to the curriculum. He justified his doing so by the congruence, as he perceived it, between Christianity on the one hand and Republicanism on the other. "The history of the creation of man, and of the relation of our species to each other by birth," Rush wrote in 1798, "which is recorded in the Old Testament, is the best refutation that can be given to the divine right of kings, and the strongest argument that can be used in favor of the original and natural equality of all mankind." In fact, said Rush, he would sooner include Confucianism and Islam in the curriculum of his proposed university than see students "grow up wholly devoid of a system of religious principles." Rush did not intend to argue for the truth of Christian revelation; "my only business is to declare that all its precepts and doctrines are calculated to promote the happiness of society, and the safety and well being of civil government." Jefferson and Rush held common views concerning religious liberty, but not on the proper place of religion in the university.

After Jefferson wrote to Priestley in 1800, two terms as president of the United States delayed further germination of the university idea until 1814. At that point, Jefferson accepted an appointment to a secondary school board in Charlottesville — Albemarle Academy, presided over by his nephew Peter Carr. The school had no students and not much vision of just what its future development should be. Never lacking in vision, the uncle set about immediately to transform the academy into a college, then into a university, and to indicate in striking detail the nature and scope of its curriculum. In 1816, the Virginia legislature did change Albemarle Academy into Central College — still without students — and authorized it to begin raising money from lotteries and subscriptions. Jefferson no doubt took satisfaction in the fact that some monies would come from the sale of glebe lands, formerly the property of the Anglican church of Albemarle County. The governor appointed a Board of Visitors for the college, that action giving the institution (if and when students did show up) more than merely local significance.

The quality of the Board of Visitors likewise gave greater visibility and potential to whatever might emerge, for it included two former presidents, Jefferson and Madison, along with another Virginian who had since become president — James Monroe. When these three distinguished Americans gathered in Charlottesville for a meeting of the board in May 1817, a curious public might have concluded that momentous happenings were afoot. From such a triumvirate as this, John Adams wrote that same month, "the world will expect something very great and very new." But perhaps it should not be too new, Adams tactfully suggested, for "prejudices are too deeply rooted to suffer it to last long." He then sensibly cautioned that Jefferson's grand scheme "will not always have three such colossal reputations to support it."

Jefferson needed those reputations and much more as he tried to keep the political wheels moving, the political jealousies and competitions at bay. Not even the location in Charlottesville had been fixed for certain, as Staunton, Lexington, and Williamsburg all argued for consideration. In August of 1818 an enlarged commission, consisting of twenty-four members representing all the senatorial districts, met in the Blue Ridge Mountains at Rockfish Gap. Recognizing the significance of this meeting, Jefferson labored strenuously to have everything in order, both educationally and geographically. On the latter point, Jefferson, making use of the latest census data, recorded the population of every county, then prepared a map showing Charlottesville to be the precise geographical and population center of the state. Further adding to his cause, Central College had earlier voted that if Charlottesville were the selected site, its property and funds would be turned over to the proposed university. When the vote was tallied, Charlottesville had sixteen affirmatives, Lexington three, Staunton two, and Williamsburg none.

Regarding Jefferson's careful educational plans, the commission's vote was unanimously in favor. The group agreed with the author of the Rockfish Gap Report "that the advantages of well directed education, moral, political & economical, are truly above all estimate." Jefferson took the opportunity to ring the changes on some of his favorite themes: education promoted the love of virtue, the mind of man was capable of great improvement, the sciences and the arts had made enormous strides in the previous fifty years and would make similar strides in the fifty years ahead. The widespread notion that "the condition of man cannot be ameliorated" and that "we must tread with awful reverence in the footsteps of our fathers . . . is the genuine fruit of the alliance between Church and State." If he rarely passed up an opportunity to beat up on Plato, neither did he allow many occasions to slip by without underlining the vices of church-state alliances or the virtues of church-state separation.

Jefferson then outlined his thoughts regarding the first professorial appointments to be made, but observed, "We have proposed no professor of Divinity." The essentials of religion — that is, the proofs for the existence of God as "supreme ruler of the universe [and] the author of all the relations of morality" — could be handled by the professor of ethics. The ancient languages could be taught, since they presented no controversy. Beyond that, "We have thought it proper," Jefferson affirmed, "to leave every sect to provide, as they think fittest, the means of further instruction in their own peculiar tenets."

The legislature published Jefferson's report along with its unanimous approval, a suitable preamble to the legislature's own approval in January 1819 of a real university for the state of Virginia. At the same time, the first board meeting following legislative approval appointed Jefferson as rector of the university. These hurdles behind him, Jefferson jumped into action — at age seventy-five — with all the vigor of a young man.

Adrenalin pumping, he wrote to Madison the next month about what was "immediately necessary," what had to be done right after that, and what admitted no delay.

Indeed, the letters flowed at a furious pace back and forth between Monticello and Montpelier, and when the letters did not get written or delivered fast enough, Jefferson sometimes rode his horse to Madison's home, about thirty miles away, and on other occasions James and Dolley Madison journeyed to Monticello. The correspondence between the two ex-presidents revealed a total trust between them — Jefferson, the master stylist, even inviting his younger colleague to change his drafts both in substance and style. In that more innocent age, they dared to sign their letters to each other "Affectionately yours." The affection was real, the cooperation close, and the mutual respect — formed in the 1770s — undiminished. In the flurry of letters concerning the university, Jefferson and Madison covered every topic conceivable, from the number of bricks to be purchased to the qualities of the professors to be appointed.

By July 1819, Jefferson's impatience to get everything moving, and moving now, spilled out. "Our works have gone on miserably slow," he reported in some dejection. "Not a brick is yet laid." To prepare students for entry into the university, Jefferson persuaded a graduate of Trinity College in Dublin and a highly recommended teacher of Latin and Greek to establish a preparatory school in Charlottesville. This good man also taught French, so Jefferson arranged for a boarding house where only French would be spoken to open its doors to eager applicants. All this frenzy of activity took its toll on Jefferson's health; he reluctantly reported to Madison early in 1820 that illness kept him "low, weak, able to walk little, and venturing to ride little." Even before that confession reached him, Madison had written his friend, "I must intreat that your health may be more a primary object than you have hitherto allowed it to be."

But if Jefferson could neither ride nor walk well, he could

still worry. The Panic of 1819 could not have come at a worse time for those seeking to get an ambitious educational undertaking on its way. Jefferson had to wheedle the legislature for loans — loans unlikely to be paid back. Annual grants from the legislature, designed to last all year, would be exhausted by February. Private subscriptions dried up, and penny-pinchers seized on Jefferson's grand Rotunda (in his Palladian plan for an "academical village") as an unwarranted and intolerable extravagance. One legislator, regarded as a friend to the university, vowed that he would "never vote another dollar to the university but on condition that it should not be applied to that building." Even though Jefferson's son-in-law, Thomas Mann Randolph, served as governor from 1819 to 1822, Jefferson felt besieged.

As some objected to his architecture, others objected — yet again — to his religion, or to his religious views as they seemed destined to be reflected in the appointments to the university. Certainly, if the first professorial choice was indicative of what would follow, one can detect the grounds for objection. Central College authorities had in 1817 appointed Thomas Cooper as professor of chemistry and law, but the college as a private institution had more latitude than might be true of a state university. When, in taking over the assets of Central, the university Board of Visitors reaffirmed Cooper's selection, much hell could and did break loose.

A close associate of Priestley's in England, Cooper joined his friend in emigrating to America in 1794. He practiced law and medicine in Pennsylvania and emerged as an ardent supporter of Jefferson during the campaign of 1800. After a term as a state judge, he turned to teaching: chemistry at Carlisle (now Dickinson) College and applied chemistry along with mineralogy at the University of Pennsylvania. Well qualified as an academic, he won this praise from Jefferson in 1810: "There is not a stronger head in the U.S. than his." But Cooper was a Unitarian — outspoken, opinionated, unyielding, and since 1789 abundantly on record concerning his religious views. (In fact, when Priestley had earlier nominated Cooper for membership in the Royal Society, he was turned down as being too radical.) Cooper quickly became a symbol of what was wrong with Jefferson's religion, and what, unless nipped in the bud, would be wrong with the infant University of Virginia.

Virginia's Presbyterians took the lead in condemning the Cooper appointment and in warning that they, along with all other orthodox Christians, would apparently be excluded from any participation or voice in the affairs of the university. For example, one Presbyterian clergyman who had been a supporter of the school read Cooper's *Memoirs of Dr. Joseph Priestley*, published in 1806, and on that basis pronounced Cooper to be "rash, dogmatic, and preemptory." Some might call Cooper a liberal, but, if so, "all his liberality is reserved for his own party." Other friends of the university thought the whole enterprise too delicately balanced to risk its crashing against sectarian shoals because of this first professorial choice. In any contest of voting strength in Virginia, the Unitarians could never hope to match the considerable strength of the orthodox opposition.

Jefferson, however, was both offended and infuriated over this early breach of academic freedom — and of his freedom as well. His anticlericalism, never far from the surface, erupted again, this time focused on the Presbyterians. He believed that they were after more than just a voice in the new institution: they wanted control. In an angry and intemperate letter to Cooper in 1820, Jefferson lashed out. The Presbyterian clergy, not the laity, he wrote, "are violent, ambitious of power, and intolerant in politics as in religion." They wished nothing more than to plant the spirit and sword of John Knox in this tender Republic. Because the Presbyterian clergy had a bit more learning than the Baptists and Methodists, they opposed the university, "lest it should qualify their antagonists of other sects to meet them in equal combat." And to his former private secretary, William Short, he wrote the next month with a temper that had not cooled. "The Presbyterian clergy are the loudest, the most intolerant of all sects, the most tyrannical and ambitious, ready at the word of the lawgiver, if such a word could be now obtained, to put the torch to the pile, and to rekindle in this virgin hemisphere, the flames in which their oracle Calvin consumed the poor Servetus."

Obviously, Jefferson was prepared to fight. It soon became equally obvious, however, that if he won this battle he would likely lose the more significant war. Joseph C. Cabell, his strongest ally in the state legislature, called on Jefferson, famous for his allegiance to Reason, to apply here some calm and quiet reflection. The Presbyterians, said Cabell, made up "a large and respectable part" of the state's tax-paying public. They desired to "participate in, not to monopolize" the affairs of the university; and, surely, "it was both natural and proper that they should enquire and judge of the characters and sentiments of those who were to be the future instructors of their sons."

On 6 March 1819, Madison gently added his caution: "I begin to be uneasy on the subject of Cooper." So did many others on the Board of Visitors, who concluded that as public opinion turned against Cooper, it would surely tend also to turn against the university. The board first postponed the effective date of Cooper's appointment from 1820 to 1821. Then Jefferson gave Cooper an opportunity to resign, assuring him of $1,500 for the breach of contract. And then, most happily, Cooper received an appointment at the University of South Carolina; he did resign the Virginia assignment in 1820, and a much-relieved board quickly accepted the resignation. Jefferson was not much mollified. Writing to Cooper in November 1822, he made it clear that he had neither forgiven nor forgotten the Presbyterians who "aim, like the Jesuits, at engrossing the education of the country, [and] are hostile to every institution which they do not direct." A decade later, Cooper faced his own difficulties with Presbyterians and with national Unionists in South Carolina.

In this same letter to Cooper, Jefferson indicated some constructive steps that might soften sectarian suspicions. After reminding Cooper that it was not anticipated that the university would have a professorship in divinity, he wrote that some had made a "handle" of this to spread the word that "this is an institution not merely of no religion, but against all religion." And that story, somehow, had to be squelched. So the Board of Visitors proposed an ingenious scheme to encourage "the different religious sects to establish, each for itself, a professorship of their own tenets, on the confines of the university." On the confines: sectarian religion would not be built into the central structure of the university but kept at some remove from that curriculum supported by the taxpayers as a whole.

Students studying with their own denominational teachers would, however, be free to attend university lectures, to use the general library, and to receive "every other accommodation we can give them; preserving, however, their independence of us and of each other." This, said Jefferson, should help fill the vacuum so widely complained about; moreover, by mixing all the students together, "we shall soften their asperities, liberalize and neutralize their prejudices." Jefferson even permitted himself to hope that in this indirect and subtle fashion, the University of Virginia could make the pervading religion of the campus "a religion of peace, reason, and morality." Could it possibly be that the "essentials" of religious instruction might survive after all?

The Cooper fiasco behind him, Jefferson turned to the recruitment of other faculty with the same gusto with which he had laid out the details of his "academical village" and selected titles for its library. With respect to faculty, Jefferson aimed high: George Ticknor of Harvard for modern languages, Nathaniel Bowditch of *Practical Navigator* fame for mathematics, Frances Walker Gilmer of Virginia for law and government. But these heavens exceeded his grasp. He then turned to Europe for "the best minds" there, but those approached at

Oxford and Cambridge initially declined. From Edinburgh, he sought the help of Dugald Stewart, the eminent Scottish philosopher whom Jefferson had met in Paris, for counsel and assistance. Slowly, painfully, the empty faculty ranks begin to fill, mostly with younger men, in their twenties, and therefore not with established reputations. But Madison thought their youth an advantage: "they will be less inflexible in their habits" and would be able to give many years of service to the university. George Tucker, a close friend of Madison and a Virginia lawyer, assumed the professorship of moral philosophy, a post that Jefferson was determined not to let a clergyman fill.

Many other details occupied the aging and increasingly arthritic Jefferson. Writing with "crippled wrists" to Adams in October of 1823, Jefferson indicated that the excitement of founding the university counteracted to a considerable extent the weariness and burdens of old age. "I am fortunately mounted on a hobby," he wrote, "which indeed I should have better managed some 30 or 40 years ago, but whose easy amble is still sufficient to give exercise and amusement to an octogen[arian] rider." Though the amble was far from easy, Jefferson would not be diverted. In 1824, he even had the pleasure of showing Daniel Webster around the nearly completed buildings, and in that same year he spent at least four hours a day for months drawing up "a catalogue of books for our library." When it came to divinity, however, he asked Madison for help, "knowing that in your early days you bestowed attention on this subject." Madison replied that he would "endeavor to make out a list of Theological Works, but am less qualified for the task than you seem to think."

No detail escaped Jefferson's attention. The gifts for organization, tabulation, measurement, and precision evident in the *Notes on the State of Virginia* were repeatedly pressed into service in every stage of planning and execution. Also, without the gift for breadth of vision and depth of commitment, nothing at all would have happened. Finally, in March of 1825, one month before Jefferson's eighty-second birthday, the university opened its doors to about thirty students. Some, delayed by heavy spring rains, trickled in during the next weeks. By May, seventy-nine had arrived. Jefferson still scrambled to get the last professor in place: someone for government and law. With respect to this position, Jefferson commented to Madison in 1825 that "there is one branch in which I think we are the best judges." Here a kind of political orthodoxy would be imposed — namely, a Jeffersonian-Madisonian brand of politics. No Federalist need apply. John Tayloe Lomax, jurist of Fredericksburg, Virginia, accepted the appointment in April of 1826.

To a degree, Jefferson also sought a kind of religious orthodoxy — that is to say, heterodoxy. He, of course, would not have seen it in those terms: he only wanted persons whose religious views were rational, moral, undogmatic, and sternly nonsectarian. Whether from at home or abroad, he was determined to choose only those who clearly would never cramp what he called "the illimitable freedom of the human mind." To be sure, what sounded like freedom to Jefferson could sound very much like Unitarianism to others.

Few statesmen in American history have committed themselves so unreservedly, so unceasingly, to the entire educational enterprise. That enterprise had a breadth that extended from the primary grades through the professional schools, and it had a depth that called for common moral pursuits grounded in an understanding of and commitment to the Author of that morality and of all creation besides. As Robert Browning wrote, "Ah, but a man's reach should exceed his grasp,/Or what's a heaven for?"

7 The Eternal Vigil

"For I have sworn on the altar of God eternal
hostility against every form of tyranny over the
mind of man." (1800)

George Washington was given his National Monument in 1884, Abraham Lincoln his by 1922. The cornerstone for Jefferson's, laid by President Franklin Delano Roosevelt on 15 November 1939, contained a copy of the Declaration of Independence along with Jefferson's "Life and Morals of Jesus." (The Virginia Statute for Establishing Religious Freedom would be inscribed on the interior of the northwest wall.) Then on 13 April 1943, the two hundredth anniversary of Jefferson's birth, President Roosevelt dedicated the striking marble rotunda, designed by John Russell Pope, in his honor. "Today, in the midst of a great war for freedom," Roosevelt said, "we dedicate a shrine to freedom. To Thomas Jefferson, Apostle of Freedom, we are paying a debt long overdue." In this celebration of Jefferson's birth, Roosevelt concluded his address by quoting the words inscribed around the inside of the Memorial's dome: "For I have sworn on the altar of God eternal hostility against every form of tyranny over the mind of man."

Wrenched from any immediate context, these famous words serve as a stirring manifesto condemning any and all tyranny: England's in 1776 and again in 1812, Germany's in 1914 and again in 1939, Japan's in 1941, or whatever unwarranted military aggression might follow. But Jefferson had not written against military tyranny, nor even against political tyranny; in his letter of 23 September 1800 to Benjamin Rush, he passionately protested against religious tyranny. For, according to Jefferson, this tyranny provided the foundation for all other despotism by destroying that most precious of all human liberties: the freedom of the human mind. Given convictions this deep and passions this strong, one cannot wonder that in the realm of religious liberty Jefferson never relaxed, never let down his guard. Vigilance here must be eternal.

JEFFERSON AND RUSH — AGAIN

That Jefferson would convey such defiant sentiments to Rush was no accident, nor was the year of this conveyance, 1800, in any degree accidental. By the time this letter was dispatched, Rush had been a fellow patriot and close friend for a quarter-century. Indeed, in the later years of his life, Rush signed more than one letter, "Your sincere old friend of 1775." He did so not only as a warm reminder of their long friendship but also as a kind of reassurance to himself that his life had really amounted to something. He continually regarded the years "1774, 1775, and 1776" as the emotional climax of his entire life. Despite almost another half-century of significant professional service as a medical doctor, a period that included service as the country's first surgeon general, a heroic if misguided effort to treat yellow fever, a solicitous concern for and advice to a President Jefferson on his own health, and an original investigation into mental disorders, for Rush nothing ever measured up to those intoxicating days in his thirties when patriotism made each moment count for so much.

As Rush grew older, his religious views turned increasingly conservative, though he never wholly abandoned his mother's Presbyterianism, or that of such close evangelical friends of his youth as Gilbert Tennent, Samuel Davies, and Samuel Finley, his maternal uncle. While he participated in the intellectual ferment of the Enlightenment, he searched steadily for common ground between those fresh ideas and the more traditional tenets of evangelicalism. In the strictly theological arena, therefore, he found himself often resisting some of Jefferson's heterodoxies. On the other hand, he saw in Universalism, which taught the ultimate salvation of all, the religious equivalent of an American Revolution that stood for the political equality of all. Republicanism and Universalism would together enfranchise and redeem all humankind. In the Christian tradition, all men were condemned by Adam's sin. Was it not just as reasonable to believe that all men would be saved by Christ's love? For Rush, if not for Jefferson, theology could be thoroughly republican, but still unmistakably evangelical. And so Rush instructed his medical students in the palpable merits of a Christianity still presided over by a divine savior.

But on that great question of liberty, be it political or religious, Thomas Jefferson and his "sincere old friend of 1775" continued to march to the same drummer. Writing to Jefferson in 1796, Rush also revealed his sympathies with the former's wariness of Alexander Hamilton. "We have been much struck of late," he pointed out, by the remarks of "a late officer of state" regarding all that the United States owed to Great Britain for "their happiness." Well, thought Rush, for those of such short memories, let consideration be given to "all" that we owe this former enemy. That country's political institutions include "a cruel and absurd system of penal laws" along with "a cruel and absurd code of laws with respect to debtors" — all of this topped off with "oppressive religious establishments" and a failure to abolish primogeniture and other features of a landed aristocracy. Hamilton notwithstanding, perhaps England did not serve as the exemplary model of liberty — political or religious.

The next year saw Rush writing to offer his congratulations on Jefferson's election to the vice presidency, even more congratulations that he escaped being named president. "In the present situation of our country," Rush declared, "it would have been impossible for you to have preserved the credit of republican principles or your own character for integrity" as long as Alexander Hamilton continued to call the signals from New York. Rush also lamented the passing of the astronomer David Rittenhouse, who had served as president of the American Philosophical Society from 1791 to 1796. Rush indicated that Jefferson would be named as Rittenhouse's successor, and "we shall expect you to preside at our winter meetings." Jefferson not only agreed to assume the leadership of this, America's first learned society, but he continued to hold that post until 1815.

If it made sense for Jefferson to express his strong views on religious tyranny to Rush, it also made sense that he did so in 1800, for this year marked Jefferson's clamorous campaign and narrow victory. If one wished to learn of religious tyranny, what more was required than to read the furious Federalist press and listen to the strident sermons cascading down from Federalist pulpits? Jefferson escaped this tyranny only because it was not absolute. A month before his now-carved-in-stone reply to Rush, the latter had written a chatty letter that, among other matters, urged that Virginia be as diligent as Philadelphia had been in ridding itself of all the royal place names. Most of your counties, Rush noted, still "bear the names or titles of several successive British families." The Philadelphia patriot thought that this simply would not do, and a presidential candidate should have some influence in the matter. Such obsolete English titles represented "the disgraceful remains of your former degraded state as men"; therefore, the names of republican worthies should forthwith replace royal unworthies.

When Jefferson replied a month later, however, he had more than nomenclature on his mind, though he thought that names given in honor of those who had rendered a distinct service to the colony might be retained. "Perhaps, too, a name when given should be deemed a sacred property." Jefferson then congratulated Rush on the fact that Philadelphia had, for the time being at least, escaped the scourge of yellow fever. This plague, which erupted chiefly in the cities, could have the beneficial effect of discouraging urban sprawl, for "I view great cities as pestilential to the morals, the health, and the liberties of man." But then, once more, to religion.

Jefferson recalled that he had promised Rush sometime earlier "a letter on Christianity," but he still needed more time for reflection. He hoped to arrive at some solution that would "displease neither the rational Christian or Deist." But one thing remained certain: whatever he came up with would never satisfy the Federalist clergy of New England, that "genus irritabile vatum" — that irritable tribe of priests. If a people could be provoked into passing the undemocratic Alien and Sedition Acts, perhaps all of the First Amendment was in jeopardy — even the freedom of religion. Not, however, while Jefferson had breath or life. Every sect, he told Rush, thinks its own church the true one, and worthy of special privilege in the nation — "especially the Episcopalians and the Congregationalists." They lust after becoming the national church; also, "they believe that any portion of power confided to me will be exerted in opposition to their schemes." Then Jefferson added this short sentence of great force: "And they believe truly." So he carefully set the stage for the pronouncement that heads this chapter, that appealed to Franklin Roosevelt, and that millions of visitors to the Memorial wonderingly read.

Congregationalists and Episcopalians had nothing more to fear from him, Jefferson said, for he would never interfere with their own doctrines or their own liberties. He would simply prevent their assumption of power over others. Yet that, he wryly observed, was quite sufficient to justify their im-

185

placable opposition to his candidacy. "But enough of this," Jefferson apologized to his steadfast friend. "It is more than I have before committed to paper on the subject of all the lies which have been preached or printed against me." When Rush replied in October, with the election still in doubt, he hoped that the nation might see in the next few weeks "a few lucid intervals" that could atone for the frustrations and follies of many years.

Less than three weeks after his inauguration as president on 4 March 1801, Jefferson again demonstrated his watchful resolve. Writing to a former governor and chief justice in Vermont, Moses Robinson, Jefferson recognized that not all citizens would rally to his leadership, despite the irenic tone of his First Inaugural. New England, because it continued to be dominated by the clergy, "will be the last to come over," for that irritable tribe "had got a smell of union between church and state." Once charmed by that seductive scent, they sniffed here and there for any hint of a possible union even more powerful than that found in New England. This may sound fanciful, Jefferson conceded, but these clergy "indulge reveries which can never be realized in the present state of science." At length, even they "will find their interest in acquiescing in the liberty and science of their country."

When Jefferson wrote to Rush two years later (21 April 1803), he intended chiefly to send along that more detailed statement of his religious views already discussed in Chapter 5. But even here, his concern for religious liberty asserted itself once more. "It behooves every man who values liberty of conscience for himself," he reminded Rush, "to resist invasions of it in the case of others." If one acted as though outsiders had a perfect right to invade the private sanctuary of conscience, then sooner or later such intruders would conclude that, in fact, they did possess such a right. The laws of this country, Jefferson asserted with some pride, have left all matters of religious opinion between the citizen and his God, not between citizens and other citizens, and surely not between citizens and sheriffs or magistrates or even presidents. So, said the ever-wary president, please keep the contents of this letter and of my Syllabus between just the two of us, between trusted and trusting friends.

At the same time that he communicated with Rush, Jefferson informed Edward Dowse, a Massachusetts friend since 1789, that he, too, must protect the president's privacy with respect to his religious reflections. "I never will, by any word or act," Jefferson warned, "bow to the shrine of intolerance, or admit a right of enquiry into the religious opinions of others." All liberty-loving Americans were bound "to make common cause, even with error itself, to maintain the common right of freedom of conscience." "Conscience" was a word that Madison had tried to get into the First Amendment, but failed. That word remained, however, much in the mind and heart of both Jefferson and Madison, as it had been much earlier on the minds of both Roger Williams and John Locke. The rights of conscience, as Daniel Carroll of Maryland said during the First Amendment debates, "are, in their nature, of peculiar delicacy, and will little bear the gentlest touch of governmental hand."

Having watched Jefferson suffer from reckless political charges and having had unhappy experiences himself with George Washington as the commander of the Continental Army, Rush was dismayed to find his own son Richard interested in pursuing a career in public service. He thought such a life hard and the fickle public ungrateful. "The time, I fear, is past in our country," a disillusioned Rush told Jefferson in 1804, "in which happiness or even usefulness is to be expected from public stations." And then Rush returned, as in his thoughts he so often did, to those far happier days of yore. "How different were our feelings in the years 1774, 1775, and 1776, and how much did the words *country* and *liberty* import in those memorable years!" Jefferson's congenital optimism did not permit him to share his friend's gloom, and, in fact, Richard Rush went on to a distinguished diplomatic career in both England and France; he even helped secure the Smithson bequest that resulted in the now-famous museum in Washington, D.C.

If Jefferson did not slip into melancholy concerning the future of his country or its public servants, neither did he allow himself to bathe in a soft sentimentalism regarding human nature. He may have rejected the doctrine of Original Sin, but he never doubted that depravity could be found in abundance on all sides. In June of 1806, he learned of the death of his honored friend George Wythe by poison, presumably by the hand of Wythe's grandnephew. Later that year he received reliable word of the conspiracies of his former vice president, the mercurial Aaron Burr, against the United States. During the next year, England embarked on a campaign of impressment of American seamen and defied the Jefferson administration to do anything about it. When the president responded with an Embargo Act curtailing trade between Britain and America, New England responded in turn with attacks not on the British but on Jefferson! Yes, plenty of depravity to go around.

Early in May 1809, Rush wrote his beleaguered friend to congratulate him on his "*escape* from the high and dangerous appointment which your country . . . *inflicted* upon you during the last eight years of your life." Rush anticipated with joy, as no doubt Jefferson also did, the return of the ex-president to Monticello, there to renew his acquaintance with his "philosophical instruments" and with his treasured library, where, said Rush (citing Voltaire), everything was subject to the humors of the reader, unlike public service, "in which we are subject to every man's humor." In retirement, Rush added, the two friends could dismiss politics and similar "little subjects" in order to concentrate "only upon those topics of science and literature which are calculated to increase the agricultural, domestic, and moral happiness of our fellow citizens."

Unfortunately, Rush did not have that many years left to correspond with Jefferson on those larger issues. He did, however, as previously noted, have enough time to bring John Adams and Jefferson together in a remarkable renewal of friendship. Posterity, Rush asserted confidently, "will revere the friendship of two ex-Presidents that were were once opposed to each other," and even human nature itself would be the better for it. In his last letter to Jefferson, written 15 March 1813, Rush wrote, "The few sands that remain in my glass urge me constantly to quicken my labors." In less than five weeks he was dead, but by that time the two presidents had rediscovered each other and had begun the skillful probe of each other's well-furnished minds.

JEFFERSON AND ADAMS — AGAIN

In June of the year that Rush died, Jefferson informed Adams of what he had learned at least as early as 1800, perhaps earlier, on the publication of his *Notes on the State of Virginia* in 1787 — namely, that to be a friend of liberty was to be the foe of established institutions, political or religious. Anyone who fought for religious liberty as hard as he had done in Virginia risked being seen as the enemy of all religion. The scheming clergy, Jefferson wrote, "wish it to be believed that he can have no religion who advocates its freedom." Both Jefferson and Adams knew better, of course, but at times they thought they stood alone. Adams responded (25 June 1813) by warning Jefferson — who hardly needed an alert — that affairs in Massachusetts had not improved. "I wish you could live a year in Boston," he wrote, listening to the preachers and reading their publications. "You would see how spiritual tyranny and ecclesiastical domination are beginning in our country: at least struggling for birth." For one who had sworn against such on the altar of God, Adams's words provided no balm to mind or spirit.

Nor did Adams himself find these sentiments calming. Indeed, they aroused him to a passionate condemnation of all alliances between religion and civil power. Adams had come a long way since 1774, when he assured Isaac Backus that the church establishment in Massachusetts was only "a slender thing." He trusted, he told Jefferson, neither the liberals nor the conservatives with power, neither the Calvinists nor the Quakers, neither the Methodists nor the Moravians, nor, for that matter, "Bolingbroke [or] Voltaire, Hume [or] Gibbon." The problem lay not in the specific religious or philosophical point of view but in its alliance with *power*.

> Checks and balances, Jefferson, however you and your Party may have ridiculed them, are our only security, for the progress of mind, as well as the security of body. Every species of these Christians would persecute Deists, as soon as either sect would persecute another, if it had unchecked and unbalanced power. Nay, the Deists would persecute Christians, and Atheists would persecute Deists, with as unrelenting cruelty, as any Christians would persecute them or one another. Know thyself, human nature!

After that explosive tirade, Adams offered a quieter reflection: "I am not sure that I am yet ready to return to politics."

Though Jefferson, in his relations with a recalcitrant Congress and an almost always resistant Supreme Court, had chafed over the political checks and balances, he could not agree more with the Braintree philosophe that religion must always and everywhere be checked: checked in Virginia, checked in Massachusetts, and checked in Spain, England, France, Ireland, Tunisia, Turkey, Chile, and Peru. It certainly needed to be checked wherever Jesuits roamed, the two correspondents agreed, for if there was anything that the Society of Jesus understood, it was not so much obedience as power.

So great a degree of power did the Jesuits exercise that although in the 1770s the order was abolished "forever," by 1814 they were back in business — to the evident dismay of Adams. "I do not like the late resurrection of the Jesuits," he wrote Jefferson on 6 May 1816. "Shall we not have swarms of them here?" And they appeared in so many guises and shapes: as "printers, editors, writers, schoolmasters, etc." All of the pervasive colonial anti-Catholicism now concentrated itself, in most vitriolic form, upon the Jesuits. "If ever any Congregation of men could merit eternal perdition on earth and in hell," Adams intemperately wrote, "it is this Company of Loyola." Our system of religious liberty forces us to give "them an asylum," but we must be ever on guard. It sounded as though by 1816 Adams, too, was prepared to swear his eternal hostility against any religion that lusted after or latched on to *power*.

Within the next couple of years, however, Adams and Jefferson found a homegrown power base equally worrisome. Despite the Constitution and its First Amendment, despite state after state moving toward a fuller freedom in religion, Connecticut, New Hampshire, and Massachusetts continued to protect and support their respective Congregational establishments. True, Quakers were no longer hanged, nor witches burned, nor dissenters even exiled or tossed in jail. Nonetheless, Connecticut Congregationalism retained privilege and favor in the governing bodies at Hartford, in academic affairs at Yale, and whenever a civil religion was required to perform on militia grounds, on election days, or at state funerals. By 1817, however, Connecticut dissenters, notably the Baptists, Quakers, and Episcopalians, joined with others in a ballot-box challenge to the "standing order" of the state.

Some clever soul, "no doubt instigated by the Devil," Adams slyly told Jefferson, even thought to reprint *The Independent Whig,* a 1720-21 London publication by radical Whigs John Trenchard and Thomas Gordon that called upon Parliament to sever all ties between religion and the British government. These volumes, Adams said, "have produced a burst of indignation against priestcraft, bigotry, and intolerance, and in conjunction with other causes have produced the late election." So Adams offered his congratulations to Jefferson for a victory — even in Connecticut — of his Republican party. While Adams's own Federalists went down in defeat, he in this case saw not defeat but victory for the separation of a single denomination from the control of statewide power.

On 5 May 1817, Jefferson returned the good wishes. "I join you," he wrote, "in sincere congratulations that this den of priesthood is at length broken up and that a Protestant popedom is no longer to disgrace the American history and character." The following year, in a close election (13,908 to 12,364), the final ties of church establishment in Connecticut collapsed. The Federalists had fought tirelessly to fend off, as they saw it, the calamity to religion and morals that would inevitably follow. None fought more vigorously than Congregational clergyman Lyman Beecher, who, as he later wrote, "worked as hard as mortal man could" to stem the Republican tide. He organized, lobbied, and "preached for revivals with all my might . . . till at last, what with domestic afflictions and all, my health and spirits began to fail. It was as dark a day as ever I saw." But, ultimately, light drove away the darkness. In what stands as a distilled capsule of America's religious history, Beecher confessed that this defeat of establishment turned out to be *the best thing that ever happened to the State of Connecticut.*" After those emphatic italics, Beecher explained: "It cut the churches loose from dependence on state support. It threw them wholly on their own resources and on God." While not normally in the business of counting conversions, Jefferson would happily chalk up this one.

In New Hampshire, Governor William Plumer, sounding very much like the Jeffersonian that he was, declared in an 1816 message to the legislature that "the rights of conscience and of private judgment in religious matters . . . are, in their nature, inalienable." No human tribunal had any right to step between God and the individual consciences of New Hampshire citizens. No citizen could "guard with too much jealousy against the encroachments of the civil power on his religious liberties." After the legislature ratified this gubernatorial position, New Hampshire's churches found themselves effectively on an even legal footing. Decades more would pass, however, before all vestiges of a Protestant establishment would finally disappear.

Massachusetts, as Jefferson sadly noted, did not in 1818

join in "the resurrection of Connecticut to light and liberality." When a constitutional convention gathered in 1820 to revise the state's charter drawn up forty years before, John Adams came out of his very private retirement, at age eighty-five, to try to do for his state what Thomas Jefferson had done for his: give religious freedom a solid legal footing. Among other things, Adams proposed that "attendance at public worship no longer . . . be compulsory." These and other provisions for a full liberty were submitted to the people and defeated by a not-very-close vote of nineteen thousand opposed and eleven thousand in favor. The prestige of the ex-president counted for little; he wrote to Jefferson that "my appearance at the late convention was too ludicrous to be talked of. . . . I boggled and blundered more than a young fellow just rising to speak at the bar." Adams returned to his retreat in Braintree, never to venture forth in any public way again.

The process of disestablishment in Massachusetts was complicated by the growing testiness between the orthodox Congregationalists on the one hand and the liberal Unitarians on the other. Both might attend the same church; both certainly resided in the same parish or town. In the early days of the Puritan Bay Colony, no meaningful distinction could be drawn between the parish on the one hand and the church's membership on the other, but that was not the case in the period after the Revolution. In a significant case that arose in Dedham and reached the Massachusetts Supreme Court in 1820 (*Baker v. Fales*), the church members — mainly Congregationalists — lost their exclusive right to call a minister. The court ruled that since the whole town was taxed to support the church, the whole town, orthodox and heterodox alike, had a legitimate voice in the affairs of the church. This so offended the Congregationalists that they withdrew from the original church, now being run by the town, to create their own orthodox ecclesiastical society.

But they thought to maintain the old property on the grounds that they, and they alone, had kept faith with the founders of a much earlier generation. The court said no. Those who withdrew ceased "to be members of that particular church, and the remaining members continue to be the identical church." And so throughout Massachusetts even today, one can find a sign boldly proclaiming the spired building on the village green to be the "First Congregational Church," with a smaller parenthetical identification underneath, "(Unitarian)." The orthodox who left, lost. The Unitarians who stayed behind won the land, the building, the parish funds, and no doubt some social prestige. This might not seem fair, but, as the court somewhat unkindly observed, a financial inconvenience for the orthodox "will never be felt, when a case of conscience is in question."

If Adams and Jefferson rejoiced in a Unitarian victory, they nevertheless would have preferred that Massachusetts and its courts get out of the religion business altogether and that disestablishment become complete. Neither lived to see that happen. In 1831, the state legislature voted for disestablishment; since this required an amendment to the Massachusetts constitution, the matter had to be submitted to the people for a vote. When in 1833 the vote came in, the citizens, by a proportion of almost ten to one, approved the amendment. In his inaugural address in 1836, Governor Edward Everett pointed out that the "wisdom of the ages" had taught "the mischief of an alliance of church and state." Religion, moreover, "is a concernment between the conscience of man and his creator, and exists in its greatest purity, when it rests upon the public sentiment of an enlightened community." Such eloquence would not have caused Jefferson to turn over in his grave, but it might have provoked him to sit up just long enough to welcome another convert into the fold.

JEFFERSON AND MADISON

No collaboration had more significance for America's history, or for religious liberty, than the one that kept this potent team

194

knit tightly together for half a century. Fellow Virginians, fellow Republicans, fellow libertarians, Madison and Jefferson shared each other's thoughts when they did not anticipate them. Their ample correspondence, extending from 1779 to 1826, and their friendship, going back to even three years before that, revealed a confident trust that only deepened over the years. They wrote to each other on virtually all subjects.

As Virginia farmers, they exchanged information on the weather, the rainfall, the snowfall, the wheat crop, the price of grain, the efficiency of types of plows. When the American consul in Lisbon presented each man with a pair of Merino sheep, they consulted one another on the care, feeding, and breeding of these valuable animals. In February of 1784 Jefferson expressed his wish that Madison had a thermometer; by April of the following year, Madison not only had one but could proudly report to Jefferson in the kind of detail that he knew his friend loved. "A pocket thermometer which stands on the second floor and the N.W. side of the House" registered 77 degrees at four o'clock in the afternoon of the 25th of April, 78 degrees the next day at precisely the same time, 81½ the next, and 82 "today." The weather during the period, Madison dutifully reported, "has been fair," with a southerly breeze blowing. He then relayed the latest intelligence on the price of wheat, corn, and tobacco, but he held out little hope for the cherries since on the night of the 20th "we had a severe black frost." Men of science and of Nature these were, with all advances in human understanding directly related to the freedom of religion, or freedom of the mind from all anti-intellectualism in the name of religion.

As Republicans, they wrote about the affairs of state while each was president, and long after. And as libertarians, they wrote about religion — but always and only about its liberty. Jefferson did not send his Syllabus to Madison for comment, nor did he discuss with him the puerilities of Plato or the ethical eminence of Jesus. In marked contrast to his letters to Rush and Adams, Jefferson's correspondence with Madison ignored theology altogether, as James Madison apparently preferred. Once the resident of Montpelier had finished with President John Witherspoon at the College of New Jersey (Princeton) and for only a brief period thereafter, he read little in theology and was even more cautious than Jefferson in offering any theological opinions whatsoever. When an Episcopal clergyman wrote to him in 1825 to solicit his views on "the being and attributes of God," Madison replied that he had not thought about those matters in any depth for fifty years. He therefore declined to respond directly to the query put to him. In brief, he had no interest in religious doctrines, except to ensure that they held no sway over the freedom of the human mind.

In 1773, at the tender age of twenty-two years, Madison thought that Pennsylvania had arrived at a far better understanding and practice of religious freedom than Virginia had yet managed. He wrote a college roommate in Philadelphia, William Bradford, to obtain more detail about how religious toleration — in existence for nearly one hundred years — actually worked. And in particular, he wanted to know whether "an ecclesiastical establishment [was] absolutely necessary to support civil society in a supreme government." That "liberal, catholic, and equitable way of thinking as to the rights of conscience" so characteristic of Pennsylvania, he told his friend in 1774, were "but little known among the zealous adherents of our hierarchy" in Virginia. Madison then wrote, in words that sounded as though they had been cribbed from the man he had not yet even met, that "religious bondage shackles and debilitates the mind, and unfits it for every noble enterprise, every expanded project."

Like Jefferson, Madison in 1776 worried that Virginia's new Declaration of Rights, written by George Mason, did not sufficiently ensure a complete religious liberty. Mason had written "that all men should enjoy the fullest toleration in the exercise of religion," but Madison thought the word "toleration" smacked too much of a noble concession. He favored this language: "All men are equally entitled to the free exercise of religion, according to the dictates of conscience." And even though the proposal came from a twenty-five-year-old upstart, the committee accepted it. They rejected, however, his more radical proposal summarily to cut off any assistance to the Anglican Church with the declaration that "no man or class of men ought, on account of religion, to be invested with peculiar emoluments or privileges." For a youngster, Madison learned fast. In the wide realm of religious liberty, he kept learning — and pushing — until he died.

In Chapter 3, we took note of Madison's crucial role in the defeat of Henry's General Assessment Bill and in the victory of Jefferson's Statute for Establishing Religious Freedom. Four years later, in 1789, Madison guided the First Amendment through its legislative shoals. By good fortune, Virginia became the eleventh state to ratify the Bill of Rights at the end of 1791, thereby adding those ten amendments to the Constitution. By even happier fortune, the secretary of state, none other than Thomas Jefferson, had the privilege of announcing that the amendments had been ratified. The preamble to the Constitution spoke of securing "the Blessings of Liberty to ourselves and our Posterity." Madison saw the Bill of Rights as a fitting epilogue, assuring all Americans "that their liberties will be perpetual."

In the election of 1800, Madison worked tirelessly for a Jeffersonian victory. Though his own district, Orange County, went for Jefferson by a vote of 340 to 7, the rest of the country voted in not nearly so lopsided a fashion. When Jefferson at last emerged the winner, he promptly offered the post of secretary of state to Madison, who just as promptly accepted. In this capacity, he advised his president on the complexities of the Louisiana Purchase, one of Jefferson's queries regarding that territory being "On what footing is the church and clergy, what lands have they, and from what other funds are they supported?" Madison offered assistance in drafting instructions to Captain Meriwether Lewis for the remarkable expedition to the Pacific Ocean, and, of course, he found himself deeply involved in the difficult negotiations with Britain over impressment and the embargo. In 1805, he even managed to negotiate successfully the release of a cargo of wine, seized by the British, and designated for the president, the secretary of state, and a senator from South Carolina.

In matters religious, Madison supported Jefferson in declining to call for fasts or feasts, since these "religious exercises" could "be neither controlled nor prescribed by us." With respect to the Kaskaskia Indians and the federal support to be given them, Madison urged the president not to go into details in his 1803 annual message to Congress, especially about the financial assistance being extended to a Roman Catholic priest. Such details, Madison observed, would be less noticed in an Indian treaty than in a presidential address. In general, however, the two friends thought so much alike on questions of religious liberty that no tugging this way or pulling that seemed necessary.

In 1809, Jefferson, having turned over the presidency to his neighbor, made his way back to Monticello. On 17 March 1809, he reported to the new president that he had endured a "very fatiguing journey" home. And once home, he found that "the spring is remarkably backward. No oats sown, not much tobacco seed, and little done in the gardens." But the Enlightenment farmer would soon set things right, even as, two weeks earlier, he had heard Madison setting things aright when in his First Inaugural he pledged "to avoid the slightest interference with the rights of conscience or the functions of religion, so wisely exempted from civil jurisdiction." That national wisdom, or the greatest portion of it, Jefferson and Madison could proudly claim as their own. For the inaugural occasion, Madison wore "a full suit of American manufacture, made of the wool of Merinos raised in this country." His apparel mattered little, however, for every eye turned toward Dolley Madison, who was "all dignity, grace, and affability."

In their mutual retirement, these two ex-presidents picked up the friendship that had, in fact, never been dropped. They returned to agricultural topics, not forgetting political ones, and expressed increasing concern over each other's health. Jefferson's preoccupation in these later years, as we have seen, was the University of Virginia. As late as 17 February 1826, Jefferson sent Madison a long letter in which he worried about books for the university's library that had begun to arrive from Paris, London, and Germany — "about 25 boxes" in all. Since the bookshelves were not yet ready, they could not even be opened for another two or three months. Meanwhile, he hoped to persuade Congress to forgive the $2,000 duty levied on them.

Jefferson concluded his letter with somber reflections on his and Madison's career in their common dedication to preserving the blessings of self-government, *"in all their purity,"* for future generations of Americans. "If ever the earth has beheld a system of administration conducted with a single and steadfast eye to the general interest and happiness of those committed to it," Jefferson wrote, "it is that to which our lives have been devoted." The warmest of friendships scarcely needed to call attention to itself, but this time Jefferson ventured to make it explicit. "To myself you have been a pillar of support through life. Take care of me when dead, and be assured that I shall leave with you my last affections."

Madison, who outlived Jefferson by ten years, did take care of him. He assumed the rectorship of the University of Virginia, as Jefferson had expressly wished. And he assumed the unofficial role of defender of religious liberty, as Jefferson would have also devoutly wished. In his "Detached Memoranda" written in retirement, Madison warned against the "silent accumulations & encroachments" by which ecclesiastical institutions acquired great wealth and, therefore, great power. Paying no taxes and facing no estate settlements, churches grew richer and richer. "Must not bodies, perpetual in their existence, and which may be always gaining without ever losing, speedily gain more than is useful, and in time more than is safe?" For Madison if not for others, the question was merely rhetorical.

Further, Madison thought congressional chaplains, paid for out of the public treasury, to be "a palpable violation of equal rights, as well as of Constitutional principles." True religion could only be a voluntary act, and these "legal ecclesiastics" engaged not in true religion but in "tiresome formality." Even military chaplains were a mistake, in Madison's view, mixing as they did political, military, and ecclesiastical authority. Though he recognized that popular opinion was against him, he found his unshakable bedrock in the Constitution. Moreover, was it not always "safer to trust the consequences of a right principle than reasonings in support of a bad one?" And was it not always wise to be on guard, like Jefferson, against every encouragement given to that persisting but pernicious notion "that civil government could not stand without the prop of a religious establishment?" Madison would take care of Jefferson, and of his country besides.

THOMAS JEFFERSON AND OTHER RELIGIOUS BODIES

While critical of institutional religion whenever it hungered after power or cramped the human mind, Jefferson at other times could speak in gentle tones and offer private support. He contributed not only to his Anglican parish in Virginia but to others in the neighborhood as well. He also recognized the role of Baptists, Methodists, and Presbyterians in assisting Madison in the defeat of the General Assessment Bill, thereby paving the way for his own. And in his presidential elections, he saw the value of dissenting voices, especially in New England, in helping to keep the Federalist monopoly in check. Those groups who neither had nor sought power found in Jefferson nothing to fear.

On the one hand, Jefferson admired the Quakers because they had no creeds and imposed no dogmatism on others. "I believe with the Quaker preacher," he wrote to a Delaware Quaker in 1813, "that he who steadily observes those moral precepts in which all religions concur will never be questioned, at the gates of heaven, as to the dogmas in which they all differ." After complaining to another correspondent in 1822 about Christianity's penchant for schisms and separations, he wrote, "How much wiser are the Quakers who, agreeing in the fundamental doctrine of the gospel, schismatize about no mysteries, and keeping within the pale of common sense, suffer no speculative differences of opinion." On this point, Jefferson proved too sanguine, as schism would afflict the Quakers along with most other branches of American Christendom.

On the other hand, the Quakers bothered Jefferson because they seemed still tied to England, the land of their origin. In the American Revolution, they had been pacifists, but, beyond that, many expressed loyalty to King George III, partly because another king, Charles II, had been so loyal to them in providing William Penn with a magnificent grant of land. "A Quaker is essentially an Englishman," Jefferson told botanist William Baldwin in 1810, "in whatever part of the earth he is born or lives." In the quarrels with Great Britain, both in his own administration and now in Madison's, the Quakers sided "against their own government, not on their profession of peace . . . but from devotion to the views of the Mother-society." In dealing with the Indians, we have, said Jefferson, scrupulously followed Quaker policies, as we have done with religious freedom as well. "Yet I never expected we should get a vote from them, and in this I was neither deceived nor disappointed." In the world of dogma, Quakers passed Jefferson's test; in the world of politics, they failed.

When in 1814 an evangelical Methodist wrote an eleven-page letter to Jefferson urging him to convert and accept "the gospel of our Lord Jesus Christ," the deist did not explode. Rather, he patiently explained that men should "not be uneasy . . . about the different roads we may pursue . . . to that our last abode." Jefferson agreed with what he had often heard — namely, "that there is not a Quaker or a Baptist, a Presbyterian or an Episcopalian, a Catholic or a Protestant in heaven." On

201

the contrary, "on entering that gate, we leave those badges of schism behind, and find ourselves united in those principles only in which God has united us all." He further encouraged his Methodist proselytizer, Miles King, to apply the test of Reason to all religious tenets, for that oracle alone could distinguish between what really came from God and what were the phantoms "of a disordered and deluded imagination."

Jefferson recalled the warm and strong support of Virginia Baptists in the cause of religious freedom. These sectarians also shared with him the acute concern about the absence of religious liberty guarantees in the Constitution. As the General Committee of Baptists in Virginia wrote to the newly elected President Washington, "When the Constitution first made its appearance in Virginia, we . . . feared that the liberty of conscience, dearer to us than property or life, was not sufficiently secured." While they took comfort in the integrity of Washington, they also pushed for a Bill of Rights. John Leland, the leading Baptist in Virginia at the time, ran on behalf of those who opposed the Constitution on the grounds that it had no Bill of Rights. In a debate with James Madison, he accepted the wisdom that called first for ratification and second for amendments under the new government that would ensure the cherished liberties. Leland withdrew in favor of Madison, thus giving the pro-Constitution forces one more critical voice and vote.

The Baptists exchanged letters with Jefferson because they saw him as uniquely their own, in Roosevelt's words, Apostle of Freedom. Under a Jefferson presidency, North Carolina Baptists said in 1806, "there is none that shall make us afraid." And John Leland, finding Jefferson's own words congenial rather than frightening, proclaimed that all persons should in religious matters speak freely, maintain principles according to their consciences, and worship "either one God, three Gods, no God, or twenty Gods," and let government do nothing about it except to see that such a person "meets with no personal abuse, or loss of property, for his religious opinions."

Fortunately, Leland did not run for president and find his radicalism, as well as his possible plagiarism, under attack.

For Leland, as for most other Baptists, religion was an affair of the heart, not of the state. Jefferson began his famous letter to the Danbury Baptists in 1802 with these words: "Believing with you that religion is a matter which lies solely between man and his God . . ." Pietism, on this level, won a warm Jeffersonian response. Or, as he wrote in 1809 to James Fishback, a Kentucky doctor who took up the Baptist ministry, defending one's religious views with "candor, moderation, and ingenuity" posed no threat. "If all the writers and preachers on religious questions had been of the same temper, the history of the world would have been of much more pleasing aspect."

On the other hand, Jefferson maintained his alertness, if not his eternal hostility, to Congregationalists and Presbyterians. The former maintained establishments in New England, and the latter yearned for establishment everywhere else — or so Jefferson in the last decade of his life fervently believed. With the Unitarian schism erupting in New England, Jefferson might have persuaded himself that Congregationalism was on its way out; by 1818, with the disestablishment in Connecticut, that hope took wings. But Presbyterianism was another matter. He resented it more than Congregationalism, partly because of its proximity to him in Virginia, but even more because of the Presbyterian-related troubles pertaining to the University of Virginia. Beyond that, in 1801 Presbyterians had joined with Congregationalists in a Plan of Union, the main purpose of which was to present a united front in evangelizing the unchurched West. A suspicious nature, however, might suppose that this remarkable cooperation had been secured in order to win more patronage and power in the East. At the beginning of the nineteenth century, Jefferson might never have believed in such a plot; by 1825, he was fully prepared to believe it — and worse. Likewise, Madison in his retirement worried about the churches' craving for "emoluments or privileges"; when would they learn?

Jefferson's earliest animosities were naturally directed against Anglicanism. Yet once Anglicanism lost all its political muscle in Virginia, Jefferson — presidential elections aside — could be more tolerant, possibly even forgiving. This new attitude derived to some degree from the friendship that Jefferson formed with Virginia's first bishop of the newly organized Protestant Episcopal Church, another James Madison, cousin to the president and head of the College of William and Mary from 1777 until his death in 1812. This Madison won scientific as well as ecclesiastical distinction — the former as a surveyor and mapmaker, like Jefferson's father. If a man loved science, Jefferson could forgive him for almost anything else.

In 1784, Jefferson told his Montpelier friend that he regularly exchanged temperature and climate observations with the college president in Williamsburg. Two years later, he bought books in France for both Madisons, a chore that he found more delightful than burdensome. In 1802, Bishop Madison visited Jefferson for several days in Monticello, on one of the president's frequent journeys from the White House to his little mountain refuge.

Jefferson also maintained a friendship with Charles Clay, once the Anglican minister of St. Anne's parish in Jefferson's own county; in 1815, he wrote Clay that "I have received from Philadelphia . . . the spectacles that you desired," and so Jefferson forwarded them to his former neighbor along with "a complete set of glasses [lenses] from early use to old age." And, to be sure, Jefferson kept warm relationships with many Tidewater Episcopalians whom he had known from his youth. Members of the Episcopal Church, as individuals, presented no problem in civility or congeniality to Jefferson. On the other hand, Anglicanism in England, having learned nothing from either the American or French Revolution, still enjoyed political favor, and therefore in that country, at least, still warranted a jaundiced eye.

Jefferson did not have much contact with Jews, since their numbers remained small in America; the steep growth of

Judaism still lay in the years ahead. But when Isaac Harby of Charleston, South Carolina, sent him a copy of his address on the "true principles of Judaism," Jefferson took delight in seeing the influence of Reason and Nature at work. Harby noted that in his Reformed Society of Israelites, "our desire is . . . to take away whatever is offensive to the enlightened mind." Jefferson responded, on 6 January 1826, that the reformation of Judaism, as described in Harby's speech, "appears entirely reasonable. Nothing is wiser than that all our institutions should keep pace with the advance of time," he happily added, "and be improved with the improvements of the human mind."

A few years earlier, Jefferson had written to Dr. Jacob De La Motta upon the occasion of the dedication of a new synagogue in Savannah, Georgia, that he rejoiced "in the restoration of the Jews, particularly to their social rights." The hope now, said Jefferson, was that Jews "will be seen taking their seats on the benches of science as preparatory to their doing the same at the board of government." While often deploring the tendency of religion to fragment, he understood, along with Madison, that factions can offer some benefit. To his correspondent, Jefferson observed that while tyranny reveled in religious unity, freedom flourished in multiplicity. In civil government, one repeated the words "United we stand, divided we fall." In religion, said Jefferson, the opposite was true: "Divided we stand, united we fall." Recognizing the scourge under which Jews for centuries had suffered, he declared to Mordecai M. Noah in 1818 that "your sect by its sufferings has furnished a remarkable proof of the universal spirit of religious intolerance inherent in every sect, disclaimed by all when feeble, and practiced by all when in power." The history of the Jews by itself seemed sufficient to justify an eternal vigil.

In his mature years, Jefferson maintained his closest religious contacts with Unitarians. He corresponded with many, from the days of Priestley and Price to those of Benjamin Waterhouse, a Harvard physicist and pioneer in the use of vaccination, and of Jared Sparks, minister of the First Independent Church in Baltimore and early editor of American history documents. In 1822 Jefferson complained to Waterhouse about the "tritheistic school of Andover," expressing the hope that more "missionaries" from Harvard would soon reach the hinterlands. And to Sparks, he expressed his assurance in 1820 that "thinking men of all nations" have "rallied readily to the doctrine of only one God."

Especially in the last decade of his life, Jefferson communicated with many other Unitarians on matters of mutual concern. He exchanged several letters with Francis Adrian Van der Kemp, immigrant from Holland and close friend of Adams as well as of Jefferson. To James Smith of Mount Vernon, Ohio, he spoke confidently in 1822 of the sweep of Unitarianism all across the country. Smith, a former Methodist turned Unitarian, told Jefferson of his abandonment of "priestly dominion" in favor of "the mild and peaceable gospel of Jesus Christ, the most perfect model of Republicanism in the Universe." A Yale lawyer, John Davis, sent Jefferson a copy of Aaron Bancroft's Unitarian sermons, which led Jefferson to "rejoice in efforts to restore us to primitive Christianity." A Massachusetts deist, George Thacher, in 1824 urged Jefferson to publish his liberal views on religion, but the latter, of course, refused. As previously noted, Jefferson also found in the Unitarianism of John Adams a congenial religious atmosphere in which to carry on their philosophical and political exchanges.

In addition to these associations, Jefferson acknowledged having attended Unitarian services in Philadelphia when domiciled there. In 1822 he tried to encourage Benjamin Waterhouse, who believed that Unitarianism was not spreading as fast as it should be, by telling him that Unitarian Jared Sparks had been named "Chaplain to the late Congress." As early as 1803, Joseph Priestley believed he saw Jefferson migrating in the direction of Unitarianism. "He cannot be far from us," Priestley wrote a friend; "he now attends public worship very regularly, and his moral conduct was never impeached." However, just as Jefferson never allowed his private letters regarding religion to be published, so he never formally declared his affiliation in the ranks of the Unitarians.

Thomas Jefferson had no quarrel with religion that relied on Reason or even with "enthusiastic" religion that relied only on persuasion. But for religion that allied itself with dogmatism and power, he spared no invective and relaxed no vigil. Of religion of this latter sort, Jefferson remained forever a sworn enemy.

LAST DAYS

The older Jefferson grew, the more he worried about how the strange turns of public opinion might affect the liberties of religion. Despite a Virginia Statute in 1786, a secular Constitution drafted in 1787, and explicit guarantees ratified in 1791, the freedom of religion was only as safe as the nation's citizens insisted that it be. The will of the people served as the bastion of democracy, the court of ultimate appeal. But it was regrettably true that that wavering will could turn into an inquisition. Lynch mobs, after all, represented the will of the people — some people, under some circumstances. In that instance, the people disdained Reason and listened only to passion; they also disdained law and the "will" of a wider public. Could a lynch mentality ever hang the First Amendment and its inalienable rights? "Although we have freedom of religious opinion by law," Jefferson wrote in a letter to Van der Kemp in 1816, "we are yet under the inquisition of public opinion." Matters were worse in England, to be sure, where both law and public opinion worked against religious freedom. But even in America, one must keep the public both informed and aware. As Madison observed, every instance in which the First Amendment worked had to be acclaimed with full voice, for just as virtue must become a habit, so the belief in and commitment to religious liberty needed to be habitual until it became virtually instinctive.

To his trusted Virginia friend William Short, Jefferson in 1820 again voiced his deep anxiety about this kind of inquisition. In this instance, since he had Presbyterians principally in mind, he called it a "holy inquisition." These Calvinists, said Jefferson, "pant to reestablish *by law* that holy inquisition which they can now only infuse into *public opinion*," for such opinion was now regarded as the "lord of the universe." Jefferson wrote this in the midst of his struggles to bring into existence a liberal, modern, free public university. Our mistake has probably been, he added, to allow the preachers so large a role in forming opinions. "We have given them stated and privileged days to collect and catechise us, opportunities of delivering their oracles to the people en masse, and of molding their minds as wax in the hollow of their hands." Having made such a mistake, we must now post guards to warn us, both day and night, against any and all religious encroachments. If "eternal hostility" was too strong a phrase, "eternal wariness" was hardly strong enough.

Jefferson met with James Madison for the last time in Charlottesville in April 1826. The occasion, not surprisingly, was a meeting of the university's Board of Visitors. They exchanged a few more letters, in which professions of friendship were a recurrent theme. Madison felt unworthy to succeed Jefferson as university rector and hoped more years might yet be granted to his dear friend, which years could not but help to "increase the debt which our Country owes you." And if Jefferson had found pleasure in the long years of their association, so had Madison found a similar joy as together they "discharged the trusts committed to us." Jefferson had on another occasion compared friendship to wine: "raw when new, ripened with age, the true old man's milk and restorative cordial."

As the fiftieth anniversary of the signing of the Declaration of Independence approached, the city of Washington, D.C., planned a worthy celebration. In anticipation of the event, the mayor wrote to both Jefferson and Adams hoping to lure the aged statesmen from their restful retreats. Jefferson knew his health would not permit him to attend, but he summoned his strength for one last letter, 26 June 1826; that letter marked not only a political anniversary but also a religious vigil. Jefferson saw the Declaration as a signal to all the world "of arousing men to burst the chains under which monkish ignorance and superstition had persuaded them to bind themselves." He did not restrict "monkish ignorance and superstition" to the Middle Ages or the Roman Catholic Church of that time. With that phrase, Jefferson fired a final shot at all repressive religion, at all failure to recognize that God had made the mind free and the conscience inviolable.

In his letter, Jefferson applauded the advance of science as well as of a form of self-government that heralded the "palpable truth that the mass of mankind has not been born with saddles on their backs, nor a favored few booted and spurred, ready to ride them legitimately, by the grace of God." If we are to celebrate the Fourth of July, Jefferson concluded, "let the annual return of this day forever refresh our recollections of these rights, and an undiminished devotion to them." If neither Jefferson nor Adams could attend the festivities in Washington on 4 July 1826, they did perhaps the next best thing by memorializing with their deaths on that day the awesome solemnity and splendor of the occasion — and of those rights.

8 A Religion for the People

"Our savior did not come into the world to save
metaphysicians only." (1818)

The ancient Greece that Jefferson much admired suffered from
a serious division that he would neither commend nor support:
a bifurcation in religion. Greek popular religion bore little if
any resemblance to the religion of the Greek philosophers, nor
did the two theological or liturgical worlds engage in any serious dialogue with each other. The mysteries of Dionysius or
the Great Mother moved in one direction, the speculations of
Plato or Aristotle, of Epicurus or Epictetus, in quite another.
And Jefferson would have considered that sad circumstance as
the attainment of neither a civic nor a religious ideal.

He had different hopes and expectations for America,
different hopes and expectations for religion that followed and
built upon the Enlightenment. The teachings of Jesus had relevance well beyond the confines of Christianity, just because
moral duties and moral instincts had relevance that tran-

scended any sectarian or even political structure. The issue was not so much whether Unitarianism would "become the general religion of the United States" as it was whether dogmatism and irrationality would cramp and cripple the minds and dreams of a free people. Jefferson thought that obedience to the teachings of Jesus, as well as reflection on the purity of his life, could help citizens to transcend the parochialisms and barbarisms of the past and emerge with a new and enduring "essence" of the traditions that they had known. Just as "our savior" had in mind the well-being of more than metaphysicians, so did Jefferson. In fact, on the Jeffersonian list, metaphysicians came in last.

As we have seen in previous chapters, Jefferson expressed great concern about the reform of religion in general and of Christianity in particular. His concern also extended, however, to the damage that would result from the destruction or rejection of all religion. As abusive and extravagant as Christianity had been in previous centuries, he nonetheless believed that "it is by far better to be as it is, than [to] be altogether without any." No system of morality, he told Charles Clay in 1814, "however pure it might be," could possibly survive without "the sanction of divine authority stamped upon it." This major concession, allowing that a corrupted Christianity was better than no Christianity at all, demonstrated Jefferson's belief in an intimate, indissoluble bond between religion and morality, influencing certainly the "vulgar minds," but probably all minds, metaphysical and otherwise.

But having made such a concession, Jefferson would immediately argue that little justification could be found in his modern world for putting up any longer with an inferior version of the Christian religion. All of the insights granted by the oracle of Reason and all of the universal truths communicated on the canvas of Nature joined to give humankind every necessity for reforming and refashioning a flawed religious inheritance. One must, for example, learn to trust in a benevolent and merciful God rather than a wrathful and vindictive one.

211

This more enlightened trust had the additional benefit of making the believers themselves more benevolent, more moral, more respectful of each other. Religion drawn from Reason and Nature did not separate Americans into disputatious sects but joined them together in a dedicated pursuit of the common good.

JEFFERSON AND EVANGELICAL RELIGION

So much of what happened to American religion in the generation following Jefferson's death would seem to challenge if not shatter his earnest faith. The counterrevolution of evangelical religion, much of it subsumed under the rubric of the Second Great Awakening, threatened the entire ideology of the Enlightenment. It revived enthusiasm, with its many negative connotations for all the philosophes, as it encouraged emotion to place a check on Reason, rather than the other way around. This evangelical religion, moreover, often took refuge in a biblical literalism that returned angels, miracles, and prophecies to their accustomed seats of honor. And it generally placed dogmas ("superstitions," in the Jeffersonian vocabulary) on a par with moral precepts, if not above them. Even before his death in 1826, Jefferson found much to deplore in sectarian religion; after his death, he would have found even more.

On the other hand, Jefferson would not have arbitrarily dismissed everything that did not label itself Unitarianism or everything that did come within the compass of the later phrase "the religion of the Republic." Many denominational enthusiasts, for instance, believed that they were simply extending Jeffersonian principles in quite logical ways. New England's Elias Smith serves as a useful, if somewhat idiosyncratic, example of a preacher who merely wanted the valued concept of freedom extended into all areas of life. Christians should be free of denominational labels; churches should be free of each other; citizens should be free of the arrogant tyranny of "regular" doctors, erudite lawyers, and presumptuous politicians. The epistle of James contains the nice phrase "law of liberty," and Smith found that New Testament "law" in every way congenial with the Jeffersonian inalienable right to liberty.

Jefferson had made "republican" a good word, not merely for his own party but for an entire constellation of values and attitudes. When James O'Kelly protested against what he saw as growing ecclesiastical authority in Methodism, he led a faction, explicitly named Republican Methodist, out from the parent body. For O'Kelly, liberty — in American terms — had been too recently and too dearly won to be sacrificed on some clerical altar. The same held true in Christian terms: "If Christians are free citizens of Zion," O'Kelly observed, "they should prize those liberties, seeing they were purchased with the precious blood of Christ." Baptists, moreover, made a fetish out of showing deference to no authority, and it can be no accident that Baptists and Methodists adjusted most swiftly and most successfully to the new Jeffersonian world. Jefferson's "republicanism" would not have matched theirs in every detail, but he could hardly have failed to applaud their republican spirit of equality and liberty.

The Monticello philosophe would also have found comfort in evangelical religion's devout dedication to morality, both private and public. Evangelical churches held their members to strict account in personal behavior and frequently demonstrated their seriousness through excommunication of the morally delinquent. Public morality occupied even more attention and raised the rhetoric to even higher levels. Voluntary societies tumbled over each other in an effort to meet the broader moral demands of the nation: war and peace, slavery and freedom, ignorance and education, temperance and indulgence, self-sacrifice and greed. Lyman Beecher, a one-man committee for "doing good," whether in the settled East or the frontier West, agreed with Jefferson that God made his creatures to be moral beings and that in freedom of association and earnestness of commitment, society could be redeemed, morality could be preserved. "Saving one's soul" should not be ignored, but neither should it be separated from the moral redemption of a people or of a nation.

Jefferson, who had had a good deal to say about returning to the pure and original church and sloughing off those "corruptions of Christianity" that Priestley described, would certainly have rejoiced in the attention this idea received in the 1820s and 1830s. Barton Stone, for example, led Kentuckians into a new appreciation for the primitive church and the spirit-filled ministry of the New Testament. Today's clergy, said Stone, should reject the "Reverend" title with all of the odor of spiritual class that it implied. Ministers should be licensed solely by God, to "preach the simple gospel . . . without any mixture of philosophy, vain deceit, traditions of men, or the rudiments of the world." Had Jefferson entertained any notion whatsoever of publishing his "Life and Morals of Jesus," Barton . Stone could have, on that point at least, provided a most suitable preface.

Jefferson, furthermore, would not have been horrified by the continued tendency of religion in America to create ever more novel forms of ecclesiastical expression: Latter-day Saints, Seventh-day Adventists, Oneida communitarians, Oberlin perfectionists, and more. Even though this unending fertility meant that not all rallied around the unifying standard of Reason and Nature, it also meant that a tyrannical religious monopoly need no longer be feared. In religion, Jefferson had asserted that "divided we stand" and "united we fall." By 1850, to say nothing of 1950 or 2000, he would have had little reason to worry about a denominational unity, however much he might have wished for a moral one.

In the nineteenth century, organized religion maintained a spirited optimism — not unlike that of Jefferson himself. If a whole continent begged churches for their help, no problem. If a whole world seemed ripe for a missionary message, no problem. If urbanization and industrialization created severe dislocations and recriminations, religion had solutions waiting in the wings. If immigration threatened to change the entire face of American religion, immigrants could be converted and a public school education could soften or erase the sharpest differences. God still had a destiny for America, and a kingdom of God on earth never seemed very far away.

The most significant commonality between Jefferson and the evangelicals remained their unwavering conviction that they lived in a God-centered, God-endowed universe. Jefferson's optimism, his commitment to a moral sense, his trust in Nature, his confidence in Reason, his political earnestness — all this and more rested on his assurance of the existence and beneficent nature of God. His theism constituted the foundation on which all else stood; without it, his universe collapsed. Similarly, for the evangelicals, the Alpha and the Omega of their universe was God. No aspect of society or politics or human behavior could be ultimately understood or interpreted apart from the mystery and majesty of the Divine Being. With a common base this wide, one might well expect more bridges to have been built between the Jeffersonians and the evangelicals, but they were not. Some bridges, in fact, were burned.

EVANGELICALS AND JEFFERSONIAN DEISM

Yale's Timothy Dwight, early nineteenth-century leader against rationalism, deism, anticlericalism, the horrors of the French Revolution just passed, and the potential horrors of disestablishment just ahead, viewed Jefferson with disdain. This "Connecticut high priest," as the Republican press labeled him in 1800, regarded the "touch of France" as "pollution" and "her embrace" as "death." He contended that those who, like Jefferson, spoke well of France and ill of England spread plague-like sentiments across America. Their "infidelity" must be stopped by any means, and revivalism constituted the most convenient utensil for that purpose. "Infidelity, naturally and necessarily, becomes, when possessed of the control of national interests," Dwight wrote in his *Travels in New-England and New York,* "a source of evils so numerous, and so intense, as to compel mankind to prefer any state to those evils." Federalist Dwight, regarded by his enemies as the "monarch" not only of Yale but of all Connecticut as well, showed no interest in any fine distinctions between a Jefferson and a Paine, a Palmer and an Allen. Infidels all, out to exterminate Christianity, they must be defeated in the voting booth and denounced from the pulpit. Swayed by such sentiments, Presbyterian Samuel Miller came to regard his long friendship with Jefferson as one of the great mistakes of his life.

Revivalism, indelibly identified in the first half of the nineteenth century with the name of Charles G. Finney, pervaded America's religious culture. "The terrific universality of the Revival," in Perry Miller's phrase, became the instrument for redefining the national ethos in the generation following Jefferson's death. The revivalist fought against sin, however defined, but he also fought against "infidelity," which emerged as the national sin: the wrong turn in the road that otherwise led steadily upward toward that kingdom of God on earth. To Elias Smith, Jefferson had looked like a harbinger of the Second Coming of Christ; to the Congregational and Presbyterian evangelicals, he looked more like the Antichrist.

When, in 1844, Presbyterian Robert Baird wrote the first real history of religion in the United States *(Religion in America; or, An Account of the Origin, Relation to the State, and Present Condition of the Evangelical Churches in the United States),* the subtitle of his work contained an accurate assessment of the state of things: evangelical Christianity was largely synonymous with religion in America; everything else was peripheral at best. Baird characterized Jefferson as "a very bitter enemy to Christianity," "one of the greatest enemies that Christianity has ever had to contend with in America," and maintained that his Statute for Establishing Religious Freedom essentially degraded Christianity by putting all sects — indeed, all religions — on an equal footing.

216

One of Baird's chapters bore this heading: "Whether the Government of the United States may justly be called infidel or atheistical." His answer, not surprisingly, was no. Nor was it even secular: it was Christian. The silences of the Constitution with respect to religion were easily explained. That document was written not "for a people that had no religion" but "for a people already Christian." No elaboration was required, since so much could simply be assumed. "The Bible," Baird carefully explained, "does not begin with an argument to prove the existence of God, but assumes the fact."

Unitarianism, a conspicuously "unevangelical denomination," bore the same disgrace as "infidelity" in Baird's view. Fortunately, he pointed out, it had grown very little, for Unitarian churches, requiring no creed and practicing no discipline, "often vanish as easily and suddenly as they are made." If "civil government had been invested with power to enforce religious uniformity," the unfortunate schism in Massachusetts would never have occurred. But the government lacked not only the power but the will, since the chief civil officers were themselves generally Unitarians. Baird also found fault with the congregational polity that prevailed in New England, allowing each church to make its own decisions. "Error thus had leave," he concluded, "to work its way unchecked by the oversight either of bishop or presbytery." Though the "impious doctrines" of Unitarianism were promoted "with increasing boldness," the results remained minimal. The Jeffersonian vision of a whole country turning Unitarian, Baird rejoiced to see, faded slowly and steadily into the sunset.

PRIVATE RELIGION AND PUBLIC RESPONSIBILITY

Revivalism could sometimes be a force for change in the social order. Charles Finney endeavored to make it so, and, as the Civil War edged ever closer, Harriet Beecher Stowe fervently hoped that "the great revival of 1858" would become "the great

217

reformation of 1858." It did not. Stowe, along with many others, thought that revivalism had taken too sharp a turn toward the purely personal. The question of private salvation seemed divorced from any degree of public responsibility. Stowe contended that all the talk of conversion left unclear just what one was being converted to: "Converted into a man who defends slavery — converted into one who dares not testify against a profitable wickedness — converted into a man whose religion never goes into his counting-house — converted into a man who has no conscience in politics, and who scoffs at the higher law of God?" Such "conversion" was unworthy of the name, surely unworthy of the Christian religion.

In the realm of religion, Jefferson blended the private and the public with startling success. He wrote about the private, privately; he lived the public, dramatically. From the moment his neighbors chose him to serve in the House of Burgesses, his sense of duty propelled him toward ever enlarging responsibilities. There could never be a commonwealth without a commitment to the common good; there could never be a free and democratic nation unless men and women rose above narrow self-interest and defeating self-indulgence. One had to pursue life, liberty, and happiness on an altruistic scale, if for no other reason than the pragmatic one that pursuit on a private scale ended in decay, ensnarement, and gloom. Jefferson trusted in a God who saved one *from* the self, not *for* the self.

Revivalism gained the reputation of abetting this inward turn, of encouraging persons to contemplate their sinful nature and take comfort in the forgiveness abundantly granted to each individual, one by one. Salvation became the end of the Christian life rather than the beginning. Converted to or for what? Stowe asked. Not many caught up in the fervor of revivalism had ready answers. Private religion came to be so identified with "the gospel" that when, in the twentieth century, certain theologians and preachers spoke of Christianity's social dimension, they were charged with having abandoned "the gospel." Whatever the rhetoric, the implication of this personalistic faith was that God ruled over a restricted segment of life, not over all of life. Nature, post-Darwin, was no longer God's world but something else altogether. And Reason yielded at every point to Revelation.

To be sure, revivalism cannot bear all the responsibility for this shift from the organic whole to the solitary soul. Ralph Waldo Emerson and other Transcendentalists gloried in unchecked individualism, finding in democracy a tendency to confuse equality with mediocrity, freedom with averaging. A sect, said Emerson, was a "convenient incognito to excuse a man from the necessity of thinking." Rather than take refuge in the anonymity and banality of the group, men and women should assert themselves, believe in themselves, live for themselves. "Nothing is at last sacred," Emerson wrote, "but the integrity of our own mind." "A true man," he added, "belongs to no other time or place, but is the center of things." "Every true man is a cause, a country, an age." To the extent that one seeks allies and coworkers, "he is weaker by every recruit to his banner." Emerson's advice: stand alone and thereby prevail.

Liberty, divorced from any sense of responsibility, did result in a splintering of society. Competition replaced cooperation, and individual enterprise supplanted communal undertakings. Those who mourned the passing of an old Anglican or Congregational order could not be sure what, if anything, might take its place. As one Scottish immigrant commented shortly after the Revolution, the new nation was composed "of discordant atoms, jumbled together by chance, and tossed by unconstancy in an immense vacuum." That surely did not represent the new world order; indeed, it represented no order at all. Drunkenness held more appeal than sobriety, luxury more allure than denial, and criminal activity more attraction than public service. Everyone was on the move — and on the make. Jefferson would have happily given up the notion of a Unitarian nation in exchange for a just and responsible nation.

RELIGION ON TRIAL

By the end of the twentieth century, institutional religion in America had lost much of its optimism, verve, and moral concern. A recapitulation of first-century Christianity seemed less a lively option, and pluralism created diversity without benefit and multiplicity without end. Historians could no longer follow Robert Baird in dividing American religion between the evangelical and the nonevangelical churches, presenting all the winning ribbons to the former. In the 1840s Baird could still think in terms of a Protestant America. A half-century later, observers more often spoke of a Christian America, and, a half-century after that, of a Judeo-Christian America. By the 1990s, more adjectives and hyphens: America was a Judeo-Christian–Islamic–Buddhist–Hindu–Sikh–Native American–New Age nation. Such a characterization hardly seemed worth the effort, and it scarcely pointed to either a cultural or religious cohesion.

When during England's Cromwellian period the lid of religious authority came off the sectarian pot, everything boiled over. That period of religious creativity in England lasted only a couple of decades. America, on the other hand, has kept the lid off for more than two hundred years, with the manifest result that everyone has become his or her own church, as Emerson anticipated. No long-standing ecclesiastical tradition, operating even by the mild force of inertia, reigns in this boundless proliferation. The open spaces beckoned, the liberal laws permitted, the heavy hand of tradition lifted. Utopian experiments flourished in the 1840s and again in the 1960s. When denominations did not divide, new ones arose out of nothing. Millions of members now reside in denominational homes (Assembly of God, Church of God in Christ, Jehovah's Witnesses, etc.) whose names Robert Baird would not even recognize. Personality cults, televangelism, and independent megachurches helped produce by the end of the twentieth century a pluralism beyond reckoning, beyond absorbing.

Structural diversity represents only one reason why religion, as it confronts a new millennium, is on trial. A deeper diversity is intellectual or theological. The great gaps opened for all to see in the first quarter of the twentieth century: fundamentalists and modernists squared off against each other, leaving vast portions of the churchgoing public wondering where they stood, or which pew they should occupy, or if the whole noisy business was irrelevant to concerns by which or for which they lived. Institutional Christianity had difficulty recovering from this episode, as it did from the ridicule heaped upon it by Henry Mencken and from the philosophical gauntlet thrown down by John Dewey and even Walter Lippmann. A politically involved fundamentalism reasserted itself in the final quarter of the century, with candidates for local offices running in great numbers, and candidates for national offices running in only slightly more limited numbers. Finally, widely reported statistical declines caused a painful reexamination of what had gone wrong, especially in Baird's favored churches. Who had turned off the steam?

Trends other than membership declines proved troubling as well. There were indications of a decline in the faithfulness of American Roman Catholics, for instance: church attendance declined sharply between 1960 and 1990, income donated to the parishes dropped by half, and the number of young men choosing to go into the priesthood dropped even more than that. Beyond this, Catholicism also suffered a decline in theological and ecclesiastical consensus. Polls revealed that well over half of American Catholics believed that priests should be allowed to marry and that women should be admitted to priestly orders. Nine out of ten younger Catholics believe that artificial birth control methods, divorce, and remarriage are perfectly compatible with their faith.

Judaism worried especially about intermarriage and assimilation, the consequences being not simply a statistical decline but a disappearance of Jews altogether from ethnic and religious calculations. Eastern Orthodox, even after generations in America, still appeared trapped in ethnic enclosures. Muslims in America struggled to remain free of worldwide Islamic entanglements, especially those in Algeria, Iran, and Iraq, as they worked to overcome an almost total cultural "apartness." Buddhists, especially visible on the Pacific coast, failed to break ethnic and religious linkages, except for Zen, though its appeal was more elite than popular. Hindus and Sikhs moved out only briefly from enclaves, while Native Americans fought for a status quo ante bellum — lots of bellums. Meanwhile, the most popular religious book in the latter half of the twentieth century was Hal Lindsey's *Late Great Planet Earth* (1970 and following), which represented the kind of apocalyptic musing that Jefferson, with respect to the book of Revelation, found devoid of all Reason. When a fellow Virginian asked Jefferson in 1825 for a comment on his *Explanation of the Apocalypse,* Jefferson quickly responded, "What has no meaning admits no explanation."

In America, religion has literally been on trial since the 1940s — before the courts, notably before the Supreme Court, with ever-increasing frequency and ever-increasing passion. Since the Constitution is the only text universally acknowledged sacred by Americans, the justices have served as our high priests and moral arbiters in a way hardly envisioned in 1787. In a long and spirited dissent issued in 1943, Justice Felix Frankfurter declared that "our constant preoccupation with the constitutionality of legislation rather than with its wisdom tends to preoccupation of the American mind with a false value." It is not hard to see why this is the case. Fractured in so many ways, with no long-established national church, with no long-entrenched national traditions, with no pervading moral consensus, wisdom eludes. We entertain at most some fragile hope that we might learn whether an action is constitutional or not, hardly any hope at all that we can reach agreement concerning its wisdom or its folly.

This is notably true in the area where Jefferson devoted so many anxious hours: education. Subsequent generations

222

created the sort of system of public education that Jefferson vainly tried to introduce in Virginia; but Americans have, especially in the past few decades, disagreed strongly about what should take place in that specific public arena. Prayer and Bible reading in the public schools? The theory of creationism "balanced" with the theory of Darwinism in those schools? "Moral and spiritual values" inculcated therein? Religious holidays commemorated and celebrated? Textbooks that offend religious sensibilities removed from the curriculum? Other books removed from the school library? Besieged on many fronts, the public schools find themselves engaged in religious skirmishes far more often than they would wish.

Private schools have, if anything, created even more problems for the courts to resolve, especially in the area of appropriate financing. Specifically, to what extent, if any, may public monies be used to support any aspect of the private school effort: transportation to and from? salaries in part or in whole? textbooks or tests or vocational counseling or maps or projectors or pencils? building and maintenance costs? and — thorniest of all — parental tuition costs? No consensus exists in American society, no consensus can be found in the courts. A zigzag, ad hoc quality colors the split decisions that point the public first in one direction, then another. The role of religion in education is, if nothing else, surely on trial. With acute irony, the latest Supreme Court decision, five to four once again, in this troubled area (*Rosenberger v. University of Virginia*, 1995) concerns Jefferson's own institution and the question of that school's support for a religious publication.

The contentious situation is sorely aggravated by the fact that "religion" represents no tangible unity. One must speak of "religions" in America, with their multiple and often conflicting voices. In the 1840s and 1850s, the churches divided in sentiment, some strongly supporting slavery and some strongly opposing. Then they divided in fact, as the most popular denominations (Baptist, Methodist, Presbyterian) split into separate — and hostile — ecclesiastical entities. In the century

223

since that scandal, American religions have rarely exercised significant command in addressing, much less resolving, public concerns in morals and religion. Where leadership has been evident, as in the abortion struggle, one again finds not unity but division. The nation has religious leaders; it lacks religious leadership. Worldwide, the dilemmas worsen, as religion appears far less often to be allied with Jeffersonian Reason, far more often with mindless violence.

DEMOCRACY ON TRIAL

A weakened religious structure in the midst of a sturdy civic order would not necessarily occasion alarm. But the political house, divided against itself in more ways than Lincoln could have supposed, shudders and shakes. Liberty, a radical Roger Williams tried to explain to his shocked and unbelieving contemporaries, did not mean licentiousness, did not mean endless faction and division. A Rhode Island governor a century later, while still endorsing liberty, found himself less sure of the consequences of the "livelie experiment" that created a full religious freedom. Trapped in trying to govern an increasingly ungovernable colony, Stephen Hopkins claimed to have located the solution in "the personal virtue and steady perseverance of the wise and good" among all the citizens. Two hundred years after the nation's lively experiment got under way, many Americans identify with Hopkins's predicament. Many also find the solution to moral and political disorder resting in essentially the same place: virtue, especially in the eighteenth century's sense of that term, and a steady, persevering wisdom.

In a recent book, *Democracy on Trial*, Jean Bethke Elshtain offers the rough modern equivalent of a Puritan jeremiad. Though she may call more for understanding than for repentance, the two are not unrelated. We find ourselves, she writes, ready to proclaim freedom at the top of our lungs but to speak of public responsibility only in a whisper. Freedom often relates only to a universe of one, to a narcissistic world devoid of obligation beyond the cocoon we indulgently inhabit and jealously guard against all comers. That way democracy dies. For the American form of government, she notes, "requires a mode of participation with one's fellow citizens that is animated by a sense of responsibility for one's society."

The very word "citizen" implies residence in a community larger than oneself. By etymology, it is closely related to such other honorable words as "civil," "civilize," and "civility" — qualities all too conspicuous by their absence from our public life. One can renounce citizenship, of course, and hie for the hills or the hermitages. But to claim the rights of citizens is also to assume the relationships and connections that are intrinsically involved. The Bill of Rights was formulated to protect us from a strong central government; those rights were never intended to function as "entitlements," granted to each of us in isolation from each other and from the society at large. They form part of a network of mutual obligations. The nation's founders, Elshtain points out, "counted on a social deposit of intergenerational trust, neighborliness, and civic responsibility." That was Jefferson's world. If it is no longer ours, then democracy totters.

A new form of insularity — namely, multiculturalism — threatens national community. If not hunkered down in our very private cocoon, we huddle together in a group cocoon — rejecting or at least ignoring common aspirations and common moral goods. Racial, ethnic, and gender tribalisms make it more difficult to work together or perhaps even to live together. And being a member of one's tribe takes precedence over being a citizen of a larger whole. When educational efforts are made to rise above this parochialism, charges of cultural imperialism and elitism are hurled. Students continue to inhabit their own private worlds; they fail to become citizens of the public world. As tribalism becomes a way of life, the public-spirited citizen turns out to be only another endangered species.

Totalitarianism destroys convictions and abhors auton-omy. Democracy rests on freedom and requires responsibility. The framers built the structures of democratic government by providing for representation, regular elections, limitations on and balances of power, and the like. But they could not build civic virtue into the system. "Responsibility is ours," a freed Václav Havel wrote in 1987; "we must accept it and grasp it here, now, in this place where the Lord has set us down." We cannot lie our way out of it, he added, or escape it by fleeing to another country or to some private world of our own.

Both American religion and American democracy were on trial in the tragedies that befell the followers of Jim Jones and David Koresh. In the steamy jungles of Guyana, over nine hundred devotees died in 1978, many convinced that an Amer-ican government was out to destroy them. On the semi-arid plains of central Texas, over eighty faithful followers died in 1993, many convinced that an American government was out to annihilate them. Neither church nor state emerged un-scathed in those admittedly exceptional examples. The two events, however, suggested to sobered American citizens that both their civil and ecclesiastical houses required repair.

The book of Samuel speaks of those who are "bound in the bundle of the living." Americans need to be so bound together, bound by sentiment and hope, by values and civility — bound by something more than a network of interstate high-ways.

THE RELIGIOUS LEGACY OF THOMAS JEFFERSON

In 1791 Pierre Charles L'Enfant presented to George Washing-ton a plan for the newly laid out "federal city." That plan included a proposal for "a grand church" that would be avail-able for major national events such as "public prayer, thanks-givings, funeral orations, &c., and assigned to no particular sect or denomination, but equally open to all." Nothing came of that particular element of L'Enfant's design; and regarding that outcome, or lack of it, Thomas Jefferson would have been pleased. For him, had such an edifice ever been built, it would have stood for centuries as a monument to the "loathsome" connection between church and state. For large numbers of Americans, however, such a structure might well have served as a valuable symbol of the centrality of religion in their lives and thoughts. It would also have reflected that "civil religion" or "public religion" otherwise visible chiefly in presidential inaugural addresses and at state funerals. The question now posed is to what degree Jefferson himself survives as a kind of "grand church" to which a large cross-section of citizens can rally. "Assigned to no particular sect or denomination, but equally open to all," what is the religious legacy of Thomas Jefferson?

In one respect, at least, it is unambiguous and widely acclaimed: religious liberty. Together with James Madison, Jefferson constructed a foundation of such solidity as to endure through political discord, sectional war, economic reversal, totalitarian challenge, and unprecedented religious fecundity. His Memorial in Washington no less than his epitaph at Monticello testify to this unique contribution to Virginia, and thence to America and much of the Western world. That Jefferson also thought of it as unique, and uniquely precious, helps explain the zeal with which he defended religious liberty far beyond the formal guarantees set down in law. While many areas of disagreement arise in connection with the margins of religious freedom, and while many five-to-four Supreme Court decisions reveal the difficulties of legal interpretation, few Americans would wish to return to a former and darker age. Religion with civil power meant persecution and oceans of blood; religion divorced from civil power opened the way for both conscience and mind to be buoyantly free. If this were Jefferson's only religious legacy, it would be enough.

But other legacies remain, perhaps of sufficient substance to build a few bridges between popular religion and civil reli-

227

gion, or between the metaphysicians and the people. Jefferson assumed an ordered, theocentric world; chaos was not king. He also affirmed that ours was and is a moral universe; unrestrained libertinism did not, must not, rule. In addition, he believed that free men and women could not find ultimate satisfaction in a religion devoid of Reason; phantoms and fanaticisms must not drive Reason from its proper place. And finally, Thomas Jefferson knew that he was not God. A large measure of perspective, a considerable degree of humility, arose from the keen sense that he, too, was only one of God's creatures. He, along with all other human beings, did not enter into the world booted and spurred, to mount the backs of those less fortunate. Rather, he, like all women and men, was bound in a bundle with the living, called and challenged to elevate, educate, liberate, and introduce lasting reforms in politics, morality, and religion.

Legacies can be left without being claimed. The possibilities for bridge building can exist without being seized. "What has Athens to do with Jerusalem?" an ancient writer inquired. The answer turned out to be "Quite a lot." Similarly, one may inquire what the Enlightenment has to do with evangelicalism, or deism with orthodoxy. For some, the answer will be "As little as possible." Others, however, might find in the four legacies named above bridges leading toward some degree of unity rather than chasms that continue to divide. The recognition of a universe that is theistic, moral, and rational might yet rescue humanity from both a prideful arrogance and a selfish indifference.

Jefferson did not escape his time or his place; in fact, he would likely have chosen no other. He would neither seek nor deserve canonization or fawning worship. On the other hand, as an early biographer of the Virginia statesman wrote, "If Jefferson was wrong, America is wrong."

A Note on the Sources

As a public figure, Thomas Jefferson posthumously forsook all obscurity. Every scrap of writing, both private and public, will eventually find its place in the impressive, painstaking *Papers of Thomas Jefferson,* launched in 1950 and published by Princeton University Press. The First Series (1950-82), under the editorship of Julian Boyd, took twenty-one volumes to reach 1791, a little past the halfway point in Jefferson's life. Under the editorship of Eugene R. Sheridan, this series has now brought the total number of volumes to twenty-six, and the chronology to 1793. The first volume in a topical Second Series deserves particular mention: *Jefferson's Extracts from the Gospels,* edited by Dickinson W. Adams (Princeton: Princeton University Press, 1983). This invaluable work includes not only a reconstructed "Philosophy of Jesus" and the first photographic reproduction of "The Life and Morals of Jesus" but also the most relevant of Jefferson's letters pertaining to religion. Eugene R. Sheridan's historical introduction, moreover, is of enormous value. No one interested in the religious views of Thomas Jefferson can afford

229

to ignore this volume. Nor should they ignore Douglas L. Wilson's skillfully edited *Jefferson's Literary Commonplace Book*, another indispensable entry in the Second Series of the *Papers*.

Any listing of the major biographies of Jefferson must begin with Dumas Malone's six-volume *Jefferson and His Times* (Boston: Little, Brown, 1948-81), also available in a paperbound format. Beyond that, the choices are many. I will limit myself to three of the best: Merrill D. Peterson's *Thomas Jefferson and the New Nation: A Biography* (New York: Oxford University Press, 1970); Noble E. Cunningham Jr.'s *In Pursuit of Reason: The Life of Thomas Jefferson* (Baton Rouge: Louisiana State University Press, 1987); and a multiauthored topical treatment edited by Merrill D. Peterson, *Thomas Jefferson: A Reference Biography* (New York: Scribner's, 1986). Not so much a biography as an analysis of Jefferson's life and its impact is the excellent collection *Jeffersonian Legacies*, edited by Peter S. Onuf (Charlottesville: University Press of Virginia, 1993).

Three collections of letters are notably useful: *Letters of Benjamin Rush*, 2 vols., ed. Lyman H. Butterfield (Princeton: Princeton University Press, 1951); *The Adams-Jefferson Letters*, 2 vols., ed. Lester J. Cappon (Chapel Hill, N.C.: University of North Carolina Press, 1959); and, most recently, *The Republic of Letters: The Correspondence between Jefferson and Madison, 1776-1826*, 3 vols., ed. James Morton Smith (New York: W. W. Norton, 1995). In lieu of the definitive many-volumed edition of the Jefferson *Papers*, one may conveniently turn to two collections in single volumes, both edited by Merrill D. Peterson: *The Portable Thomas Jefferson* (New York: Viking Press, 1975) and *Thomas Jefferson: Writings* (New York: Library of America, 1984).

CHAPTER 1

For the background on the settlement and growth of Anglicanism in Virginia, one may consult such old but still valuable classics as Francis L. Hawks's *Contributions to the Ecclesiastical*

History of the United States of America, vol. 1: *Virginia* (New York: Harper, 1836); William Meade's *Old Churches, Ministers, and Families of Virginia*, 2 vols. (1857; reprint, Baltimore: Genealogical Publishing, 1966); and William S. Perry's *Historical Collections Relating to the American Colonial Church*, vol. 1: *Virginia* (1870; reprint, New York: AMS Press, 1969). More recent studies include George M. Brydon's *Virginia's Mother Church*, 2 vols. (Richmond: Richmond Historical Society, 1947, 1952); the ingenious architectural treatment of Dell Upton, *Holy Things and Profane: Anglican Parish Churches in Colonial Virginia* (Cambridge: MIT Press, 1986); and the broader survey by John F. Woolverton, *Colonial Anglicanism in North America* (Detroit: Wayne State University Press, 1984).

More specialized topical treatments include the following: Wesley M. Gewehr, *The Great Awakening in Virginia, 1740-1790* (Durham, N.C.: Duke University Press, 1930); Rhys Isaac, *The Transformation of Virginia, 1740-1790* (Chapel Hill, N.C.: University of North Carolina Press, 1982); and, moving into the nineteenth century, Donald G. Mathews, *Religion in the Old South* (Chicago: University of Chicago Press, 1977). The issue around which so much passion swirled in and before the Revolutionary era — namely, the importation (or not) of Anglican bishops into colonial America — receives convincing explication in Carl Bridenbaugh's *Mitre and Sceptre: Transatlantic Faiths, Ideas, Personalities, and Politics, 1689-1775* (New York: Oxford University Press, 1962).

CHAPTER 2

The background of the European Enlightenment is thoroughly discussed in Peter Gay's two-volume interpretation, *The Enlightenment: The Rise of Modern Paganism* and *The Enlightenment: The Science of Freedom* (New York: Alfred A. Knopf, 1966, 1969). His convenient and "Comprehensive Anthology," *The Enlightenment* (New York: Simon & Schuster, 1973), offers much invaluable primary material. On the English scene specifically, one may consult the classic of Caroline Robbins, *The Eighteenth-Century English Commonwealthman* (1959; reprint, New York: Atheneum, 1968), as well as a volume oriented more specifically toward religion, John Redwood's *Reason, Ridicule, and Religion: The Age of Enlightenment in England, 1660-1750* (Cambridge: Harvard University Press, 1976).

If the European Enlightenment initially influenced Thomas Jefferson most profoundly, in the American Enlightenment he became an active participant. That latter movement, long concealed in the shadow of its Continental counterpart, has now emerged fully into the light. This was most obvious in the nearly simultaneous appearance of three insightful surveys: Henry F. May, *The Enlightenment in America* (New York: Oxford University Press, 1976); Donald H. Meyer, *The Democratic Enlightenment* (New York: G. P. Putnam, 1976); and Henry Steele Commager, *The Empire of Reason: How Europe Imagined and America Realized the Enlightenment* (Garden City, N.Y.: Doubleday, 1977). Since Scotland's seminal thinkers had a special impact on America and on Jefferson, one should also know Douglas Sloan's *The Scottish Enlightenment and the American College Ideal* (New York: Teachers College Press, 1971), as well as the work edited by Richard B. Sher and Jeffrey R. Smitten, *Scotland and America in the Age of the Enlightenment* (Princeton: Princeton University Press, 1991).

On those great words of the Enlightenment, "Reason" and "Nature," see Charles A. Miller's *Jefferson and Nature: An Interpretation* (Baltimore: The Johns Hopkins University Press, 1988); Jack Fruchtman Jr.'s *Thomas Paine and the Religion of Nature* (Baltimore: The Johns Hopkins University Press, 1993); and Daniel J. Boorstin's older but still valuable study, *The Lost World of Thomas Jefferson* (1948; reprint, Boston: Beacon Press, 1960). The focus of Boorstin's book is not Jefferson himself but his "circle," which included academicians, astronomers, botanists, inventors, medical doctors, politicians, and more; the center of that circle geographically was Philadelphia, and personally, Benjamin Rush. Jefferson's deism is effectively located in its context by Kerry S. Walters in *The American Deists: Voices of Reason and Dissent in the Early Republic* (Lawrence, Kans.: University Press of Kansas, 1992). The best edition of Jefferson's single book is that edited by William Peden, *Notes on the State of Virginia* (1954; reprint, New York: W. W. Norton, 1972). A helpful guide to Jefferson's bibliomania is offered by Charles B. Sanford in *Thomas Jefferson and His Library* (Hamden, Conn.: Archon Books, 1977), though the exhaustive treatment remains E. Millicent Sowerby's *Catalogue of the Library of Thomas Jefferson,* 5 vols. (Washington: Library of Congress, 1952-59).

CHAPTER 3

For a treatment of church-state issues in the Revolutionary years, one should take advantage of Anson Phelps Stokes's serene and omnivorous *Church and State in the United States,* 3 vols. (New York: Harper, 1950); beginning with Moses on Mt. Sinai — just to get a good running start — Stokes gathers together much and misses very little, quoting generously along the way from primary documents. From the wealth of broad histories of these critical years, the works of three historians must not be omitted: Bernard Bailyn, *The Ideological Origins of the American Revolution* (Cambridge: Harvard University Press, 1967); Gordon S. Wood, *The Creation of the American Republic, 1776-1787* (Chapel Hill, N.C.: University of North Carolina Press, 1969) and his more recent work *The Radicalism of the American Revolution* (New York: Alfred A. Knopf, 1992); and Edmund S. Morgan, *The Challenge of the American Revolution* (New York: W. W. Norton, 1976); and his lucid introduction *The Birth of the Republic, 1763-89,* rev. ed. (Chicago: University of Chicago Press, 1977).

Concerning the Declaration of Independence, see the engaging analysis of Garry Wills, *Inventing America: Jefferson's Declaration of Independence* (Garden City, N.Y.: Doubleday,

1978). For the complex political shifts leading to Madison's Memorial and Remonstrance as well as to Jefferson's Statute for Establishing Religious Freedom, see the excellent work of Thomas E. Buckley, S.J., *Church and State in Revolutionary Virginia, 1776-1787* (Charlottesville, Va.: University Press of Virginia, 1977). The complexities and ironies of applying the Statute in Jefferson's own state are authoritatively explored in Buckley's article "After Disestablishment: Thomas Jefferson's Wall of Separation in Antebellum Virginia," *Journal of Southern History* 61 (August 1995). On the Statute itself, authoritative treatment may be found in *The Virginia Statute for Religious Freedom: Its Evolution and Consequences in American History*, ed. Merrill D. Peterson and Robert C. Vaughan (New York: Cambridge University Press, 1988). *Religion in a Revolutionary Age* (Charlottesville: University Press of Virginia, 1994), edited by Ronald Hoffman and Peter J. Albert, consists of eleven suggestive essays. One of Jefferson's English correspondents is the subject of Bernard Peach's *Richard Price and the Ethical Foundations of the American Revolution* (Durham, N.C.: Duke University Press, 1979). *The Revolution in Virginia, 1775-1783* (Williamsburg: The Colonial Williamsburg Foundation, 1988), by John E. Selby, gives full attention to Jefferson's role in this turbulent time. And one book should be mentioned just because it is beautiful — William Howard Adams's *Jefferson's Monticello* (New York: Abbeville Press, 1983).

CHAPTER 4

The bicentennial of the Constitution in 1987 brought renewed attention to the work of the Philadelphia gathering. Two of the most elaborate treatments are *The Founders' Constitution*, 5 vols., ed. Philip B. Kurland and Ralph Lerner (Chicago: University of Chicago Press, 1987); and *Encyclopedia of the American Constitution*, 4 vols., ed. Leonard W. Levy et al. (New York: Macmillan, 1986). Focusing more narrowly on religion and the First

Amendment, William Lee Miller in *The First Liberty: Religion and the American Republic* (New York: Alfred A. Knopf, 1986) provides indispensable background to the achievement of 1789. Quarreling with the prevailing "separationist view" of the Jefferson-Madison undertaking is Daniel L. Driesbach, *Real Threat and Mere Shadow: Religious Liberty and the First Amendment* (Westchester, Ill.: Crossway Books, 1987). In opposition to Driesbach's analysis, see Thomas J. Curry, *The First Freedoms: Church and State in America to the Passage of the First Amendment* (New York: Oxford University Press, 1986); Leonard W. Levy, *The Establishment Clause: Religion and the First Amendment* (New York: Macmillan Publishing Company, 1986); and *The First Freedom: Religion and the Bill of Rights,* ed. James E. Wood Jr. (Waco, Tex.: Institute of Church-State Studies, 1990).

Jefferson's heavy political involvement is the subject of two valuable books by Noble E. Cunningham Jr., both published by the University of North Carolina Press for the Institute of Early American History and Culture: *The Jeffersonian Republicans: The Formation of Party Organization, 1789-1801* (1957) and *The Jeffersonian Republicans in Power: Party Operations, 1801-1809* (1963). On the Federalist party during its years of resistance to Thomas Jefferson, see the imposing work of Donald H. Stewart, *The Opposition Press of the Federalist Period* (Albany: State University of New York Press, 1969).

Religion's role in this period, sometimes subliminal but more often not, is the subject of several excellent works on national destiny and self-understanding. See, for example, John F. Berens, *Providence & Patriotism in Early America, 1640-1815* (Charlottesville: University Press of Virginia, 1978); Ernest Lee Tuveson, *Redeemer Nation: The Idea of America's Millennial Role* (Chicago: University of Chicago Press, 1968); Nathan O. Hatch, *The Sacred Cause of Liberty: Republican Thought and the Millennium in Revolutionary New England* (New Haven: Yale University Press, 1977); and Ruth Bloch, *Visionary Republic: Millennial Themes in American Thought, 1756-1800* (New York: Cambridge University Press, 1985). On the nineteenth century as a whole, Paul C. Nagel's *This Sacred Trust: American Nationality, 1798-1898* (New York: Oxford University Press, 1971) provides expert guidance. And for a full sweep from the colonial period to the present, see *God's New Israel: Religious Interpretations of American Destiny*, ed. Conrad Cherry (Englewood Cliffs, N.J.: Prentice-Hall, 1971).

The most comprehensive study of dissenters in New England who resisted both the Congregational establishment and the Federalist party is William G. McLoughlin's *New England Dissent, 1630-1833: The Baptists and the Separation of Church and State*, 2 vols. (Cambridge: Harvard University Press, 1971). McLoughlin also provides a valuable interpretation of a younger contemporary of Jefferson in *Isaac Backus and the American Pietistic Tradition* (Boston: Little, Brown, 1967). A somewhat older contemporary, John Leland, receives an appreciative treatment from Lyman H. Butterfield in *Elder John Leland, Jeffersonian Itinerant* (Worcester, Mass.: American Antiquarian Society, 1953). For a clear view of a dissenter more Jeffersonian than Jefferson himself, see Michael G. Kenny, *The Perfect Law of Liberty: Elias Smith and the Providential History of America* (Washington: Smithsonian Institution Press, 1994).

CHAPTER 5

Jefferson's own views about the proper content of a religion worthy of a free and enlightened people have received less attention than they should. Paul K. Conkin has perceptively explored aspects of this issue in two essays: "Priestley and Jefferson: Unitarianism as a Religion for a New Revolutionary Age," in Ronald Hoffman and Peter J. Albert, eds. *Religion in a Revolutionary Age* (Charlottesville: University Press of Virginia, 1994), and "The Religious Pilgrimage of Thomas Jefferson," in *Jeffersonian Legacies*, ed. Peter S. Onuf (Charlottesville, Va.: University Press of Virginia, 1993). A book-length study by Charles B. Sanford, *The Religious Life of Thomas Jefferson*

(Charlottesville: University Press of Virginia, 1984), follows an approach more topical than historical or biographical; Sanford's research was extensive and his notes are most useful, but he gives limited attention to the chronological development of Jefferson's religious ideas. Much thinner, both literally and figuratively, is Henry Wilder Foote's *The Religion of Thomas Jefferson* (Boston: Beacon Press, 1947, 1960); Foote is concerned mainly to authenticate Jefferson's credentials as a Unitarian.

In her doctoral dissertation, "The Radical Religious Ideas of Thomas Jefferson and John Adams" (University of Cincinnati, 1973), Constance B. Schulz compares those two remarkable "epistolary" comrades. Another comparison of sorts may be made via the work of Edward H. Davidson and William J. Scheick, *Paine, Scripture, and Authority* (Bethlehem, Pa.: Lehigh University Press, 1994). On the central figure in the Jeffersonian "lost world," see Donald J. D'Elia, *Benjamin Rush: Philosopher of the American Revolution* (American Philosophical Society Transactions, n.s., vol. 64, pt. 5, 1974). Many "editions" (basically simple reprintings) of Jefferson's "Life and Morals of Jesus" have appeared in this century, beginning with that issued by the N. D. Thompson Company in 1902; the book cover has imprinted on it *The Jefferson Bible*, though this appears nowhere on the title page. But "Jefferson Bible" remains a catchy phrase and so is more often used. The latest printing (*The Jefferson Bible* [Boston: Beacon Press, 1995]) is introduced by F. Forrester Church. For full editorial apparatus, however, the preferred volume remains that named in the first paragraph above: *Jefferson's Extracts from the Gospels*.

CHAPTER 6

The only book to give elaborate attention to Jefferson's religion and education is Robert M. Healey's *Jefferson on Religion in Public Education* (New Haven: Yale University Press, 1962); Healey had explicit contemporary concerns in writing the book, but these did not prevent his careful reading of the third president in the context of his own time. Donald G. Tewksbury's *The Founding of American Colleges and Universities before the Civil War* (New York: Teachers College, 1932) remains uniquely valuable. And the first volume of the documentary history of *American Higher Education* (Chicago: University of Chicago Press, 1961), edited by Richard Hofstadter and Wilson Smith, is indispensable. While Virginius Dabney's *Mr. Jefferson's University* (Charlottesville: University Press of Virginia, 1981) quickly zooms past Jefferson, it nonetheless offers an affectionate historical portrait of the state's leading institution of higher learning. For a penetrating analysis of the relationships between religion, education, and the new nation in a quite different context, see Mark A. Noll's *Princeton and the Republic, 1768-1812* (Princeton: Princeton University Press, 1989).

CHAPTER 7

Information on the Thomas Jefferson Memorial was courteously provided by the National Park Service. In *James Madison on Religious Liberty* (Buffalo: Prometheus Books, 1985) Robert S. Alley makes clear Madison's unwavering dedication to this special liberty, both during Jefferson's life and for the decade that remained to him thereafter. Jefferson's own dedication is most immediately evident in his letters to, among others, Benjamin Rush, John Adams, and — of course — James Madison.

If Jefferson could not personally be eternally vigilant, he has inspired such vigilance in a great many others. Perhaps two such guardians deserve particular notice. Leo Pfeffer, counsel to the American Jewish Congress, wrote, among many other works, the following: *Church, State, and Freedom* (Boston: Beacon Press, 1953; rev. ed., 1967); *God, Caesar, and the Constitution* (Boston: Beacon Press, 1974); and *Religion, State, and the Burger Court* (Buffalo: Prometheus Books, 1985). James E. Wood Jr., longtime editor of the *Journal of Church and State*, has authored or edited, among many other works, the following: *Religion, the State, and Education* (Waco, Tex.: Baylor University Press, 1984); *Secular Humanism and the Public Schools* (New York: National Council of Churches, 1986); and *The Role of Religion in the Making of Public Policy* (Waco, Tex.: Institute of Church-State Studies, 1991). Also certain religious bodies have maintained a special vigilance on behalf of religious liberty — notably, Judaism, Jehovah's Witnesses, Seventh-day Adventists, and, until recently, the vast majority of Baptists.

CHAPTER 8

Much attention in recent decades has been given to the nettled question of religion in America's public life, often under the heading of "civil religion" or "religion of the Republic." For a discussion of this issue in the context of the period with which this book is concerned, see Catherine L. Albanese's essay "The Civil Religion of the American Revolution," in her *Sins of the Fathers* (Philadelphia: Temple University Press, 1976). I have examined collectively the views of Benjamin Franklin, George Washington, John Adams, Thomas Jefferson, and James Madison in *Neither King nor Prelate* (Grand Rapids: William B. Eerdmans, 1993). *American Civil Religion* (New York: Harper & Row, 1974), edited by Russell E. Richey and Donald G. Jones, helpfully introduces the entire subject; note especially the essay by David Little, "The Origins of Perplexity: Civil Religion and Moral Belief in the Thought of Thomas Jefferson."

A. James Reichley presents a careful study in his *Religion in American Public Life* (Washington: Brookings Institution, 1985), while Richard V. Pierard and Robert D. Linder narrow the focus in *Civil Religion and the Presidency* (Grand Rapids: Zondervan, 1988) to a survey of the public faith of the nation's leaders from George Washington to Ronald Reagan. Sidney Mead has given great attention to this subject, meshing his thoughts with Jefferson's at many points; for a succinct statement of his views, see *The Old Religion in the Brave New World: Reflections on the Relation between Christendom and the Republic* (Berkeley and Los Angeles: University of California Press, 1977). Jean Bethke Elshtain's *Democracy on Trial* (New York: Basic Books, 1995), cited in Chapter 8, raises concerns that Jefferson would fully share. Finally, Garry Wills in *Under God: Religion and American Politics* (New York: Simon & Schuster, 1990) ranges widely and engagingly across the spectrum of American history but ends solidly with Thomas Jefferson and James Madison, carefully noting remarkable resemblances in their writings to the thought of Roger Williams.

Index